Organizational
Culture Change

Other books by Marcella Bremer

Nieuwe Helden (in Dutch)

21C Positive Change

FREE Premium Content

This book includes free premium content! To download PDFs of the Checklists for your change project go to

www.organizationalculturechange.com/go/premiumcontent

Our readers are also entitled to receive free reports about the average culture profile of certain industry groups, once they are published.

Organizational Culture Change

Unleash your organization's
potential in circles of 10

MARCELLA BREMER

kikker groep

Zwolle MMXII

Published by Kikker Groep
Vrouwenlaan 106, 8017 HS, Zwolle Netherlands
www.kikkergroep.nl
Designed by Marcel Lamers

Kikker Groep publishes its books in a variety of electronic formats.

Readers should be aware that websites given as citations and/or sources for additional information may have changed or (re)moved between the time this was written and when it is read.

ISBN: 978–90–819825–1–1

Printed in the United States of America
FIRST EDITION

Contents

Preface

Welcome to this pragmatic user's guide to organizational culture change. This book wasn't written to be read… it evolved from my pragmatic, hands–on workshops and it is meant to be **DONE**. It is a practical user's guide, audio–recorded while I was talking to my workshop students. Beyond the pile of beautifully written change management books or academic theories, I simply tell you my experiences as a consultant on culture change and what can happen in reality.

I aim for achieving sustainable, that is, successful change. You may have heard of the infamous failure rate of organizational change programs that don't deliver what they promised: between 50–75% Change programs often fail because their approach is too conceptual, too large and too wide.

My approach is to keep change small, personal and focused on specific behaviors in peer groups of 10 trusted coworkers. But nothing will happen if you don't take action. So here's one piece of advice for starters: **Just do it! Moreover: do it together, in "change circles" of 10 people.**

The basic tool I use as a starting point for change is the Organizational Culture Assessment Instrument (OCAI), developed by Professor Kim Cameron and Professor Robert Quinn and elaborately described in their book "Diagnosing and Changing Organizational Culture – based on the Competing Values Framework".

The OCAI serves as a starting point. But it is "only" a starter. Working with clients all over the world, I have elaborated on Cameron and Quinn's approach of dialogues after the OCAI survey into workshops and a 7–Step–Guide to effective Culture Change.

This book isn't simply telling you WHAT to do: we suggest HOW you could do it. But the exact detailed HOW–TO is entirely up to you and needs customization for your organization. And above all: it needs to be DONE. So, welcome to all of you fellow consultants, trainers, managers, team leaders, HR managers, executives, supervisors, students, coaches and coworkers.

Let's develop the workplace and the world!

Marcella Bremer MScBA

Acknowledgments

A big Thank You to professor Kim Cameron for allowing me to provide the OCAI online and embark on this fascinating journey of helping people and organizations to change. Thank you for the inspiration, your support and your books.

Thank you Leandro Herrero for your inspiration and excellent Viral Change approach. Thanks to all of our clients and colleagues who helped us learn more about this fascinating topic: Change!

M.B.

Praise for this book

"Your helping to make accessible and applicable 30 years of research on the Competing Values Framework is a very important undertaking. You are doing a great service to the field."

Warmest wishes, Professor Kim Cameron PhD MA MSc
Associate Dean, William Russell Professor of Management & Organizations at Ross School of Business, and Professor of Higher Education, School of Education, University of Michigan, United States of America

"This in an excellent book with an unusual achievement: solid foundations and logic together with practical implications, all in one. The book is packed with ideas and 'applications' and in every page there is something not just to read but to reflect and imagine 'the translation' in a particular organizational challenge.

I thought the author has been generous. She could have easily written two books with the same material. The book draws on a particular understanding of cultural frameworks, usually a barrier to critical thinking since readers are inevitably forced to 'accept' the model in order to benefit from the content. Again, unusually, this is not the case.

There is a very solid model behind, of course, but one could read and learn 'above and beyond the particular model'. For those of us sitting in the side of the organization as an 'organism' where there is no change unless there is behavioural change, the book provides both the intellectual grounds and practical toolkits to navigate.

Many people interested in Employee Engagement will also find the book very useful and hopefully will draw conclusions about the need to switch to a bottom–up, grass roots, small groups, activism model as we orchestrate in our Viral Change™ programmes.

I am sure there will be a second and third edition and most likely a great deal of conversations triggered by this excellent piece of work."

Leandro Herrero MD MBA FCMI FIoD FRSA
CEO, The Chalfont Project Ltd and Viral Change™ Global L.L.P and author of "Viral Change", United Kingdom

"The strength of this book is that it is inspiring as well as practical. The author avoids the pitfall of unrealistic promises that characterize many books on change management. This book is a must–read for anyone who really wants to contribute to the necessary culture changes that organizations need to make in the coming era."

Hans Wopereis, managing director ITIP Development & Consultancy, author of the Dutch book "Het licht en de korenmaat; je ziel als werkgever", The Netherlands

"Relying on Cameron and Quinn's Organization Culture Assessment Instrument, Marcella Bremer speaks to individual minds, but links them in an inclusive network of virtuous partnerships, circles and organizational fan clubs.

It does not hurt that she is our school's graduate. A reasonable and useful guide if you want to manage a change of beliefs. In Bremer's book you will find everything you always wanted to know about positive brainwashing, but were afraid to ask."

Dr. Slawek Magala, Professor of Cross–Cultural Management and head of the Department of Organization and Personnel Sciences, Rotterdam School of Management, Erasmus University, The Netherlands

"It's a pragmatic approach that will appeal to many and helps to deal with the issues that we stumble over during the change process. I feel that I have read just about every "change text" but I strongly recommend you read this book that brings together many of the concepts in an easy to digest "This is what you do format"."

Denis McIvor, President of the Organisation Development Association, Australia

"Marcella makes a great contribution to the success stories on Change programmes with her work and through the ideas in this book. This a must read for people in the Change business.

Of special note are the references to the latent Leadership potential at all levels in the organisation. This book will help your thinking on how you can help create a performance Culture that really does get the best out of the people in your organisation."

Clive Bevan, Executive Team member at New Performance Era Ltd, United Kingdom

The author

Marcella Bremer MScBA works as a consultant guiding organizational change and personal development. Her motto is: "Develop the workers, the workplace and the world."

She is a Master of Science of Business Administration from Rotterdam School of Management and she helps organizations and consultants diagnose and change culture, so they can utilize culture to create a great place to work in a very pragmatic, hands–on and engaging way.

She's been using the Organizational Culture Assessment Instrument (OCAI) for years in a great variety of organizations and she felt it was time to share practical lessons learned and experiences. All cases are based on the global database of OCAI online.

"This is the book I'd like to have read in college and when starting out as a consultant in change and organization development and later on, when I managed our own team. 50–75% of Organizational Change programs fail because their approach is too conceptual, too large and too wide. My approach is to keep change small, personal and focused on specific behaviors in peer groups of 10 trusted coworkers. Circles of 10 can change the world."

Chapter 1 What's changing this 21st Century?

In the "old" world, let's say before 1992 when the Internet got serious, change management was a separate discipline. Organizations needed to change every now and then and if it was time to improve, adjust or change, they hired a change manager or consultant to help them control the process of "unfreeze–change–refreeze". It was a clear project with a beginning and an end.

It was "exclusive change". Exclusive in the sense of excluding employees and designing change in a small project team or board. The outcome was often top–down change: telling the others to change and how to change. Forcing people from the outside, by command and control, by systems or procedures, to change their behaviors.

An infamous outcome of this process, discussed at length by change practitioners and in text books, was resistance to change or even sabotage. Last but not least, this process produced the 50–70% failure rate of organizational change programs.

If you browse through some LinkedIn discussion groups, you can see these topics are still food for interesting debates today. This approached stemmed from the factory in the good old industrial era where the boss knew best and labor could be designed and measured by people like Frederick Taylor. Employees manufactured goods and change was slow – you could see it coming.

Nowadays Taylor is dead, change has reached the speed of light with the flow of information, and no human boss can keep up with this complexity and connectedness. Our colleagues and customers hear, see and feel what we believe and what we do. That is how we're adding value in an interactive service economy.

Change is the New Normal

We have entered the 21st Century. In this "new" world life and work without the Internet is unthinkable. Technology changed rapidly and swept us along in a tsunami of new possibilities. The effects are not only technological but they permeate every part of our work–life. Social media give us 24/7 access to friends, coworkers or contractors.

The inside of organizations becomes visible on the outside by twittering employees. Information and services travel around the globe with the speed of light. Better prices, the latest updates, free bonuses: well–educated consumers demand and find them.

Globalization and mutual dependency are a fact. Change is no longer a once–a–decade operation. Change is constant. You can't afford to hire a specialist to do it for you. Managers, executives and professionals need to change and learn, adapt and improve, respond and get results all the time.

Corporations offer permanent positions as a "change manager". They establish corporate academies that teach change management. Heraclitus is more right than ever before. Change is the only constant. Change is the new normal.

♦ Who can afford to risk the 50–70% failure rate of organizational change nowadays?
♦ Who controls a corporation staffed with highly–educated, twittering, autonomous and self–confident professionals?
♦ Who really controls complex services that add value in interaction with the client and that are customized all the time?
♦ Who oversees all the complex and interdependent changes, big or small, and their future implications to the organization?
♦ Who is so intelligent and all–mighty that they can decide what's best for the others and find all the solutions?

We face rapid technological changes, global competition, financial volatility and economic interdependency, emerging markets, environmental issues. The baby boomers are getting ready to retire while the digital Generation Y, raised in wealth and self–confidence, enters the workplace, though their numbers are small.

Talent retention is harder than before, innovation is more necessary than ever before to stay in the race, world wealth is shifting and we have to find new ways of thinking, living and working.

Welcome to this new world of change. Welcome to the 21st Century (21C). You may have noticed already: Top–down, exclusive change doesn't work anymore. If it ever did at all...

This is the world of co–creation, crowd–sourcing and emergent advantages in networks inside and outside of the organization. This is the new openness. The new democracy. The coming of age of masses of well–educated workers who like to take ownership for their own lives and careers, rising to the next step in Maslow's pyramid; ready for self–actualization.

Whether you see this happen or you still have some doubts – that's up to you. The thing is, you need to do what works. You need to change successfully. That's what this practical user's guide is going to help you do.

Let's take a look at the new 21C Change. More than ever before, successful change entails:

♦ Bottom–up and inclusive change: Engage everyone
♦ Personal and collective change at the same time
♦ Entice people to change their beliefs and to change behaviors
Oh come on – we don't have time for that! We're not therapists. We don't like the fluffy stuff!

I don't have much time either, we're all busy. I'm not a therapist and I'm not comfortable with fluffy stuff. But I do want to make a difference, instead of merely making a living. That's why I change the 21C Way. Even if it takes a little more time in advance, it returns this investment big time.

That's why I use the OCAI tool: depart from a quantified starting point, engage everyone and focus on specific behavior to produce the performance we need. To co–create change that is successful.

I learned this the hard way. Of course, I had heard about resistance and the 70% failure rate of organizational change. But when I earned my Master's degree in the Science of Business Administration, with a major in Change Management, we didn't learn many practical tools on human behavior. We had the academic perspective, like: organizations are systems. And: when people define things as true, they become true. Interesting and true. But how do you apply such knowledge?

In my first post–graduate assignment, I presented a plan with the "best" solution to this particular organization's problem. I remember the board meeting where the top executives agreed on this plan. Great! But they never implemented it... My hard work ended up in a drawer.

I was hurt at that time, because I took things personally then. I was so much younger. I was frustrated. It wasn't enough for me to make a living. I wanted to make a difference. But in order to do so, I needed the others. And they just wouldn't do like I said... Why weren't there more people just like me?!

I remember employees nodding Yes but not keeping their agreements. Because they never intended to. Because there were hidden advantages to the old behavior, or on the contrary, hidden objections to the new behavior. Or because no one else was doing it. Or because they were scared. Or simply, because they didn't contribute to the plan. They didn't co–create the change.

Yes, all those complainers are right: Change is difficult. People will bounce back to their old habits like rubber. If the boss turns his back on them, they will stop doing the new behavior. This will happen because we can't change the others. We can't exclude them. But we can invite them to the change!

All successful change is inclusive change. It engages people. The CEO can't change the company. The HR Manager can't either. And this brilliant but expensive outside consultant can't succeed on his own. No thoroughly validated off–the–shelf method will do the work for you. No step–by–step recipe is the solution. Forget ticking the right boxes.

Change is a customized group effort. What will work within this organization? What will not? You have to do the work together. You have to get creative collectively.

It was not until I started to engage people more and respect their ideas and diversity that I achieved to bring about real commitment and change. I took courses in NLP, body work, psychology, Psych–K and a trainer's education to learn how people think, feel and behave. I learned to work on beliefs, how to strengthen new habits, how to help people practice specific behavior.

I found that the fastest and most successful way to change is by engaging your coworkers and employees: they have lots of interesting information, insights and ideas to improve culture, leadership, engagement, strategy, diversity, innovation, performance and even fun. They might stick with such co–created change much sooner than in the old–fashioned commanded change (though nothing is ever certain).

They co–create feasible change together, in peer groups of 10 people. These "change circles" help them to stick with the change and support each other. In small groups people are able to know, see and trust each other while they support each other.

Group patterns where people copy one another's behaviors, while they coach and correct each other emerge. This way we bypass the "stickiness of culture" that exists because people copy each other and newcomers try to fit in and adjust. We use this copying mechanism in another direction – to stir change – once we have all agreed which behaviors we need for successful change.

Change is not about the ultimate "best" plan but about what gets accepted within your organization. It is not command and control, it is **collaborate and co–create** these days. It is not about "being right", it is about getting it right. It is all about **fans and followers** these days!

This book is about organizing such co–creation and collaboration. It is about winning fans and followers. It is about employee engagement in small groups. It is about co–creating successful change.

By the way, if you want to read more about our fascinating 21st Century: jump to Chapter 23 where I've collected more specifics on what differentiates 21C Workplaces from the past.

Chapter 2 Did you check your 7C's and Steps to Culture Change?

Before introducing the 7–Step Guide to Culture Change and the outline of this book, let's take a look at the 7C Framework of Change that helps identify the conditions that will make the difference to your project. After struggling in several projects, I summarized the prerequisites to co–create change in the

7C Framework of 21C Successful Change:

1. Commitment from the top
2. Clarity on current and desired situation and goals
3. Consensus and commitment from workers
4. Continuous communication
5. Copy–Coach–Correct: Consistency
6. Create critical mass
7. Carry on

Before, during and after the change process, I check if these conditions are met. It may seem tempting to skip one of them, because you're busy, your client doesn't want to spend more time thus money on the project or people question the importance of these particular C's. Don't give in to this pressure.

Always check on your 7 C's if you aim for real, lasting change

C1 The top executives need to be committed, not only to the change and its expected gains, but to personal change as well. They must be so committed that they are willing to change themselves if necessary and endure the discomfort of adopting new habits.

C2 Without clarity, efforts tend to diversify, diffuse and confuse. We need to know where we stand, where we need to go and why we have to move now. Clarity lacks more often than you think. Ask the team leaders or employees to explain your organization's strategy. And you will have your answer if there's clarity for starters.

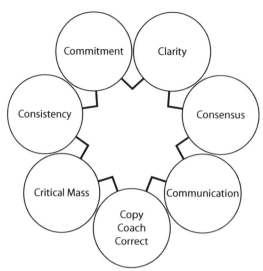

7 Conditions for Change

C3 Consensus and commitment, engagement if you will, are vital to change. The CEO can't change 1,000 others, not even 10 of them. He can try to influence them, role model, be the change he wants to see. But enough others have to change their behaviors or nothing will change in the organization as a whole. You can only achieve consensus and commitment in small teams (the power of 10, see Chapter 13, "change circles").

C4 Communicate, have dialogues, ask, explain, exchange. True communication creates meaning and connection. Without communication there will be no understanding, respect, confidence and will to really make change happen this time. Communicate and support each other in small teams.

C5 Respond to all behaviors all the time – this is a major leadership skill that seems to be often lacking. Utilize the copy mechanism: people will do what you do. Be the change so others can copy you. Coach them and if necessary, correct old or undesired behaviors. Be consistent and the change will become clear. People might check if you are for real. Small behaviors can have huge impact. Consistently keep doing it: copy, coach and correct. Organize the change in small teams (the power of 10, see Chapter 13) of people who support each other.

C6 If the behaviors are spreading through the organizational system, you are on the right track. Reach that famous critical mass when enough people are executing the new behaviors and it becomes profitable for everyone to do so, even for the ones who resisted so far.

C7 Last but not least: Carry on. Never, never give up. The minute you let go is the minute people are tempted to go back to old habits and rest in their comfort zones. Help them through the "messy middle" to a happy ending, when "new" has become a habit again. Until the next change...

7–Step Guide to Culture Change

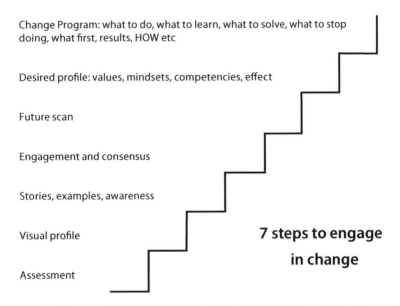

Change Program: what to do, what to learn, what to solve, what to stop doing, what first, results, HOW etc

Desired profile: values, mindsets, competencies, effect

Future scan

Engagement and consensus

Stories, examples, awareness

Visual profile

Assessment

7 steps to engage in change

Don't worry if this 7C list raises questions for you at this point. This is a short introduction and during this book, you will start to see what I mean. This Culture Change Guide is engaging you to BE the change and to just do it.

So, how do you change an organizational culture...?

Now here's the **7–Step Guide to Culture Change**.

It's an easy–to–follow framework of 7 steps:

1. Assess the current and preferred culture (15 minutes)
2. Diagnose the quantified, visual profile
3. Understand culture better by adding qualitative examples, stories
4. Raise engagement and awareness and create consensus of where we are
5. Assess the future, vision and strategy to see where we need to go
6. Understand and customize the necessary, preferred culture to thrive in this future. Agree and see this new culture, from values down to behavior and outcomes
7. Together, create a How–to–change plan that people take ownership for because they co–created it. Work in small teams, ocai–workshops or change circles of 10 people max.

Steps 1–6 represent the WHAT to change. This is the easy part, in a way. You can assess the "what" to change. Where are we now and where do we want to go. Define A and B. Where we Are. And where we want to Be.

Agree on the best feasible B, given your market, your challenges, your people. You can use logic and dialogue with the OCAI survey and the subsequent OCAI workshops that I share in this book. It can be planned in time.

Step 7 is the magical HOW. This is where you need to puzzle and find out what works in your system and what doesn't. How do you actually, truly, get from A to B? This is tailor–made for each organizational system.

This is the part where situational intelligence is necessary because no off–the–shelf road map can take you there. This is your work, as a Culture Consultant or leader. Engage the others and find out what will make a difference in your workplace.

Though there is no fixed road, in this book I share my tools to help solve this puzzle, to find leverage in the organizational system, to identify and engage key stakeholders and discover what will work to help them change behaviors that will last.

For all consultants and change guides out there: this is the puzzle part that yields the fun – and often some frustration. But don't worry – just keep securing your 7C's – and you will get there in the end. This is the part that can't be planned in detail. This might be beyond logic, full of surprises and it must be experienced without total control: to reach the magic shores of B. Where you want to Be.

The biggest obstacles against success with the 7–Step Guide are listed in the 7C's. Now that you know them, you can check them all the time and adjust your approach. What stands out for me, lately, is the common desire to have fast, painless, easy change. Today's pace is high: "We want it all and we want it now". But beware of 7C: Carry on. Habits and cultures take time to grow.

Stay in for the long run. Failed change projects are often aborted too soon. After the fresh beginning, people get tired and frustrated in the messy middle. This is where many organizations, CEOs and change guides give up – turning to another priority, trying to forget the effort, time, money and expectations spent in vain.

We all long for happy endings, but in real life, they aren't guaranteed and they take much longer than in the movies. Never forget: we are working with behavior. It took years to raise you – but it was worth it, wasn't it?

The same counts for organizational behavior. You have to keep trying and adjust your approach until you find the key behaviors that will make the change real – and then persist. If you manage your expectations and you are prepared to puzzle your way out of this maze in the middle, it can be engaging and fun and it's easier to persevere.

And the winners are...

If you follow the 7–Step Guide, you will co–create a great place to work! It is an ultimately engaging process, enticing everyone in the organizational system to contribute and change.

It is inclusive and will appeal to your highly–educated professionals. Generation Y yearns for autonomy and participation at the same time. They are confident enough to like challenges and flexible to thrive on change. If you engage them, you might unleash a great potential. As goes for all of your employees or, should we say, stakeholders.

Culture is the ultimate difference between failure and success. It can make or break your organization. It's more important in our service–oriented, information economy than ever before. Your customers will hear if your help desk really cares or not.

Social media is revealing the inside of corporate culture to the public out there... Change is the only constant – and at a much higher speed than good old Heraclitus could ever imagine. Culture and change are key to overcome today's organizational challenges.

The competitive advantage of the future is the organization's ability to adapt quickly and to connect people... because that is turning relationships into results while servicing your customers. Collaboration stirs innovation and engagement and performance.

The winning organizations are those who develop a people–oriented and results–focused entrepreneurial culture at the same time.

If you want the full vision now, jump to Chapter 23. If you like to see how this process of co–creating a great culture is done, stay right here and take it chapter by chapter.

What you will learn in this Culture Change Guide

How to guide engaging, successful 21C change and become a great place to work!

More specific, learn how to:

- Diagnose and change culture with a validated approach to change,
- Engage coworkers and have them take ownership,
- Utilize everyone's energy and ideas,
- Work with positive energizers and change agents,
- Become aware of resistance and assess satisfaction
- Align mission and values with performance, strategy and behaviors,
- Align different departments and the board with the shop floor.
- If you like, to relate the MBTI personality test and management styles to culture types
- Conduct workshops and truly engage your organization, team by team...

Step 1 Assessment Current + Preferred Culture

This is where we decide to start working with culture, because it makes all the difference in today's world and to organizational effectiveness. Check out Chapters 3, 4, 5 and 6 that introduce the concept of culture, the Organizational Culture Assessment Instrument (OCAI) and the Competing Values Framework.

Step 2 Diagnose the Quantified Culture Profiles

Time to understand the outcome of the assessment with the OCAI tool. Chapter 7 shows a lot of different industry profiles that give an idea of what these quantified, visual profiles look like. Chapter 8 and chapter 9 discuss practicalities of organizing the assessment and communication in the process, while Chapter 10 focuses on organizing the workshops after the OCAI survey.

Step 3 Understand and Add Qualitative Information

In Chapter 11 the OCAI workshop starts! It's the exciting point when participants gather and start discussing their outcome and add qualitative information to better understand their current culture and agree on where they Are (point A). This is where they get involved... We join the Care Center for Disabled People to see how this works.

Step 4 Raise Awareness, Consensus and Engagement to Change

The workshop participants become aware and enthusiastic about where we Are and where we want to Be. Engage them to contribute to the organization. To share their expectations, ideas, improvements, objections and solutions.

To take ownership for their workplace, because it concerns their daily activities. Because it is all about them. The CEO can't do it alone. The consultant can't make it happen either. Change is a collective endeavor. You need the big majority. Skip this step and you're on a failing mission, or cosmetic change if you're lucky.

Step 5 Future Scan, see the Why, the Vision and Strategy

In Chapter 12 we explore the future and where we want to Be (point B). Why is it necessary to change now, and in what direction? The workshop continues to reach an interesting point where consensus and true engagement is vital to change success.

Step 6 Understand and Customize Preferred Culture

Now it gets personal. What will I change as of tomorrow? Which habits to abandon? Which new behaviors to practice? What will make a difference in our organization? How can we customize general logic into specific behaviors that will do for us? How will team members support each other? Join in as the group explores the will and skill to change the details that matter.

Step 7 Co–create: How to Change Plan... and DO it

Chapter 13 shows what this group came up with. This is the magical How. How do we change, once you know your preferred future and culture, once you've committed yourself. What precisely will every one of us do next? How do we carry on when we get tired or start to doubt the change process..? The Care Center managed to create successful change, though it was not painless.

Cases: How did the others do it?

Now you know everything. But there's more to it. Though every organization and team is unique, we can learn so much from their change experiences. So join us in these cases: the Rehab, the University Library, a Machine Maintenance company, a National Bank and this Merger of five mental health institutions. Each case shows different angles and lessons learned to organizational culture change. Check out Chapters 14, 17, 18, 20 and 22.

Extra explanations, experiences and lessons learned

Meanwhile, our understanding of culture, change and leadership deepens. We discuss "dark" and effective sides of culture in Chapter 15 and show examples of interventions in Chapter 16.

We dedicate Chapter 19 to the crucial role of leadership during the change process; some personality traits and management roles that align with the culture types.

We discuss an amazing example of "positive change" in Chapter 21 and positive energy networks that can fast forward your culture change.

Last but not least, Chapter 23 explores the future of organizational life. In the online, global OCAI database with culture assessments we see an interesting desire for more adhocracy and clan cultures in the future, across countries and economic activities. What does this mean...?

Let's explore the desire for innovation, mastery and autonomy in our 21st century. Let's meet Generation Y and dream of the future. Let's see how many organizations still work in an old–fashioned way, while the "only way is up" in the Competing Values Framework.

Change has become a core competence and culture is more important than ever before in our service/experience economy to add value to customers and to provide "flexible glue" to remotely working, autonomous employees – while still providing shelter, belonging and a meaningful, collective purpose...

Chapter 3 What is organizational culture and why should we care?

In this chapter we cover what organizational culture is, what its functions are and why it matters to organizations, managers and employees. It is incredibly important, as Lou Gerstner, former CEO of IBM knew from experience, when he said: "I came to see in my time at IBM that culture isn't just one aspect of the game, it is the game."

What is organizational culture?

What is organizational culture? There are a lot of definitions and I don't intend to repeat all the theories and culture gurus here. A common, operational explanation is: "It's how we do things around here". That certainly is an important part of culture. It's visible on the outside.

When you enter a building, you get a glimpse of corporate culture right away from what you see – how the office looks and what people are doing. But it's not the whole story. "How we do things around here" is a simplification. A very important aspect of culture is not visible from the outside right away – that part is: "How we think about things around here." When I enter and the receptionist feels that visitors are keeping her from doing her "real" work and I disturb her completing some planning schedule, she will not greet me warmly. The way she thinks immediately directs how she behaves.

Culture is not just "How we do things around here." The other part of culture is under the water's surface and that is how we think and feel about "what we're doing here." Why are we doing these things in this particular way? It represents who you are as an individual or an organization. It's what you believe. It reflects your assumptions, your values and priorities, your convictions about reality, about customers, about the competition, what is okay and what is not.

These beliefs are expressed, consciously or not, when we do things in a certain way. These behaviors are reinforced when people work together in a group: the team or

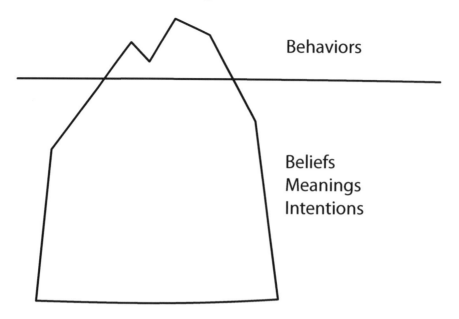

organization. Our shared values and beliefs become visible in the corporate environment. They direct our behaviors, our competencies and thus results and performance for the organization as a whole.

Moreover, because people tend to copy each other and like to belong to a group, beliefs and behaviors are likely to spread through the organization and sustain over time. In summary: shared beliefs and behaviors are the two main components of organizational culture. They are the factors that we are going to work with when we want to bring about successful organizational change.

2 Sides to Change

Change that is sustainable over time walks on these two legs: beliefs and behaviors. **There is an inside–out, from thinking to doing direction.** People can change their values, norms and beliefs. Then they start to do things differently because that is in line with their new beliefs. Imagine the receptionist.

She used to feel that visitors at the desk disturb her. One of her tacit beliefs was that people tend to be selfish and that they always want immediate service and that it's never enough. She feels like she's giving and serving while she's never acknowledged.

Another belief she held was that she can only do one thing at a time, she's not too quick, didn't they always say that to her when she was a kid?

But since she's got a new manager, things have changed. He's had several one–on–ones with the receptionist, which was very scary at first because she expected to be scaffolded or why else would he spend time with her?

To her surprise, he asked her how he could help with her job! He gave her the feeling that she mattered. She doesn't have to service all the time, he's supporting her as well...

His talks made her more confident. She decides she's not stupid because she's learned a lot since childhood. She remembered the compliments she got for her excellent presentation from their former CEO.

She had forgotten about it, since the organization restructured and the workload got so bad that she couldn't handle everything and she felt her shortcomings all the time. Talking with the new manager made her think. And it feels different now!

She enjoyed the recognition from this new manager. When she received the customers warmly, she found out that some are nice people who will wait for a minute and who thank her politely – when she smiles.

It feels different so she keeps practicing the new way. She prefers friendly visitors above impatient, unpleasant encounters. And she changed those encounters herself...

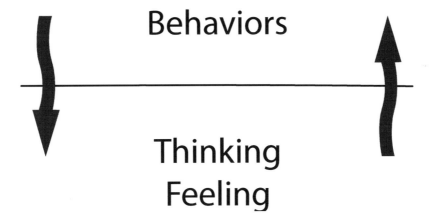

The other direction of change is outside–in, from doing to thinking. People do something new because they had training on certain skills. They start to practice. While doing things differently, they start to think about it differently. It's a new experience that influences some beliefs or norms they hold.

He's the receptionist and he's had a customer focus training. He feels more confident now that he has learned how to be assertive and polite, while processing three calls at the same time. He gets better at multitasking and he even finds it a challenge to be on the phone while he's checking his boss's agenda and a new visitor shows up at his desk.

No one is disturbing him here. He feels alert and alive and he likes to handle three things at the same time, mastering his job, now that he has had the training. He has changed his beliefs about himself, about the visitors and about his job.

An outside intervention may make him change his behavior as well. His manager may come up with a new procedure to enhance the customer focus. He has to pick up the phone within three times or otherwise the call is directed to the call center and this will be visible in his call records.

That doesn't look good, so he makes sure to pick up the phone immediately. Because he is "forced" from the outside to do something different – he starts to think and feel differently. He didn't want to do it at first because he was used to chatting.

His coworker likes to gossip and she is a great storyteller. They got a bit angry about their manager and his stupid procedure, but on the other hand, they noticed that there were many customer complaints lately.

They want to keep their receptionist jobs and frankly, the complaints produce negative energy and stressful one–on–ones with their manager. So they follow the procedure reluctantly and it's awkward at first but then they both get used to this new way of handling calls.

They chat after the calls and they're more pleased with their manager's compliments than they will admit. It starts to feel good, competent and professional. They're the most customer focused receptionists they know.

There are two ways in which a culture evolves. It's how we do things around here and it's how we think about it. If you want successful culture change, it's best to use both sides – outside and inside. Above and below the water line. Behaviors and Beliefs.

Cameron & Quinn have a quotation in their book in which they acknowledge these two levels of change that are very important. "When the values, orientations, definitions and goals stay constant, even when procedures and strategies are altered, organizations will quickly return to the status quo. The same is true for individuals. So without an alteration of values and expectations, change remains superficial and short of duration."

"Failed attempts to change often produce cynicism, frustration, loss of trust and deterioration in morale. As our research has shown, organizations may be worse off than if the change strategy had not been attempted, so modifying organizational culture is key."

Then Cameron & Quinn say "a change in values and mental models and targets should therefore be combined with the change in context of how people work together." Here you see that you have to work inside–out and outside–in to change "the way we do things around here."

Beliefs and behavior in groups

Now let's move from individual beliefs and behavior to groups. Behavior in groups is determined by 3 Cs. Culture is stabilized in groups because people interact with each other at work. The three Cs of culture on the behavioral group level are that people copy, coach and correct each other.

So if you are the new hire as a receptionist, for starters you copy what the others are doing because "that's the way we do things around here." Your coworker is going to coach you on your first day.

She explains: "When you pick up the phone, be a little more polite to the customers," or "Pick it up within three rings," etc.

But when you're not doing good enough, your coworker corrects you. She says "You really should be doing better. You can pick up the phone within three times. Be so polite to the customer that they feel you care. Otherwise I'm afraid you can't stay after probation time."

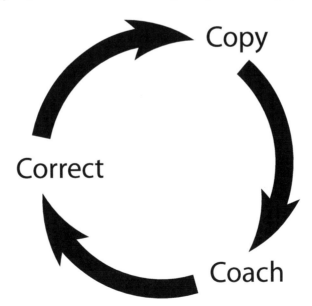

A culture tends to stabilize to "the way we do things around here," because people copy each other, correct and coach one another all the time, in various ways. That's the sticky part of culture. Beneath our reinforced, collective behaviors are the beliefs that we collectively share, tacit or not. They determine whether we value our customers, our coworkers, who gets promoted, what criteria are for a job well done, when to collaborate and when to compete, how to address the CEO or the receptionist, who is important, what we care for, etc.

Culture is why one team achieves great results in spite of weak processes and tools while another team that has the best possible processes and gear fails to meet their targets. "The way we do things around here" is directed by the way we think about things. If you think you can't do something, you probably won't try it. If you feel confident on the other hand, you're more likely to try something new.

If your team believes that they are a great, trustful team, they will share lots of information. If your team doesn't trust the other departments, they hoard information. The connection between beliefs and behaviors is as simple as these examples...

What does culture do for a group?

Culture evolves in any group, whether you're aware of it or not. People tend to copy, coach and correct each other. Culture is sticky. People tend to hire people who are just like them and (sometimes unconsciously) prefer to work with others who resemble them in beliefs and behaviors. If you don't use culture, culture will use you, because it will mold you to show a certain behavior that is appreciated in the group. In short: Culture is our collective comfort zone!

Culture is stabilized and reinforced because colleagues will copy, coach and correct each other. But why does this happen? What are the functions of culture? A lot of research has been done on the topic. Let's explore five important functions that culture has for a group of people:

1. Culture provides reduction of collective insecurity. It gives the group a shared view – "this is how things are." When I start working somewhere, I copy their behavior and I adopt or comply to important beliefs even when they don't explain them.

Their perspective may be that the customers are the most important to the company. Or it may be that they value employees and if they have to choose, it's first people and then profits. It's a world view. It makes life easier to comprehend, it's their "way we do things around here and what we believe in." It gives certainty – "this is how things are."

2. Culture determines social hierarchy. It gives people a position. When I'm the new hire, I know I have to work my way up and that gives a certain peace. It's clear who the leaders are.

We don't have to spend much energy on determining positions while there's so much work to do. That's a stabilizing feature of culture in a group.

3. Culture provides continuity, because we share these values and standards and we copy them and we coach others to adopt them too. It doesn't matter if people are leaving and new hires are coming in, culture gives continuity because on the behavioral level we are passing on "the way we do things around here".

It enhances speed as a group because we all know what we mean when we use certain words. It's straightforward because we share our common language, our world view, our beliefs and our behaviors and what they mean.

4. Culture provides a shared identity and familiarity. If you start working at this company, you belong somewhere. Belonging is a very basic human need, so that's a very important function of group culture. If you'll copy the others and fit in, you'll be appreciated.

5. Last but not least, culture gives us a vision of the future. It gives us a purpose. If we value customers most then – we should take care of people. We pick up the phone quickly because we care about the customers. This gives us a purpose in life and work. It makes our behavior meaningful. Today, we contributed to the world by helping our customers. You made someone smile who had a bad day – until they met you at the reception desk.

Why should we care about culture?

Why does culture matter? Why would you read this book instead of doing business as usual?

Culture directs many factors that are relevant to CEOs, HR Directors and others in an organization. Let's take a look at those factors and you can sell culture – whether it's to your client or your executives and coworkers.

Let's face it: we often have to "sell" the topic because of many prejudices. We've heard them all before. Culture is not tangible, it's the soft side, it's "fluffy stuff", it takes too much time, you can't manage it and we're not psychotherapists, are we?

Let's stick to our key performance indicators and focus on the hard results. Well, that's exactly what we're doing – when we work with culture. Culture is directly influencing organizational performance or team performance. It's the reason why organizational change fails – or why it succeeds.

Culture affects recruiting and hiring. A lot of workplaces nowadays are concerned about diversity and aim for an inclusive culture. That's interesting when you realize how we are inclined to hire people who are just like us... Here you see culture work directly in recruiting and hiring.

Employee retention is another important topic. It takes a lot of money, time and energy to hire new people and teach them how to work in your organization and then they leave again in three months. Employee retention saves a lot of time and money and you want to keep the best employees. What is keeping them here is not just the salary, it's the culture. It's whether they like it or not – the challenges, the values, the leadership, the culture in their team. Culture provides very important "glue".

Attrition or motivation, absenteeism or engagement are directly influenced by corporate culture. Turnover and profits, innovation, production, customer satisfaction, market share, the image, the brand, how the stakeholders think of your organization – it's all affected by culture. Culture, in effect, is about everything. It directs behaviors all the time so it produces outcomes. Every day. In every field.

Culture is a multiplier to misery or magic. It has a great leverage effect. You can't afford not to be aware of culture because it produces your results. Culture evolves anyway within a group, so you'd better influence it consciously and utilize culture to meet the targets of the organization. We can also define culture as how you behave when you're thinking and when you're not thinking... Culture guides automated, subconscious behavior but also your consciously pursued goals and behaviors.

Compare culture to the water in a fish tank that determines whether the fish will thrive or not. The fish are not aware of the water quality but it definitely determines how fast and effective the fish can swim.

Knowing what culture effects, makes it easier to sell. Culture is the missing link between hanging your mission statement on the wall and making the mission come true. That should appeal to CEOs and HR Directors...

In the Netherlands we have train compartments that are meant for working, reading and concentration. There is a sign "Silence" on every window pane, comparable to an organization's mission statement. Whether it's really silent in the compartment or not depends on the people who sit in it. What is the way they do things around there?

What do they value? Politeness, taking care of other people, tolerance, individualism, their own needs? What are the norms in this group? How do they copy, coach and correct each other? If there's a group of loud teenagers coming in – what does the individual business person do?

Does she copy their behavior and pick up her cell phone to make that one important call? Or does she correct them and point at the Silence–sign? And when they start chatting again, does she coach them to try again – or is she scared to address a group with different values?

What if one cell–phoning person gets in, while there's a group of others silently working? What if she gets negative feedback, while phoning? Will she end her phone call – apologizing and acknowledging the value of respect for others and rules?

Will she start a scene, placing her highly–valued personal needs above the rights and needs of others? Will someone call the conductor to solve this issue with her authority? Or will the group as a whole unite against this newcomer who violates the rules?

Every scenario is possible. What makes it interesting is that this is a metaphor for culture, though the travelers in the compartment don't share deep collective beliefs and behaviors (unless it were a very long journey and they were allowed to exchange words).

What happens depends on personal values and norms and which values the majority embraces. Next to these beliefs, every one's behavior makes a difference: how do we interact? Is the group pressure strong enough to copy, coach and correct?

Can culture be changed?

Can culture be changed? The question stirs a lot of debate. Maybe change is a too strong verb to use but we could agree that you can influence culture. There is never 100 percent control because we're dealing with human behavior and we can only entice people to behave in a certain way. We can influence culture. Maybe change is also a bit too abrupt. When you influence a culture, there is evolution and development.

Changing or developing a culture takes a lot of will and skill. In organizations, it's not just individuals but we have group change. That can be either easier or harder than individual change, because the majority in the organization needs to change certain beliefs and behaviors. That is both an individual and a collective process. The current culture can either enhance or hamper this change, because of its stickiness and stabilizing effects.

Summary

All organizational change is about changing beliefs and behaviors to some extent. Without new, different behaviors, nothing would change. People need to do things differently, or there is no sustainable, long–lasting change.

Culture tends to be sticky because it fulfills important needs for individuals as well as the group: reduction of insecurity, social hierarchy, a purpose and vision, familiarity and continuity. It is stabilized by the 3C mechanisms: copy, coach and correct.

Culture determines organizational performance because it directs individual and group behavior. This is why culture eats strategy for breakfast. It is great to make new plans and intentions. But to walk the talk is a completely different game. The good news is: culture can be influenced. Let's find out how...

Chapter 4 What are the 7 Conditions for Successful Change?

Before we turn to using the OCAI, let's talk about culture change in general. We'll discuss some of the conditions for successful change and culture change in particular. Let's reflect on the will and skill that you need for culture change, revisit our 7 crucial Cs and look at the "chariot of change" as well as the "ABCDE" of culture change.

Culture change takes will and skill. These are two elements that you need to assess before you start culture change. As a consultant or an HR manager you first need to check if the top is really willing to do it. This means that leaders need to walk their talk and practice what they preach.

Here's a possible pitfall for consultants, because we all need to pay the rent. When you enter an organization you want to win the assignment. But what if they're not really willing to change…? A CEO more or less tells you: "I'm so happy that you are here. Please change my organization for me." Leaders may believe, unaware or not: "I'm okay, but the others need to change. They have to change their culture."

One of the things I learned in my work as a consultant is that CEOs and top executives often feel that they are themselves not part of the culture. They have such a different perspective, their position is unique and they don't feel part of the "common culture".

However, they are a very important part of culture. They shape culture, even when they're not aware of it. People will watch their actions and interpret what they mean – leaders play an important role in culture. But not solely. Culture is ultimately a group process. We need to engage everyone in the process of change.

If you want to conduct successful change, be sure to work with the CEO and be sure that she or he's really willing to DO it. This counts for all executives, managers and team leaders in the organization. Everybody has to change their "way we do things around here." But it starts with the leaders.

They must BE the change they want to see in their organization. This is the will that needs to be present at the start. Of course you cannot be 100 percent sure that people are willing to change all the way. They might encounter some resistance to change within themselves, sooner or later in the process. But this is your first check: the will to start a change process.

Assess players and necessity

♦ How are you part of the old culture...? (They probably have become leaders in the current culture so they did something right according to the current norms. In that case, they are rooted in this culture. Here's the question whether they are aware of this and whether they believe that they can change.)
♦ What changes are necessary according to you?
♦ Have you ever successfully changed your behaviors before?
♦ What should you do differently to help the others/organization make the change?
♦ Are you open to training and coaching...?

The responses, including non–verbal cues, will give you a clue about their true will. Another important factor, mentioned in every change management course and book: people must feel that there is a **necessity to change**. It must feel urgent like the infamous burning platform; "We must do it now." Otherwise you might not have enough motivation to change and not enough will to see it through the hard parts.

Assess the necessity to change now

♦ Why must we change now?
♦ What would happen if we didn't change?
♦ Can we postpone it until next year?

The second part you need to assess is the skill. Skills can be acquired if there's enough will. If you're willing to do it, you will go all the way to learn whatever is necessary but you must be willing...

Often, change programs and training focus on the skills level but that's not enough. People must be willing to change further including reconsidering their beliefs if necessary – all the assumptions, everything that they believe is true about their world, about their work, etc. If they're willing to change crucial beliefs, they can also acquire the new skills and they will stick.

We must be realistic: There are skills that some people cannot easily learn. Picture really introverted people who may not be able, no matter how many training sessions they follow, to learn to behave more extroverted and to be excellent call center employees. Take a look at the future skills that seem to be necessary. Do they think they can acquire these...? Assessing skills may be difficult, just as assessing their will. Some leadership tests may shed light on this topic. (More in Chapter 19).

I have seen how change fails when there's not enough will and when you only focus on skills – like some change programs that assume that you're done once you provide enough communication and training and tick the right boxes in your change project plans.

Focusing on training new behaviors is not enough. You have to change crucial beliefs as well and adopt new ways of thinking to turn new skills into habits and create lasting change.

7 Crucial Conditions for Culture Change

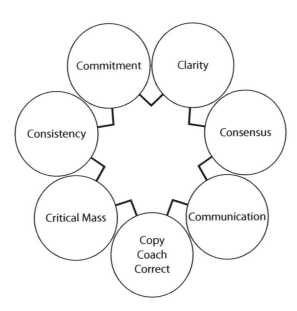

Remember the 7C Framework of Change Success in Chapter 2? Let's check them again before we start our culture change process.

1C: Commitment from the top. The leaders must BE the change as they are the pullers of the culture change. The top executives need to be committed, not only to the change and its expected gains, but to personal change as well. They must be so committed that they are willing to change themselves if necessary and endure the possible discomfort of adopting new habits.

2C: Clarity on current and desired culture. It must be very clear "where we are going" and why. And moreover: why now?

Without clarity, efforts tend to diversify, diffuse and confuse. We need to know where we stand, where we need to go and why we have to move now. Clarity lacks more often than you think. Ask the team leaders or employees to explain your organization's strategy. And you will have your answer if there's clarity for starters.

3C: Consensus. People need to reach consensus about the change. If I just tell you that you have to change, you may feel some resistance. But if we engage in a dialogue, we might both learn and reach true consensus – why we need to change and in what direction and how much. If we agree, we'll have a much better chance at sustainable change. We both have committed ourselves.

Consensus and commitment, engagement if you will, are vital to change. The CEO can't change 1,000 others, not even 10 of them. He can try to influence them, role model, be the change he wants to see. But enough others have to change their behaviors or nothing will change in the organization as a whole. Consensus is created in small teams of people who trust each other. The OCAI–workshop is such a group, but you can work with existing small teams or change circles of maximum 10 people.

4C: Continuous communication. Communicate, have dialogues, ask, explain, exchange. Without communication there will be no understanding, respect, confidence and no will to really make change happen this time.

It's incredibly important to keep telling "Why we're doing this, what direction we're going, how far we are already," and keep a dialogue going on. This is something you can never do enough. Change brings about so much insecurity and uncertainty. Change means that you're entering a situation that you are not accustomed to.

People may need extra explanations – reassurance even and that it might feel awkward but they are going to be just fine. They need to know what's going on at the top of the organization and in other departments. It's really important to keep communicating in various ways about what you're doing and why. Again, use small teams to communicate intensely.

5C: Copy–Coach–Correct. We have seen that people copy, coach and correct each other to do it "our way." This is very important to start off the change: people start copying each other.

Some people start with the change and others might copy them if they are:

- ◆ informal leaders
- ◆ who are very visible and

◆ well–connected and
◆ their new behavior seems to be rewarding.

It's important that people can copy a few role models, who could also be formal managers of course. This is why it's important to work with the formal and informal leaders and people who have a position in which they interact with lots of others – a CEO's secretary can be a great **change agent**.

As a leader, informal or formal, respond to all behaviors all the time – this is a major leadership skill. Utilize the copy mechanism: people will do what you do. BE the change so you can inspire the others. Coach them and if necessary, correct old or undesired behaviors.

The copy–coach–correct mechanism happens in small teams of people who work together. Make sure to work with small teams of people who are visible for each other, who influence and interact. Be consistent and the change will become clear. People might want to check if you are for real and test you... Will you look the other way if I...? Don't.

Show consistency and do it kindly. Explain. But above all; do it. Small behaviors can have a huge impact. Consistently copy, coach and correct. Do this in peer groups of 10 people who work together on a daily/frequent basis – co–create in your change circle of 10.

6C: Continue to Critical Mass. If the behaviors are spreading through the organizational system, you are on the right track. When you keep reinforcing this process of practicing new behavior and more and more people start to think and act in new ways – then, at a certain point in time you achieve critical mass.

There's enough people who have adopted the new behaviors and the system can reach that magical tipping point, when it becomes favorable for the others to change as well. Now it is attractive for the majority to do it, too. Most small teams have made the major changes... At last, even for the people who resisted the change at the beginning – they adjust. The organization is living a new culture and starts to create sustainable change.

7C: Carry On. Last but not least: Carry on. Never, never give up. The minute you let go is the minute people are tempted to go back to old habits and rest in their comfort zones.

Once you've created critical mass – there's a large number of people who are doing things in the new way – you have to keep doing it. This is a matter of discipline, reinforcement, perseverance – no matter what. It takes some time to acquire new behaviors and to get really accustomed and turn them into "automated" habits.

For instance: It may be easy to start on a diet the first day, the second day – but the third day it's getting harder. We need a period of time to keep doing it. We need to tell ourselves why we bother at all – we need to reinforce our beliefs about what is healthy behavior. This is why you have to persist and keep motivating people to do it the new way.

It's like Rosabeth Moss Kanter once said: Everybody likes new, promising beginnings and happy endings. But we sometimes have to struggle through the middle of change. Turning new behaviors, a new culture, into "business as usual" again.

Chariot of Change

How does this magical tipping point work? Let's take a look at the metaphor of the "chariot of change".

When you're introducing a change process in an organization, there are some people – and let's hope they are the executives and the team leaders – who are enthusiastic about change. These people see that this particular change is necessary, but they may also like change in general.

They like adventures, they like to try out new things, they are open to new experiences. These people can become the pullers of the change. They pull the chariot. They inspire everybody. They can be called "positive energizers". They're the change agents (more about them in Chapter 19).

There's often a passive majority. They are not early adopters, they are not particularly fond of change, but they are willing to go along if it's really necessary and the change is persuasive. They'll think: "Okay, I'll try." But they can be passive at the beginning, more or less neutral, waiting to see if it's really worthwhile. They are sitting in the chariot and they are being pulled.

Some people don't like change. They like everything to stay the same. They are okay with the status quo. They have habits they're attached to. Others may have had some bad experiences with change. There may be mistrust or fear, attrition or skepticism. "There's another change program … whatever."

Some are opposed to this particular change initiative because they have a better idea. They are the people who are reluctant to the change – the resistors. They can be real hard critics, openly fighting against the change. But silent sabotage at the back end of the chariot is an option too. Some people might even be pulling it back.

When you try to move the chariot of change, it is tempting to go to the people at the back end and give them a lot of attention. You try to convince them and say "Please, stop pulling it back. It's important. We have to go that way," or "Sit down in the chariot and we'll pull you."

It's an understandable reaction to pay attention to people who are not satisfied and to respond to problems. Our brains are wired to look for things that are not okay, for things that can cause problems – those things will stand out.

Many people were trained to analyze problems in their education, especially managers who have always been warned about the infamous resistance to change and here they find it...

However, the most effective way to start change is to focus on the "positive people" who are pulling the chariot and to support them as much as you can. When the chariot starts moving the passive majority who waited to see if it was worthwhile can come to think "I can see where we're going," and they jump off the chariot and start pulling too.

In the end, you might have a lot of people pulling, a few in the chariot and maybe some people at the back end of the chariot. Now is the time to see if they're willing to come along or not and take measures if necessary.

Keep this chariot in mind when you start a culture change process. In the beginning, the leaders provide the purpose, the necessity and the vision of the change: you paint the dream. Give your organization an image that is appealing.

Persuade with a focus on the positive aspects of change.

Facilitate the ones who pull the chariot of change, support them and they will become change agents and will convince the others to come along. They will be energizing and inspiring. It's your job to facilitate them, because our goal is that they take ownership. It is their culture, not yours alone.

As an outside consultant I may be pushing and pulling to get the change process started, but I can't do their change. They have to take ownership themselves. It's not my chariot – I will leave eventually. As a consultant, you facilitate people to "own" their culture change, to get engaged, inspired and energized and come up with ideas, improvements and really make the change as a group.

Your first attention in change goes to these positive change energizers, then to the majority. Help them persevere. Help them through the middle part – when the excitement of a new beginning fades and the happy end seems so hard to reach.

Show the benefits that become visible along the way, entice the majority. Keep practicing, practicing, practicing – just keep doing it. Finally, you will turn the last resisters around. The people who really can't live with the change might leave the organization in the end.

Group learning

Culture change is an interesting process because it involves individual and group learning at the same time.

As an individual

I have to change the way I think to develop lasting new behaviors. I may hold assumptions about my work and my workplace that I have to adjust more or less.

For example, I will never give my boss feedback on a new process that didn't work – if I believe that being open and sharing failure will damage my career. If I'm rewarded for being compliant and smiling at every new process my boss designs, I have to make a conscious decision to disagree or share unfavorable facts with my boss.

I may have to train my competence to be assertive and provide negative feedback in a non–alarming way. If you just send me to a skills training "Assertive feedback" I might acquire the capacity, but never use it if I still hold this belief about my boss.

I have to be willing to change, or I won't be open to change my belief. After reconsidering my belief, I can change my capacities and change my behavior by applying the new skills.

I tell my boss that it didn't work this time – but he doesn't take me seriously and responds irritated, waving my feedback away. My boss doesn't believe that the new process is not producing the required results. But I persevere. Every time something doesn't happen according to plan, I'm brave enough to present the facts. I know he has a right to know – it's my job to be open with him to improve our processes.

Doing what is best for our organization will advance my career. I'm convinced that this will be rewarding in the long run, somehow, even if this particular boss thinks that I'm a critical person.

If I always share information that may not be nice to hear but is accurate, my coworkers start to copy this openness and we see culture evolve. When we develop new automated routines that are typical for the way we do things around here – we have anchored a new culture.

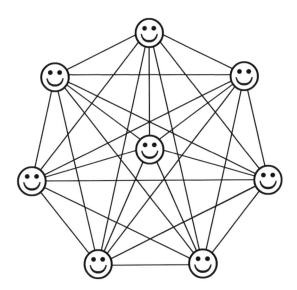

As a group

We need leaders as role models. Brave people who demonstrate the new behaviors, true believers who think that certain habits must change, people who challenge the status quo. Action speaks louder than words. Individuals can support each other to change, especially in small teams – they support each other to think in new ways, to learn the skills, to practice the new behavior, to stick with it when it gets hard.

Then you get leverage – it gets easier when you have more people who do it and others who copy them. You need enough individuals who have gone through this individual change process – adjusting some beliefs if needed, adding the capacities, feeling secure enough to practice the new behavior. The others can follow.

Teams of up to 10 people are a perfect vehicle for change. Small enough to see each other and feel comfortable practicing, big enough to copy behaviors and feel supported. Through the teams, the organization changes. We can reach critical mass. The individuals change, one at a time, but in a group they support each other and make changing faster and easier for others who follow.

However, the same group process may work against the desired change. If you have a group with very strong opinions and the (informal) leaders lack enough will and skill to change, it may be hard. If the majority can't or won't – your change effort will be unsuccessful. The informal leaders may pull the early adopters back. You won't reach the tipping point to the new culture and an organization may fall back into its old habits.

Early adopters may give up without support. It's not easy when you're the only one in a team who is doing new things. If you come back to the office with new skills after an individual training, but the rest of your team hasn't changed – you might give up. They might try to correct you: "Come on, what is this being–assertive thing? You used to cooperate and we liked you better when you did…".

It's a very interesting and subtle process – the individual and the group learning can stimulate or hamper one another. These two factors (individual plus group learning) decide whether your change will be successful in the end. That's why we assess the will and skill of key individuals before we start, and work with the 7Cs as well to ensure group learning, critical mass and persistence.

Easy as… ABCDE

We have seen the iceberg and the two important Bs: Beliefs and Behaviors. If we elaborate on these two levels, we can utilize the "logical levels" of reality. You can use them as levels of change and even levels of personality. They were developed by Gregory Bateson and adapted by Robert Dilts. They provide a foundation to define change in more detail, and you can use these levels when developing your culture change in more detail. I use the elaborate ABCDE scheme mainly with boards and managing teams, while I use the 2Bs with workers and other employees. (I'll tell you more about that later).

The logical, ABCDE levels are:

♦ Spirituality – What do we mean? Your broader meaning as an organization to the world. Though important, this level is not included in the ABCDE scheme for practical purposes.

♦ Identity – Who Are we? Self–image, your mission and your purpose as an organization.

♦ Beliefs – What do we Believe? What do we value and prioritize? Values, norms, convictions, assumptions and feelings that you're collectively sharing in your organization.

♦ Capabilities – What are our Competencies? Skills, resources, planning and people of an organization – everything you can do.

♦ Behavior – What do we Do? Services, processes, products and structures of an organization. This is where they produce outcome and results.

♦ Environment or the Effects of all these behaviors– What do we effect? Look at your building, your market, your clients? What outcomes do they effect?

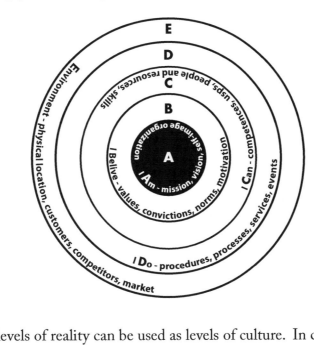

These logical levels of reality can be used as levels of culture. In culture change, we use them as:

A, we Are – Identity;
B, we Believe – the values, norms, feelings;
C, we Can – the capabilities, the people and resources;
D, we Do – the behavior, services and processes;
E, we Effect – the location, market, clients and results.

It's an easy to remember scheme of ABCDE. Defining culture on these levels can help people gain insight into where they are now and where they want to go and how they might get there, including on which levels they must solve any obstacles.

As discussed in Chapter 3, effective change comes from two sides. The ABCDE levels are presented as a circle. On the inside, you have the invisible identity – we are. The next circle represents the beliefs – conscious or not. The next circle shows the capacities – things we can do (but maybe we don't).

The level of behavior finally becomes visible: "the way we do things around here". This produces effects. It has an outcome. That is the environmental effect circle on the outside. Successful change comes from within, working from beliefs to capacities, from will to skill, to finally the level of behavior.

Successful change also emerges outside–in, from changing things in the environment, like sharing desks, changing your office design, using a new system or device. These kind of interventions visible on the outside will "force" people to act differently. They change behavior.

Outside–in and inside–out: When designing change, think of measures and interventions that support these two directions. They work together to produce change at the behavioral level of what we do. And that's crucial, or nothing will really change. We're going to use this ABCDE scheme to help define and implement culture change and we work our way from identity and "abstract" values down to specific, daily behavior and results. We need to create real, behavioral change that sticks.

Summary

We have noticed that real change takes a lot of will. Leaders must BE the change they want to see in their organization. They must walk their talk; if they don't, they might sabotage the whole process in a minute. Apart from the will, we have to assess the skill to change and check our crucial 7C's time and again. Before, during and after the change process...

We recommend a positive approach – focusing on the people who want to pull the chariot of change and who may enthuse the others until the tipping point is reached. Change from two directions, using the ABCDE scheme or the 2Bs (Beliefs and Behaviors) to help your change succeed because it emphasizes and rewards the new, desired behaviors from the inside and the outside. Does this sound interesting? If it is still complicated, bear with me. We will get to the point where I will show you how to do this after the OCAI. First, let's explore the Organizational Culture Assessment Instrument.

Chapter 5
What is the power of the Competing Values Framework?

Culture seems to be about "everything" in an organization. So, where do we start? It's to the credit of Cameron and Quinn that they made culture feasible and operational with the Organizational Culture Assessment Instrument (OCAI). It provides a great, practical starting point for change. Let's take a look at the Competing Values Framework, the four culture types of the OCAI and how to assess culture with the OCAI. The extensive explanation can be found in the book by Cameron and Quinn: "Diagnosing and Changing Organizational Culture".

Competing Values Framework

The Competing Values Framework was developed by Professors Kim Cameron and Robert Quinn of the University of Michigan. They did extensive research on the effectiveness of organizations. They were curious as to what makes the difference when it comes to organizational effectiveness. They found that there are two dimensions that matter most. You can see them as two polarities or competing values – two choices that determine organizational effectiveness.

Those two polarities are, on the one side, internal focus and integration and on the other side, external focus and differentiation. Cameron and Quinn saw organizations who were looking inward, busy with themselves and integrating their activities. Other organizations were primarily looking outside and differentiating their activities to meet external demands. Either an internal or an external focus is one important choice for organizations. The second focus that was found to be very important, is whether you value stability and you like to keep things under control and stabilized or, as an organization, you value flexibility and discretion. In flexible–focused organizations, behavior is more allowed to vary according to differing circumstances.

Two competing values

Those are the two choices that determine organizational effectiveness. Cameron and Quinn put these "competing values" in a framework:

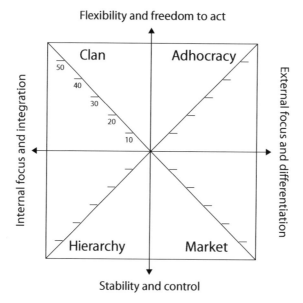

The vertical axis shows flexibility and discretion at the top. At the bottom, you see stability and control. On the left–hand side you've got internal focus and integration and on the right–hand side you see the opposite: external focus and differentiation.

Four culture types are defined this way. At the top right is adhocracy culture – valuing flexibility with an external focus. Their defining verb is to create. At the top left is clan culture. They like to collaborate. They also value flexibility but they have an internal focus and they like to integrate their activities.

At the bottom left is hierarchy culture. Hierarchy culture likes to control. It likes stability and it's busy with improving efficiency and procedures. At the bottom right is market culture. It has an external focus, looking outwards and seeing what the market demands of them. But they value stability, so their response to the market might be controlled, well–planned and if possible, research–based.

These are the four "archetypes" of culture in the Organizational Culture Assessment Instrument, based on the Competing Values Framework. The convenient thing about working with this framework, is that it's easy to remember and it provides a clear framework of reference that people can use to understand their culture and change their specific organizational situation.

Four Culture Types

Now that we have the overview, let's review the specific qualities of each culture type in more detail.

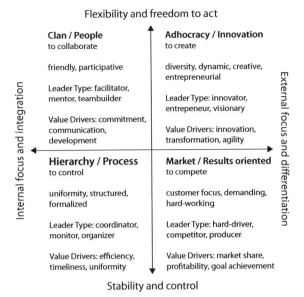

Flexibility and freedom to act

Internal focus and integration

External focus and differentiation

Clan / People
to collaborate

friendly, participative

Leader Type: facilitator, mentor, teambuilder

Value Drivers: commitment, communication, development

Adhocracy / Innovation
to create

diversity, dynamic, creative, entrepreneurial

Leader Type: innovator, entrepeneur, visionary

Value Drivers: innovation, transformation, agility

Hierarchy / Process
to control

uniformity, structured, formalized

Leader Type: coordinator, monitor, organizer

Value Drivers: efficiency, timeliness, uniformity

Market / Results oriented
to compete

customer focus, demanding, hard-working

Leader Type: hard-driver, competitor, producer

Value Drivers: market share, profitability, goal achievement

Stability and control

Adhocracy culture

Their verb is to create. This is a very dynamic, entrepreneurial, visionary environment. If you walk into their building, you get a glimpse of these characteristics. Leaders or executives act as innovators and also have a broker role. They balance any conflicts over resources and try to stimulate and manage innovation and entrepreneurship.

Their value drivers are agility, innovation and transformation. They really like change. They're always on the move, looking for new ideas and inspiration. They believe that innovation and vision and new resources produce effectiveness. This is their theory of effectiveness.

They like surprises, new standards, improving things, finding new solutions, experimenting. It's okay to take risks. Even occasional failures are accepted, if you learn from them. It's a dynamic environment where people learn, experiment, innovate and create.

This is the culture of an organization at their start – there is a new idea to meet an external demand, an entrepreneur sees a market opportunity and jumps in, starts pioneering, experimenting and innovating and what evolves is an adhocracy culture. Examples are Internet Start–ups and technological firms.

Clan culture

In this culture type people like to collaborate. This culture is focused on flexibility, but it has a more internal focus than adhocracy. You notice clan culture when you walk into their offices – you experience a very people–oriented, friendly environment. People are engaged. They are involved in their work and with their coworkers.

The leaders value people and they often play roles as facilitators and mentors. Sometimes they can even act like father figures, checking if everybody's doing okay, monitoring how human resources could be further developed, coaching employees and stimulating participation. People matter.

Clan culture values commitment, communication, participation and teamwork, development of people. This is what produces effectiveness in their opinion. Human development and participation are key. They like empowerment, team building, employee engagement, doing things together, collaboration. There's a lot of clan culture in health care and education because these sectors are people–oriented and this seems to match very well.

Hierarchy culture

To control is their verb. Focused on stability and control, they have an internal focus. Think of a formal and structured environment, everything perfectly organized if you walk into their office. Their leaders are functioning as coordinators to the work in process and they have a monitor role. They check if everything is going okay, if processes run smoothly. This is very important in a hierarchy culture.

They value efficiency, consistency and reliability. When you start a process the outcome should always be the same. Every customer gets the same package of products or services, the same treatment. They also value timeliness and uniformity. Everything should be running smoothly according to fixed procedures and have equal quality and be efficient.

They believe that control and efficiency with capable processes will produce effectiveness. For instance, Lean Six Sigma is a nowadays popular process re–engineering method aimed at improving the efficiency of processes. This fits into hierarchy culture. They like error detection, process control and measurement. Other examples are fast food chains with standardized hamburgers and government organizations that need to deliver reliable services.

Market culture

This is a very results–oriented, "getting things done" environment. You feel it the moment you walk into their offices. The leaders have roles like directors and producers. They are hard drivers of performance themselves. Everybody's working hard. It's very important to get things done. They value market share, goal achievement and profitability. To compete is their favorite verb. There may be competition between departments or coworkers ("Who is the best?") but above all competition with other firms. They like to achieve targets and score well.

Their theory is that competing and customer focus produce effectiveness. They like external partnerships, involving clients, doing surveys, improving productivity, setting ambitious targets and trying to meet them. They like to out–compete the others and win. Think of Philips Electronics in earlier days or General Electric, which were very big organizations focused on market share and performance.

Organizational life cycle

The life cycle of organizations is related to the Competing Values Framework. Most of the time an organization starts up in adhocracy culture – they start with an idea. They have a great innovation. Some pioneers are confident that they will bring something great to the market so they start working on it, from their typical garage. If they have some success, they will grow and need some coworkers.

They develop into a clan culture when they grow. They still value flexibility but they have more coworkers so their focus shifts from the external market to the internal organization because they are busy coordinating their tasks, consulting each other for decision making and collaborating.

This will go for a certain period of time until the organization grows further because they are successful. Then they need more hierarchy culture because they need to organize further and control processes and outcomes. When they get many staff, there's no time to consult coworkers all the time. They make procedures, they set up a clear structure and organize their processes. This can be a painful transition from clan culture, when we knew each other well and collaborated closely. "If I do you a favor, you will help me later on." Now things become fixed and they are organized in structures. It may feel like losing something dear, transforming into a professional business rather than a family.

Then, as a big organization having organized their work, they need to stay successful in the market – after some time of integrating activities and improving control processes, it's time to look outside and see what is happening in the market. What are our competitors doing? What do our customers want from us? They need to know what the customer wants in order to sell their services or products and make money. They set targets that the sales people have to achieve, they need to get things done. So they shift to market culture and focus on profits and targets and market share because they have to. They gain external focus and differentiation, responding to the market.

This is the life cycle of organizations from adhocracy to clan to hierarchy to market culture. But it doesn't end here. Operating as a mature, well–established organization in market culture, you may need to innovate after some time because you face new challenges in your market. You have to start a new life cycle and renew as an organization and start all over in adhocracy culture. It's time to spice things up and to stir innovation and creativity again.

This is one of the challenges all organizations are facing in this rapid, exciting 21st Century. No one can afford to do the same thing for years and years. Change, the new normal and the way to spark the yellow flame of adhocracy culture again, becomes a key feature for successful organizations of this era, that have change built within.

The right mix

There is no good or bad culture in the Competing Values Framework. The culture types are meant to be neutral, every one of them having specific qualities, based on competing values that organizations can focus on. The only thing to assess is whether you have a good fit with your environment.

If you're working in health care, a dominant clan culture aligns with the people–oriented work you're doing and the collaboration we need as medical staff. For patient safety it would be best not to adopt a total adhocracy culture. You need elements of hierarchy culture to ensure quality and reliable processes in health care. Last but not least, some touch of market culture helps finish appointments in time, but too much of it would put too much performance pressure on your shoulders and could harm patient safety.

So it's important that your culture aligns with your employees, your leaders, but also with your customers and the kind of service or products you're offering to the market. Every organizational culture is a mix of these four archetypes. It never happens that an organization has a 100 percent clan culture for instance. They need some contradictory behavior to be successful and respond adequately to different situations. They can have a dominant culture type, which is their main focus, but sometimes they need to vary their approach and you'll find elements of other culture types in their organization as well. If their culture mix suits their situation, this organization will be successful.

The culture archetypes are neutral and generalist. Not good or bad, they present an overview of a culture type and typical values and likely behaviors – but the details differ in each organization. You can see different expressions of market culture depending on the organization.

One organization could have a market culture that focuses more on competition between teams ("Who is the best?"); while another is focused on competition in their market and a third organization is dedicated to working hard and achieving your goals no matter what. All three organizations might have the same high score on market culture. But they have different angles and details within each culture type and the specific expression of the culture archetype varies in each organization. We will discuss this further in Chapter 15.

Assessing the culture types

Let's take a look at how to assess these culture types. When you use the Organizational culture Assessment Instrument (OCAI), how does this tool determine your culture? Cameron & Quinn did extensive research and found six aspects that define culture. Culture comprises many aspects, but these six qualify to determine culture. These six are enough to serve the validity of the model and represent a reliable image of the current and preferred culture type. This way, the assessment takes only 15–20 minutes to complete.

The six aspects are rated in a questionnaire. You assess them once for the current culture and then you assess them again for preferred culture. If you need to change, you can see the difference between current and preferred. For each of the six aspects, you have to divide 100 points over four competing value statements.

Cameron & Quinn designed the survey this way because it resembles real life – you only have 24 hours a day and a specific budget and you have to choose between competing values and goals all the time. If you have to divide 100 points you have to make up your mind what is most important – you can't give high scores to everything. You have to set priorities. We would probably all love to "have it all at the same time" but hey – welcome to reality.

The six aspects of culture that are assessed are:

1. The dominant characteristics of the organization – it's the general overview that you get when you walk into the buildings, when you call us, when you see, hear, read us, it's what stands out immediately.
2. The primary leadership style and the leadership approach that is used within the organization.

3. The management of employees – how are employees and the workplace treated, what stands out?
4. The organizational bonding mechanisms that hold the organization together – the organization glue – why do we work here together?
5. The strategic emphases – what drives the company? What are our consciously–pursued purposes? What is it that we aim for?
6. The criteria of success that determine how victory is defined and what gets rewarded and celebrated and what doesn't, who gets promoted and who gets fired etc.

After you've done the questionnaire, as a result you get a quantified, visual profile of current and preferred culture and the difference between them. You see the Competing Values Framework with that black graph as the current culture and the dashed graph is the preferred culture. What does this culture profile show us in one glimpse? It shows the dominant current culture and its strength. It also pictures the gap between the current and the preferred culture. You can read this as a measure of readiness for change or, if you like, discontent. It shows the dominant preferred culture – how much do we want to change and, if so, in what direction? What are the values that we need to emphasize in the future?

Congruence

The outcome will also reveal your organization's cultural congruence. Cultural congruence means that the six aspects of culture are aligned in the same dominant culture.

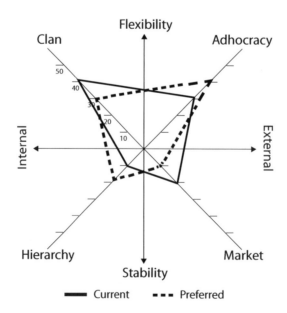

For instance, if I'm working in education and our dominant culture is clan culture, then it is congruent if all six aspects score highest on clan – dominant characteristics, criteria for success, leadership style, management of employees, organization glue, strategic emphases – they must all be people–oriented, focused on collaboration and participation.

If not, we might experience discomfort and discussions and confusion. "What is most important over here? The annual performance review focuses on and rewards me if I meet targets but our managers stress that we need to innovate? I can't do both to the same extent."

Culture incongruence, when the six aspects are not aligned, is often the trigger to change because it doesn't feel good. It takes time and money, irritations, debates and meetings to figure out what is most important.

If the dominant characteristics are clan culture, for instance, but the criteria for success and strategic emphases are rooted in market culture – they focus on targets and production and competing – people get confused. "My boss values targets but our culture and my coworkers are people–oriented. I don't know what to do… should I focus on my achievements or could I take time to relate to colleagues and collaborate better?"

Compare

Your culture profile shows how you relate to your industry group or economic sector, to your country and to other competitors. Do all of the high schools have clan culture, for instance? Or, does a particular successful company differ from other organizations in their economic sector?

If your organization is in jeopardy, does that show from your profile? How is your industry group working? It can help to compare. Though the details of a specific culture make all the difference like we have discussed, the general profile can reveal in what direction successful competitors or economic sectors are moving.

Analyze this profile

Let's go back and take a look at the culture profile again. In this specific profile they have a very strong clan culture in the current situation – it's almost 44 points on a scale of 100 points. When a current culture is very dominant, it may be harder to change it. It will take more energy to make the shift.

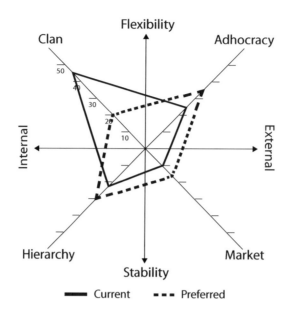

Secondly, you see a very strong desire to change in this particular profile because the preferred culture is a very strong adhocracy, innovative culture. They desire to work more entrepreneurial and look outside. They want more external focus and differentiation. We can check the congruence of the culture if we look at the profiles for each separate culture aspect and see if they are congruent or not, finding the urge to change from this incongruence and its associated discomfort, confusion or conflicts.

You can relate the profile to the organization's life cycle. If we look at this particular profile you could argue that they are growing because they are now in clan culture – and we assume they have started in adhocracy. They'd like to move back to the earlier phase of more innovation and freedom, like when they were smaller and could be more flexible. What would be best? To answer this question you would have to look at what is happening in their industry group, what is their organization size and so on. Some interesting points for reflection.

An OCAI culture profile shows a visual quantitative outcome that provides a quick impression of culture and the desired change. This is an excellent starting point for change. To really change however, you need to do some more work than just do the assessment with your organization.

Because the culture types are generalist – you have to define the outcome with your specific details. You have to customize your result. 44 points of clan culture – what does that mean in your situation? The qualitative part of assessing corporate culture begins when you start to work with the visual profiles and you use the OCAI workshops. Instead of collecting qualitative information the old–fashioned way and doing lots of culture interviews with many individuals who are all sharing their wide variety of personal associations, you now have a framework – a reference for everybody. The OCAI workshops are a great vehicle to start working on change and begin with understanding the generalist outcome with adding important details.

44 points of clan culture are the bones: dress those up with qualitative details – the stories, the examples, the incidents, the typical behavior: what does it mean? Clan culture in one team could mean that we are all friends and we share a lot of private information. Clan culture in the other team could mean a focus on coaching each other because we value human development. So you'll find different details in each situation, though we could both score clan culture at 44 points.

This is done in the workshops afterwards because the assessment is only a starting point to change. In these workshops you become aware of the meaning, you get to work on consensus, you can develop engagement, improvement of your plans and achieve sustainable change – but we'll cover that later on. **Remember the 7–Step Guide to Culture Change** and see how the OCAI fits in:

Step 1 Assess Current + Preferred Culture
This is where we decide to start working with culture, using the Organizational Culture Assessment Instrument based on the Competing Values Framework.

Step 2 Diagnose Quantified Culture Profiles
Time to see the outcome of the assessment in one glimpse.

Step 3 Understand and Add Qualitative Information
The OCAI workshop starts! Participants start discussing their outcome and add qualitative information to better understand their current culture.

Step 4 Raise Awareness, Consensus and Engagement to Change
Participants are enticed to engage and take ownership for their culture.

Step 5 Future Scan, see the Why, the Vision and Strategy
They explore the future, building even more change readiness (whether the platform is burning or not... here they find the answer Why change is necessary now).

Step 6 Understand and Customize Preferred Culture
To achieve the preferred culture, we have to become personal as well. What will I change as of tomorrow?

Step 7 Co–create: How to Change Plan... and DO it
Collectively, customize a plan of How to change – for everyone personally as well as a group, prepare for obstacles and mutual support and then: Just do it!

Summary

We have discussed the Competing Values Framework and how the OCAI assessment provides a validated, visual and quantitative profile on current and preferred culture, based on these competing values. We have seen the development cycle of organizational culture, its congruence and the six aspects that determine culture. These six factors are assessed in the OCAI that is done within 20 minutes.

No culture type is good or bad in itself – it depends on the fit with the products or services, the leaders and employees, customers and competitors of an organization. Every organization has its specific mix of these four culture types and its own expression in typical behaviors and other details.

Because the archetypes of culture are rather generalist, they should be further refined and customized into these details that make the difference for the particular organization.

The OCAI works fast while it gives a lot of information. This is an excellent starting point to change. So, why not try the assessment yourself? Don't just read this, but start doing it... You can check out the free version of the assessment at

www.ocai–online.com/ocai/one/introduction

Bring your personal profile to Chapter 7 when we compare some industry profiles.

Chapter 6 Can you recap the (dis)advantages of OCAI?

Now that you know how the OCAI operates, let's focus on the features and advantages of this culture assessment and its disadvantages. This will help you decide whether the OCAI is the right instrument for now. If it is, this chapter might help you convince the others because you have its features nicely listed.

Validated, focused, fast & feasible

The Organizational Culture Assessment Instrument is a validated tool. It's used by over 10,000 organizations worldwide and that number is still growing since OCAI Online provided it online and added translations in various languages. It's developed after extensive research by Cameron & Quinn and very focused because only six aspects of culture are assessed. From their research, Cameron & Quinn found that these six are enough to cover an organizational culture.

Because it's such a focused tool, you can do it very quickly. People can participate in 15 to 20 minutes and that means they can participate even if they're busy. That makes the OCAI tool very feasible – it's not lengthy and it's not complicated – people can remember the four culture types easily. They do one quick assessment and then they participate in a workshop. The process to change is very clearly structured.

The OCAI tool is available online which saves a lot of work compared to doing the assessment by hand. Using pencil and paper, you might get user errors when people find it hard to divide 100 points or they forget to score one of the statements. The online version of the OCAI tool has a calculator to show how many points are left to divide. Users can't proceed if they forget a statement. The results are reliable in that sense.

Aware & share reference

The OCAI tool makes people aware of culture because they start to think about culture when they do the assessment. Culture is often experienced subconsciously. Things you never think about in your busy workday become conscious and clear when you rate the OCAI statements.

In what way does your manager support you...? ("Never thought about it, just doing my job here.") Do coworkers spend too much time chatting? What is not appreciated here? Remember your first day on the job; how surprised you were when everyone was late for meetings? (Now you are used to it as well).

People might talk about culture to their coworkers. It enhances a general awareness of corporate culture – what is our way of doing things? It gives a shared reference because everyone participating in the assessment gets a sense of the four culture types and takes it from there.

Quantitative basis with qualitative customization

Another important feature are the quantified scores. This can help "sell" the necessary culture change to people from a technical background – technically educated executives or CEOs who like to work with figures and facts, for instance.

It takes the "fluffy stuff" out of culture. It gives culture a quantified basis of how people perceive the current and preferred culture, presented in a visual profile. It's not a subjective feeling of one individual or something that the HR manager made up. This is based on research and a validated tool.

It's easy to add qualitative information in workshops because everybody is sharing the same reference framework. In the old–fashioned way, you used to do interviews throughout the whole organization and people would talk for 30 minutes, expressing personal associations.

Using the OCAI tool, everyone can organize the stories, the incidents, the examples to relate to the culture types. The framework makes it easier to analyze all those stories and understand what makes up our specific culture.

Engage in workshops

Because you ask for the meaning of the profiles in the OCAI workshops, it is very involving and it's a great starting point for change. The OCAI tool is quick and easy but the biggest added value emerges afterwards when you join the workshops and you create consensus and more.

People engage in dialogue to agree on current culture and preferred culture. They understand and specify "Where are we now?" and "Where do we want to go? Why must we go there now? And what does that look like exactly?" True consensus is really important to get people to move and change together.

Conducting workshops and working with your results, people from all levels work together. They engage in the process of becoming aware of culture, understanding the necessity for change and finding specific ways to make the change happen and committing themselves to it.

Collect insights and improve plans

With workshops throughout an organization, you collect a lot of information from all levels in the organization. It's like doing a jigsaw puzzle – you put all those pieces together and you get a great image of your organizational culture, because everybody has their own point of view – the CEO has different insights than the people on the assembly line or your help desk employees who talk with customers all day.

They all bring their information and their points of view to the workshops. They start to make their own plans to change from current to preferred culture. They're adding all this information and they improve the change plans.

If only the management team or board comes up with a great change program (the old–fashioned "exclusive" change way) – and they don't consult the shop floor, finance, marketing, help desks, IT department – their change program wouldn't be as successful or realistic as it could be. All these pieces of information can improve plans with relevant insights from all levels. This can be a great feature of the OCAI workshops.

Engage! Inspire! Energize! And really change...!

Because you're working on consensus and because you ask people to work on a plan, you entice them to take ownership. Maybe they were opposed to the survey at first, but once they see the outcome, they may recognize it and see the opportunity.

Employees can respond like: "Maybe it's interesting. It feels great that you're asking me what my opinion is about culture and that you're sharing strategy and future goals with me. You're asking us what we would do to move toward our preferred culture. I'm going to give my best."

It might become so engaging that you diminish resistance and tackle second thoughts. You might improve plans while adjusting them to justified objections and finding solutions. Because people come up with their own ideas, you can prevent resistance later on in the change process or even sabotage and damage – like in "old–fashioned" top–down rolled out change programs. You can avoid people saying "yes" but doing "no".

This is a great opportunity of using the OCAI tool and workshops. If you're successful in engaging everybody in the workshops and blending it all together in a good change program that the majority can agree on, you enhance momentum for change. You gain so much more than just improvement of plans. If you do it right, this is your chance to engage employees and enhance inspiration, energy and successful change.

Disadvantages and caveats

Are there any disadvantages to the OCAI tool? Of course, because nothing is perfect for everyone all the time. Participants with a lower education sometimes find the wording of the assessment difficult. It can be too academic or it can be hard to relate to for people who are not used to verbalization. This could be something to think about before you start the survey.

In one organization we thought it was valuable to include everybody – also the shop floor, with a low education. So, they had trusted members of the Works Council who helped them understand the statements and they could participate in the OCAI.

We also encountered highly technically–educated people who found it hard to use their imagination. They were surgeons or engineers – but they had a hard time to imagine what was meant by the statements. They were not trained to see human behavior or meaning. They were focused on the contents of their profession.

Some people respond literally and are not used to perceive the meaning that derives from the context or the relationship. (This is why in the online environment of the survey, you can find tips and tricks on how to perceive culture. Just check the sidebar of the online assessment.)

Some people think very specifically. These 'specific' thinkers can experience difficulty to vote for a certain statement or to divide the points. They object: "I like the first part of the statement but I don't agree with the second part," or "The words are just fine, but the adjectives are not good. I'm in favor of competition but I don't like aggressive competition."

Our general guideline is to follow your first impulse. Don't be as accurate as you can be and don't take every statement literally. Just follow this first impulse – try to see an image or relate to a feeling when you read the statement. Don't focus on single words.

Survey attrition

Beware of questionnaire attrition and an overload of surveys. It's not a specific disadvantage of the OCAI itself; it's something we should beware of as executives, consultants or HR people. People are so busy and here is another questionnaire…! Some organizations have a culture (!) of applying and trying several methods one after another – they begin but never see it through.

They like new beginnings and dismiss the method before any results become visible. They love to tick the right boxes, fill out the forms, complete surveys and research – but don't intend to or cannot take action.

So, check any possible overdose of activities before you start. And don't start the OCAI if you're not intending to work with your results.

Don't use the OCAI if you're not intending to take action based on the outcome

This is not the obligatory (bi)–annual employee survey to see if everybody's still happy or not. Too often these surveys are just a legal obligation while the results are thrown in a drawer and they're not looked at anymore.

The OCAI is intended to be a starting point for change. If you discover that the board is not really willing to take it this far, then maybe it's better not to get started at all. Respectfully decline the project. This can be hard because we all have to pay the rent – but it's very important that consultants, executives and HR people remain credible and that we value our integrity as professionals. Let's not raise expectations when the results are likely to end up in a drawer. This can damage trust; the social capital of an organization.

No command–and–control

We should also take into account that there is no **100 percent** control over culture. The OCAI is really a great tool. It gives you a generalist, quick overview of current and preferred culture. You can compare six different aspects. You can divide between subgroups in an organization.

Culture starts to look controllable because you have quantified scores. But you can't change culture all by yourself. We can influence the others and guide them, entice them, finding change agents and tipping points, but we are dependent on the people we work with. We can't change the others top–down, by mandate. Change is the opposite of command–and–control. Sometimes, no matter how skilled and experienced you are, you won't get it done... (Learn from it!)

Collective or personal profiles?

Working with large groups, you have to work with **average profiles** because you cannot work with 500 or 1,000 individual profiles. The average collective profiles are convenient. They share a lot of information. They're not square (like some critics of averages fear) and they look familiar to the participants. I haven't met a group yet who didn't recognize their collective profile.

If you have any doubts about the collective profile, just check on the individual profiles to see what they look like. In the online OCAI version, these individual profiles are delivered to the participants by email. Simply ask people to bring their personal profiles to the workshop.

I have a hammer, so where is the nail?

Beware of the consultant's bias. The OCAI tool could be your hammer. So, everything looks like a nail. We like to use the OCAI tool in many different ways and it can be used for different purposes, but always check if the OCAI is really the best tool to use with this particular organization in this situation.

Having reviewed these caveats, let me share my enthusiasm with you. I'm a dedicated OCAI user, that comes as no surprise. I like it because it is generalist and quick and it provides quantified and visual profiles that are recognized in the blink of an eye. It sells to executives who like figures and facts.

It's very easy to add qualitative information, like anecdotes, stories, examples that illustrate culture: all the details you need, without time–consuming interviews. People can take ownership when you invite them to the OCAI workshops to work on the results. They define and customize their own change process, exchange ideas, gain insights, improve plans or get a better understanding of other groups in the organization. They change their minds and can adopt new beliefs. The workshops serve as a first intervention or a first "new culture" example when employees are not used to being consulted by management.

I like to make the workshops as practical and operational as possible. We work from values, which are very abstract concepts, down to daily behavior. Behavioral change is what you need to bring about real change – you need to specify new behavior and find ways to practice it, spread it and turn it into new routines. Working on behavior, culture becomes operational and personal. It's no longer an abstract entity, but it relates to daily workplace experiences and produces new outcomes in the end.

When is the OCAI tool useful?

You can use the OCAI in various ways and make the change process as extensive or short as necessary. For instance, you can use it quickly for one single issue in one department – that you spend one afternoon on with a team. But it can also be the foundation for a comprehensive change process in a big multinational company as well. For what reasons do organizations, consultants and HR directors use the OCAI tool? It serves as a **zero measurement before or after an intended change**, in the case of downsizing, restructuring or regaining a competitive edge, customer focus or innovation.

The OCAI tool can facilitate **troubleshooting**. If there's a lot of absenteeism in your organization, employee attrition, customer complaints, too many safety issues or you have a feeling that staff is dissatisfied, you can use the OCAI tool to quickly see what people think of current and preferred culture. This can be a starting point to work on those trouble issues.

Of course the OCAI tool is used in **merger and acquisitions**, to assess if two organizations fit together and if the merger would be successful or not. It's been used to assess the readiness for innovation because organizations need innovation to survive in this rapidly changing global market. Evaluate how much adhocracy culture is already present and if people are ready for more innovation and develop plans to enhance innovation in the workshops.

The OCAI has been used in **selecting vendors** for long–term outsourcing. An organization that needed vendors for very complex high–tech services needed to sign long–term contracts – five or 10 years – to ensure this service with a qualified, reliable partner. They found that in the phase of signing these contracts, the vendors promised "We will meet your standards and targets. We'll do whatever you need."

But after the contract was signed and actual collaboration started, they found that the vendor's culture was different. They valued different things. The organization had a dominant market culture, they had to work on time and meet specified quality standards. The vendors often turned out to prefer adhocracy and be creative – "We do this later and we'll adapt this…" The organization used the OCAI to select the best match and partner with a vendor that adhered to the same values and norms.

OCAI is considered in the **recruitment** of employees. If you want to hire a candidate – the receiving team of direct colleagues does the assessment. They use the OCAI tool to assess their current culture profile – "What is our workplace culture right now?" The new hire scores the OCAI tool for how they expect their new team to work. Compared to the actual team's profile, this can be an interesting topic during the job interview that raises awareness with both parties. How well do they match?

Summary

We have discussed the features of the OCAI tool: a quick, quantified, validated culture assessment that serves as a starting point for engaging change, giving the opportunity to improve plans and gain momentum and change readiness.

However, some people find the survey difficult while others are not intending to take action based on the survey. In those cases, the OCAI may not be your right tool at this moment.

Check this carefully before you proceed.

So, have you tried the assessment yourself? Remember: Don't just read this, but start doing it... You can check out the free version of the assessment. Bring your personal profile to Chapter 7 when we compare some industry profiles.

Chapter 7 How much can Culture Profiles differ?

In this chapter we compare some industry profiles to get a better look and feel of different culture types. The financial sector, health care and government stem from our research in the Netherlands. We'll discuss the quantified scores. We take a separate look at the manager's and the worker's views because their profiles tend to differ.

Sector profiles from research in the Netherlands

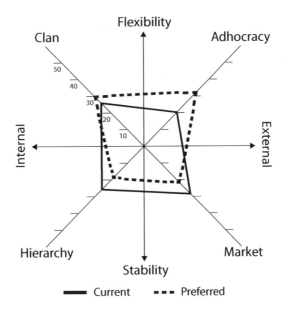

Financial sector

Here we are: the financial sector. This is the profile from our research in 2009, about a year after the credit crunch, based on 133 random participants. The black graph is the current culture and the dashed graph shows the preferred culture: a visual image of "financial culture". They have a pretty high score on hierarchy culture and also on market culture. That seems to align well with how banks are working. They have to follow certain procedures and good governance rules, while bank employees have financial targets to meet as well.

We asked a few bank employees to add stories to this quantified profile and they recognize their culture. They described many procedures to follow – everything is very well structured – and they have to achieve financial goals. Performance is valued in banking. The dashed graph shifts upward: what they would prefer in the future is more clan and adhocracy culture. The increase in especially adhocracy culture is interesting, because one could argue the banking sector had too much freedom and innovation when they developed certain creative financial constructions that partly caused the credit crunch in 2008.

Why would they want more adhocracy culture? What does this mean exactly? When we talked to bankers, they said: "What we mean is that we need a little more professional space. The freedom to do our jobs in our professional way. We currently are stuck in procedures that we have to comply to, even when it doesn't make sense." What they meant was not more creativity, but simply to regain some personal freedom at work.

Health Care sector

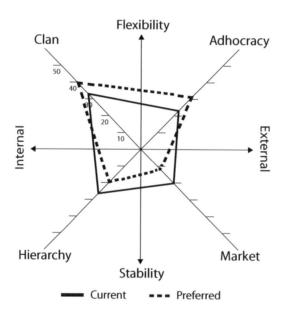

Above you see the profile of the health care sector. We did research in the Netherlands in 2008 and more than 1600 people participated. The black graph shows the dominant culture type for those working in health care: hierarchy culture. They tend to have a very people–oriented culture. They value people and this aligns with health care.

The second important culture type is hierarchy culture, because health care has many procedures and regulations to obey as well. There are very clear structures and practitioners have their position with accompanying authorization to provide specific medical treatments. Legal regulations seek to protect patients by high quality standards. That's the explanation for clan and hierarchy culture currently. Health care workers, from nurses to doctors, recognized this profile as their culture at work.

Also, they recognize the upward shift to clan and adhocracy culture. They'd like to give more attention to individuals, HR development, facilitating and mentoring by leaders. They'd like to be appreciated and acknowledged a bit more. This is their explanation for more clan culture.

As for the adhocracy culture shift, it's the same as in banking – they sometimes feel stuck by procedures, administration (filling out forms) and standardization while they'd like to differentiate between patients. Of course health care should always be safe, but every patient is a different individual. They could spend extra time with particular patients and maybe work a bit faster with the next patient. They'd like to have their professional accountability to decide – instead of getting detailed instructions like "Spend 7 minutes on each case".

They want to diminish market culture in the future. This is partly a reaction on a huge reorganization in the health care sector at that time because hospitals needed to work much more cost efficiently and make more money. As a result, nurses, surgeons and almost everybody in health care felt that they had to work too hard. It's a response to work pressure. They felt: "We cannot give more than this."

Small is beautiful?

Another conclusion from the health care research: We found that the smaller the organization, the smaller the gap between current and preferred culture. On the other hand, the bigger the organization, the bigger this gap. This could mean that people are less satisfied in large organizations.

This we discussed with respondents. They explained that in a large organization you tend to be hampered by procedures and management layers. If you want to make a change or improve existing health care practices, it's very hard to get anything accomplished at all because of the organization's size. You have to pass it on through the layers, push it through departments, convince many others, endure long meetings and wait for final signatures of approval. That is not stimulating to change initiatives. This is where the need for more adhocracy culture derives, to be able to innovate on a small scale within reasonable time frames.

We divided health care in different sub sectors and found that employees in care homes were the least happy workers, followed by those in large hospitals. The happiest workers were the health practitioners who could work individually or in small groups. This is an illustration of the autonomy that today's highly educated professionals value and that seems to be harder to achieve in large institutions.

However, as a reaction to the demand to be more efficient, many hospitals started to merge to share cost and gain large–scale advantages and out–compete other hospitals. They thought that bigger was better. That was an assumption. Later on, it turned out they weren't able to compete any better because they were bigger. Even worse, employees got dissatisfied in these large, merged organizations that lost their identity.

Public Administration

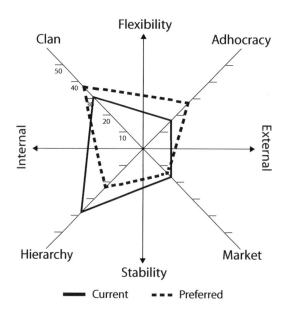

Welcome to the Dutch Public Administration in the year 2010. 451 random government employees participated in this research. They have an extremely high score on hierarchy culture currently. That's a recognizable feature in a government workplace. You can imagine that they have to obey many legal regulations. Procedures, quality and treating every citizen the same way is very important.

Their hierarchy culture is followed by clan culture, because government agencies used to have an internal focus (no external competition) and according to the old prejudice, you could take your time, secured by lifetime employment and chat with your coworkers on the job. But that is now changing. Government agencies are run like businesses more and more.

They prefer more adhocracy culture in the future. In fact, you can see the same shift as we have seen in the financial sector and health care. People explained they want a bit more appreciation at work (more clan culture) and more professional space to work in their own way. There is also a movement in government that fosters innovation – to use social media and web 2.0 applications in serving citizens. Young government employees are preparing for the 21st Century.

Shifts from current to preferred culture

So far, we have seen an upward shift for preferred culture in those three industry groups. In fact, we see that shift almost everywhere in corporations, institutions and economic sectors. We'll discuss what that might mean in Chapter 23. Sometimes the shift is substantial, showing a huge gap between current and preferred culture. When should you take action, based on these profiles?

Professor Kim Cameron shared his rule–of–thumb based on his experience with the OCAI. **If you have a gap of 10 points or more**, it's a "call for revolution". If you have a difference of 10 points or more, based on a substantial number of participants, you need to take action. Change is strongly desired, so you need to do something quickly, starting with finding out what your participants mean and what they need.

If you have a **5 to 10 point shift**, it means that you need to take action. You have to find out what the score really means, why people want more adhocracy culture for instance, and then take action.

From 1 to 5 it doesn't mean that you're doing perfectly well. If you have a difference of 3 points between current and preferred, make sure to check the foundations – what do people mean with this score and what's going on? The details and the stories behind the numbers may ask for some action.

When you have little shift – people seem to be very satisfied and current and preferred profiles tend to be the same, try to find out if this is really the case. 2 points may not be a lot on a scale of 100, but details can make the difference – the divine and the devil are in the details.

So we strongly recommend always checking what the numbers mean, and discover the qualitative information behind the profiles.

The three sector profiles made an upward shift, some of more than 10 points. People seem to be dissatisfied and they desire change, but we don't know why exactly. We have to check on the stories behind the quantified scores. We have to customize this outcome to the specific situation and ask people "Do you recognize the profiles? Can you give some examples? What do you mean if you want 10 points more adhocracy culture? How could that be done? etc."

This is what we're going to do in the OCAI workshops and this is why it is so important, once you've done the assessment and you have the profiles, to work with the outcome and add specific examples and find out what this outcome means.

More about numbers

The health care sector research had a lot of participants – more than 1600 – while the collective profile was not square. From a statistical point of view, you could argue that if you have more participants the profiles tend to get square because all extreme scores are averaged. Large numbers of participants could theoretically produce squares and won't provide any real information. However, in our experience, this hasn't happened (so far). Even with a large number of participants, the averaged collective profile yielded interesting insights that individual participants recognized as their culture.

Managers and Employees

Now let's compare two sub–profiles from one research population. On the left is the profile of the managers and on the right is the profile of all those who don't have a management position – the employees.

The managers experience hierarchy culture but also see some clan culture – that is the black graph. The **staff has a lower score on clan culture**. This is an interesting difference that we see a lot. Managers tend to score the clan culture higher than employees.

Maybe this is because managers feel more comfortable leading their own departments and their self–image is that they are people–oriented leaders. When you ask their staff, you can see that they rate clan culture much lower. They would like to get more appreciation at work, maybe to be facilitated more or simply receive more attention from the management team.

Another explanation is that staff might feel less comfortable because they are not in charge. They may be insecure about what is going to happen or they fear that they are judged – possible explanations why staff rates lower on the friendly, comfortable clan culture.

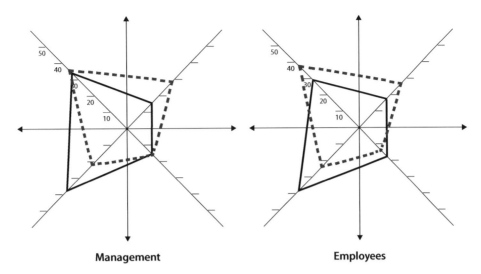

Management   **Employees**

On the other hand, if you look at the score for market culture on the right–hand side, you can see that **staff experiences more market culture** than the managers. It may not be an extreme difference, but it is a difference.

The people who are doing the actual work and who add value to customers (like front office employees, shop floor, factory employees, nurses, teachers, care takers etc.), experience more market culture than executives, boards, managers, supervisors who control, plan, coordinate and create vision and strategy. This might mean that "the workers" experience that they have to work hard and they face performance targets and challenges. Managers perceive work pressure as less than their staff is actually experiencing.

Different groups within an organization all have their own specific emphases; depending on what they value and how they perceive culture, depending on their position in the organization, their profiles may differ. It provides some insight in how different "sub–cultures" perceive their organizational culture.

You can compare different locations, or different departments – marketing, sales, finance, shop floor or management. You can also compare different professions within an organization, for instance surgeons and nurses who are working in the same department but still have a different view on their workplace culture.

Some organization's profiles

Let's browse past a few profiles of individual organizations from different industry groups. You get a better look and feel of what these profiles look like.

We start with the culture profile of a **bank**. You can see that they are currently mainly in hierarchy culture – very high scores. It's a higher score than we just saw in the banking sector as a whole.

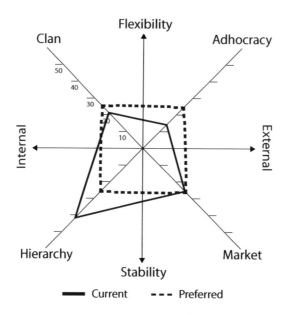

They have to follow a lot of procedures and legislation. In this particular bank, you can see that they want more clan and adhocracy culture. Their profile looks like a call to action Their "pain" is in hierarchy, their "gain" is in adhocracy culture.

The next is a **high school**. This is a totally different image. You can see that they have a people–oriented clan culture.

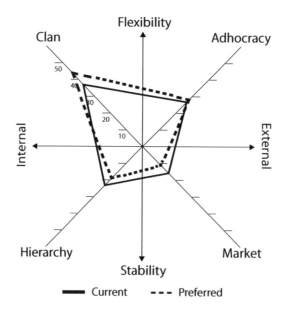

They have to follow regulations – hierarchy culture – and they have to teach their classes and deliver educated children according to results–oriented market culture. Sometimes teachers can explain courses in their own way and leave the textbook, which could be a touch of adhocracy culture. The main feature here is the people orientation.

Clan culture seems to fit well when you're working in education. Their preferred profile focuses on even more clan culture – they like to go on with that.

Below is the profile of a **consultancy firm**. You can see that they have to work hard and compete because their highest score is on market culture. This aligns with stories from consultancy where you have to work long hours and perform really well to make a lot of money, preferably.

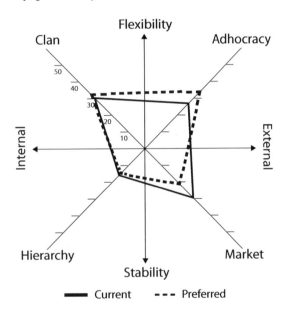

You can see that the consultants in this particular firm would like to have a little less targets. They'd like to have a bit more professional freedom so their highest shift is toward adhocracy culture, while they abandon the competitive market culture somewhat.

Next is a profile from an **engineering company**. You can see the same pattern – they have to work hard because their highest score is on market culture. They'd like to make an upwards shift to clan culture. Their challenge is to shift from results–oriented to a people–oriented culture. Such a shift along the diagonal axis is not easy. We'll get back to this in later chapters.

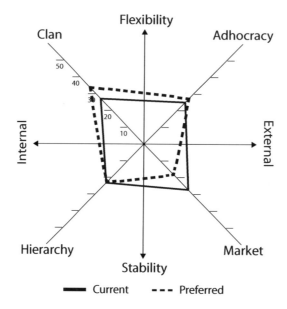

A firm of **IT consultants** shows a different profile because their highest score is on adhocracy culture. In this particular case, they had to solve very complex software problems while every problem was unique so their IT consultants faced many challenges. Employees needed to be intelligent and innovative, experimenting, even risk–taking, to solve those complex problems. That's why you see this dominant adhocracy culture.

They were pretty satisfied, but sometimes it turned out too chaotic. It may be sometimes too creative. Their biggest shift was from adhocracy culture to a bit more order and structure, following procedures, taking notes, doing it the same way again and

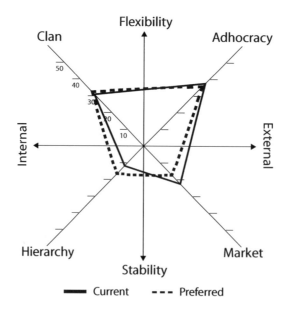

utilizing lessons learned and knowledge management, because they voted for more hierarchy culture in the future. This was their challenge.

An **IT maintenance company** looks different. Maintenance problems are more straightforward and employees have to solve the same issues over and over again. They just follow the steps of the procedure to help their customers when they have IT problems. Dealing with "standardized" problems that you could solve just following the procedure, they didn't have to be very innovative and creative.

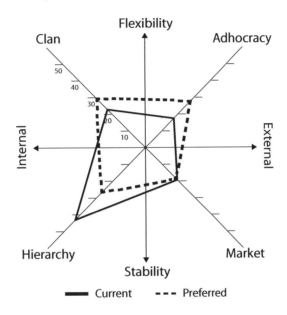

However, the people in this organization were not satisfied. There is a huge shift away from hierarchy culture. They wanted to be more creative and have some professional freedom, next to more of a people focus.

Last but not least, look at an individual profile of one participant from an insurance company. This individual profile is very extreme. Sometimes the individual profiles look just like the organization profiles, but some people tend to score on extremes.

Maybe there's something extraordinary going on in this organization that they respond to. This person was fed up with a dysfunctional hierarchy culture and feeling stuck in procedures. They wanted to be seen as a human being at work, hence the high score on clan culture for the future.

If it is feasible, we recommend to work with the individual profiles as well. If you use the collective average profile you have a convenient reference and overview of what everybody is feeling. But if you have enough time and not too many participants in a group, you can compare the individual profiles.

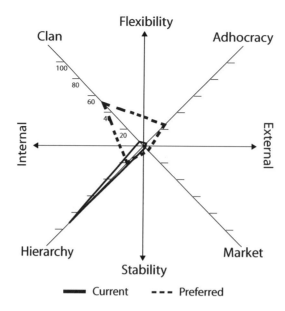

It can bring interesting discussions and great insights because people can differ so much and a dialogue about their perspectives may add to better understanding and even team building. But this can't be done with large numbers of participants.

Separate profiles for 6 culture aspects

We have compared different profiles and browsed past some typical profiles from varying economic activities. In the Organizational Culture Assessment Instrument, not one but six culture aspects are assessed. They can be profiled separately. Let's take a look:

The **Dominant Characteristics** is the first culture aspect that is rated in the OCAI tool. This organization below has a hierarchy culture. When you walk into their buildings, you see that they are formal and structured. Everything happens according to plans and procedures, people conscientiously follow the rules and the receptionist will make sure that you wear your badge and sign the entry form as a visitor before you can enter their building. Moreover, you might have to sign again when you leave and hand in your badge.

You might see many meetings going on and people quietly working behind desks, while every department has their own office and things look very well organized. The secretary brings you coffee – the boss makes you wait...Just some examples of the impression you may have meeting them. You can also see that they'd like to get a completely different outlook in clan and adhocracy culture for the future – they'd like to aim for more flexibility.

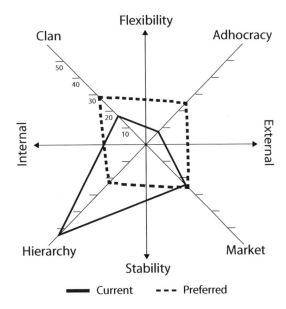

The second culture aspect is **Organizational Leadership**. Look at the profile below – it's rated highest on market culture. The leaders of this organization tend to be hard drivers, working hard themselves and expecting the best results of their staff. They tend to be competitive.

So while the first glimpse in dominant characteristics is hierarchy (focus on formal procedures and efficiency), the organization as a whole is led in a very results–oriented way. Profit and getting things done, making your targets, is valued. Decisions by the top executive team are based on competitive criteria and targets.

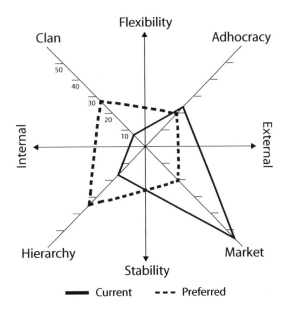

Management of Employees – the highest current score below is on both hierarchy and market culture. Employees are managed by their team leaders with a focus on both procedures, efficiency as well as targets, results and accomplishments.

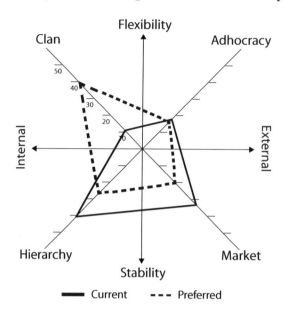

In daily business life, it matters to get the right signatures and approval, follow the formal procedures as well as make sure you achieve results. There is little space for improvisation, variation or situational flexibility. For example, you can't make a deal with a customer to close the sale. You'll be rewarded to follow the normal sales script and guarantees, delivering conformity. If you lose the customer because of the strict approach, that's too bad. You are managed according to stability, uniformity and certainty.

Organization Glue – what bonds people in the organization. It's again hierarchy culture: the process focus. They relate to each other by position, procedures and process. They feel bonded by their functions and positions in the same organization, by their joint efforts to make the process operate as efficiently as possible. They are not primarily bonded by friendship, personal interest, innovating or learning or improvising.

Strategic Emphases show an interesting polarity. They focus on efficiency, timeliness, reliability – achieved through formal procedures, a clear structure and maybe quality control (Hierarchy culture). But their strategic goals aim for innovation, growth and renewal as well (Adhocracy culture). They'd like to have the best of both worlds. Keep reliability as well as achieve innovation.

Third, they need to make money and achieve results too (Market culture). The official strategy focuses on other aspects than the Organizational Leadership for

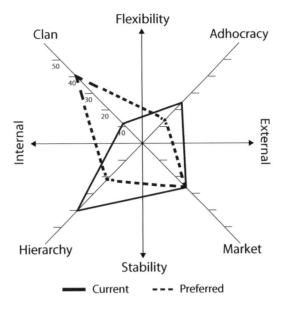

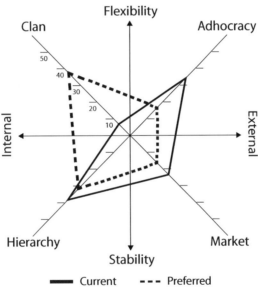

instance, sending out a mixed message: We need you to innovate and grow AND keep efficiency and reliability at right levels. Meanwhile, we lead this organization towards results... targets are sacred. You start to feel the confusion, the competing values, the discussions: what is more important when...? Culture trumps strategy, so there's a chance that this organization has created a paper tiger with their strategic emphases. It could be wishful thinking to aim for this much innovation. We could expect conflicting visions judging by these profiles.

Last, but not least, below are its **Criteria of Success**. They are rated highest on hierarchy culture. When it comes down to what is rewarded and who is having success

– they are the employees who are reliable and conscientious, those who make sure to follow the procedures, tick the right boxes at quality control, wait for permission (the right signatures), show up at the appropriate meetings, those who know their place and contribute to the processes that matter.

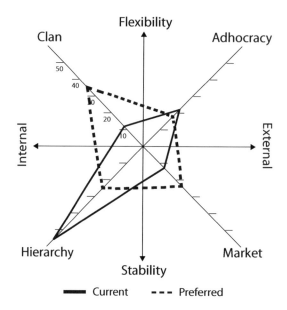

The score is very high, indicating that these success criteria come from way back and are deeply rooted, maybe the remains of an earlier leadership style. So, the six culture aspects can turn out to have different profiles. They supply more information on specific aspects of an organization.

Congruence

Currently, this culture is not completely congruent. They are not scoring in the same dominant culture type. Though hierarchy culture provides a sound basis in focusing on processes and reliability, their Organizational Leadership is driven by results and competition, while their Strategy and Goals aim for innovation and dynamic improvisation.

Congruence means each of the separate profiles has the same dominant culture type. When your organizational culture is congruent, it is comfortable because everything is based on the same values. There are less misunderstandings and confusion; there are no contradictory values that you have to discuss all the time. You don't need time–consuming debates about what is most important. Everything is aligned. Your manager is working from the same values as you are and it's very clear what is successful and what is not.

In case of incongruence, it means that you might have a people focus when it comes to Organization Glue, so "We are collaborating and we are loyal to the team." But when it comes to Criteria for Success, the ones who meet their targets and have a competitive angle get promoted.

Contradictory behavior emerges when a culture is not congruent. However, you do need contradictory behavior to be successful. The most effective organizations vary their approach if necessary to respond to changing circumstances. It doesn't mean that incongruence is bad, but it can feel awkward, stimulating discussions or confusion.

The six profiles above are not congruent. You can have a total of 24 differences in six profiles with four culture types. These profiles have 10 out of 24 differences to the average score. That means it's not congruent but it could be worse.

What needs attention in this culture are the Strategic Emphases with their extreme score on adhocracy culture as well as the Organizational Leadership with its focus on results. The question what this means, is worth a dialogue in the OCAI workshops.

Summary

We have seen that different industries produce different culture profiles. Individual organizations differ from each other, and within organizations differences exist as well.

These can be functional differences if they're not too deviating, depending on department, profession and position, aligning to the nature of the accounting department or the sales force. Small accents can be different as long as the main values of the organization are collectively shared.

We've also seen that large and small numbers of participants can both produce extreme scores. Now you know to mind the 10–point gap – that means change is necessary. Congruence means that all six culture aspects rank in the same dominant culture type.

And what did your personal profile look like? Compare this to the profiles we've just discussed. What do you expect to see in your (client's) organization...?

Remember: Don't just read this book, but start doing it... Without doing, nothing ever changes.

Chapter 8

How to use the OCAI in your situation?

Once you have decided to use the OCAI tool, there are practical choices to be made before starting the assessment. We will discuss a project group for change; the objective, the target group and definitions for the assessment; the choice of profiles that you want to have calculated; issues of participation, privacy and openness; and some matters about the planning and duration, progress and ending of the assessment.

The Change Project Group

Every change initiative needs guidance. And especially in culture change, you need to involve everyone or nothing will change. This calls for the organization of many practical matters.

Setting up a guiding group is not necessary when you work with one team, say a maximum of 20 people. The team can do the assessment themselves and then start working with the results. However, when you're working with a large organization, you need to organize things and you might install a project group to guide the change process.

This change guiding group has several tasks:

◆ They represent staff, from CEO to shop floor (including the Works Council)
◆ They define the purpose of the assessment
◆ They organize practical matters and monitor the process; they guide the change process
◆ They take care of internal communications about the assessment and the change
◆ They act like change agents: explain the necessity of the assessment and subsequent change process
◆ Preferably, they can BE the change. They entice others to participate and change.

Who should participate in this project group in a large organization? It is important that the members are voluntary members of this project group. It shouldn't be obligatory – that would not provide the right energy to get started on a successful change project.

Preferably the members are from all levels and they are interested in organizational culture, change and behavior. They have affinity with the topic. Make sure that they are engaged people who care about the organization and its future.

It is useful to include informal leaders because they are able to persuade their coworkers to participate in the assessment and to keep a positive attitude towards change. Next to the CEO and the HR manager and a representative from the Works Council (who are very often a part of this group), you could invite some executives that you need buy–in from, but also "positive energizers" with lots of connections in the organization. (More about positive energizers in Chapter 21).

The composition of this project group, with such important tasks – to entice people to participate and to change – is important. You want to make sure that you can work with them and they are able to guide this process.

Selecting the members is a subtle and sensitive process because people can easily feel excluded. It is essential to be able to explain very well why these particular people are participating in the project group for change. Beware of the appearance that they are all friends of the CEO and it's a handpicked fan club.

Consultants: a warning

In the hurry of getting started or the euphoria of winning the contract as an external consultant, this sensitive but essential process of inviting the right members to the change guide group is easily overlooked.

However, as an outside consultant you may be hired after the Culture Committee or Change Group is already launched and you'll have to deal with them. The first step has been taken already and this is your first encounter with organizational culture...

It is important to check if you can work with them – or, in what way you can. It is often more damaging to dismiss a group once it is formed. For your own sake, for your results, reputation and work pleasure, resign when you can't work with the situation you encounter or when you discover one of the success conditions (Remember the 7Cs: Chapter 4) is not sufficiently covered.

The objective of the assessment

An organization chooses to work with the OCAI for a particular reason. We have to define the objectives clearly and make sure that everybody understands its purpose.

For instance, the objective could be to check if a merger or acquisition is feasible. Or, there could be internal differences that you'd like to solve. Another purpose could be employee contentment and checking readiness to change. Or maybe there are certain symptoms, like absenteeism or attrition, that indicate that change is necessary.

Target group

Once we clearly know the purpose of the assessment, we're able to choose the target group: the people who will be invited to participate. The target group depends on the objective. If you see a lot of absenteeism company wide, make sure to include all employees. But when you're going to work on a brand new strategy, you might begin with the board of directors or the top management team only.

If you want to compare two locations, because one is performing well and the other isn't, you could just include the two locations. If there's one team with certain problems, just include them.

Explain the objective and its associated target group carefully, so no–one feels excluded. It may cause damage not to include a whole organization because people may feel excluded. Sometimes it ignites mistrust or lessening motivation when people feel they are not important enough to be invited...

Inclusiveness

We generally recommend to include everyone if possible. It engages people and enhances the general awareness of corporate culture. Using the online tool, it is easy to invite everyone while it only takes 15 minutes of their time and there is no extra cost involved.

This inclusiveness matters. Remember the critical mass that you need for change and the chariot of change. Culture won't change if you're not including everyone. We cannot demand a sustainable change by tomorrow top–down; we need to include everyone, bottom–up and give them a chance to co–create and prepare.

The decision to use this assessment now may be a top–down initiative, but it is aimed at emerging bottom–up change, when you invite employees to work with its outcome in the OCAI workshops.

However, some organizations don't want to include everyone.

This decision might damage the social capital in an organization, but if you don't want to raise expectations or the assessment is not relevant for all departments, it can make sense.

Some organizations prefer to work with random samples because they fear that allowing everyone to spend 15 minutes on the OCAI, adds up to many lost working hours. My answer to that is that sabotage, resistance or demotivation during a change process will add up to much more lost work time. This time spent in advance, will return its investment during the change process.

If you prefer samples, you have to make sure they are truly random.

Another reason to use a sample can be to use the OCAI tool as a pilot study to see how it goes, before deploying it in an organization.

The best is voluntary participation. Make sure that it's not an obligation to do the assessment. Mandatory participation may produce doubtful results – like participants scoring all four culture types at 25 (adding up to 100) to get it over with, without displaying any real information.

Their boss tells them but they don't feel like it – for various reasons (e.g. a lack of trust, fears of privacy and career damage if you speak your mind). If you put so much pressure on, it could damage relationships at work. It's better to find out why people wouldn't want to join the survey – and try to solve those issues.

Voluntary participation however, could be biased as well. The majority could be people who are dissatisfied and like to make their point about everything that's wrong within the organization. On the other hand, the assessment could also attract the positive people who like to contribute to their organization – while the dissatisfied people have lost their faith in change or their interest in the organization.

Voluntary participation can go either way. The only way to find out is to take a look at the overall participation rate, check on the scores (any interesting deviations?) and to ask participants in the workshops what the profiles mean to them. In our practice, this possible bias hasn't been an issue (so far). Mostly, people recognize their profiles and are willing to work with them.

Define key concepts and units

Before starting the assessment, we have to make sure that all participants are thinking about the same unit when they read "organization" in the survey. You have to set the definitions clearly. What do we mean by "organization" – is it our own team, do we focus on the complete department or the entire organization? We have to tell people in advance what unit to focus on.

The same counts for preferred culture. Should people focus on the next two years? The next five or ten years? You could specify with future events: "The preferred culture is the situation after the merger," or "after the product launch," etc.

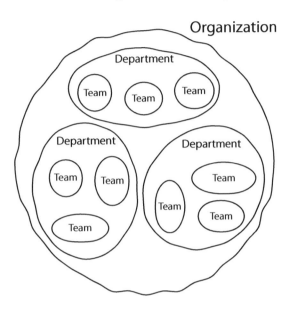

You can explain this in your instructions when you invite participants to the assessment by email. You can also repeat it on the online instruction page: "Please focus on this unit; please focus on this future, in this timeframe."

Decide on the profiles

We also need to make a decision about the profiles that we need.

For instance, if your organization experiences employee attrition and absenteeism, a profile of all employees is relevant or at least of the particular units with high absenteeism rates. But you might also want to check the profile of their team leaders or managers to see whether there are substantial differences in how they perceive workplace culture.

In case of a merger, you would at least need the two collective profiles of the merging companies to compare. If there are conflicts, you can do the same for two arguing departments.

In case of a zero measurement before change, you could work with one collective profile or make separate profiles for departments and see the internal culture differences in the organization.

It depends on the purpose and the information you need, how many and which sub–profiles you'd like to get from your organization's population. Common sub–profiles are different departments and management as well as employees separately.

Planning and Duration

Another topic to think about is the time schedule and duration of the assessment. My recommendation is to take at least two weeks for the assessment. This enables everybody to participate, even when they're busy or when they're traveling for work. As a rule of thumb, we use four weeks as a maximum.

If the assessment would be open for three months, for instance – the first participants might assess a different situation than the last participants three months later. If it's open too long, interest might wane and a sense of upcoming change will fade.

A time slot of two weeks, with a maximum of four, helps to create momentum and expectation. Especially if you have already announced and scheduled the OCAI workshops to look forward to...

Privacy and Openness

When they do the online assessment participants have to enter their full contact details. This might scare some people. But their privacy is guaranteed. This is necessary to identify them – and prevent abuse of the system.

The demographics serve to identify participants who belong to particular sub profiles, e.g. managers or workers, department A or B. The contact details are used to send people their individual scores. The individual profile by email is a confirmation that the results were stored in the database correctly and is a way to thank people for participating.

Another important purpose is to make people more aware of their culture at work. It enhances an active attitude when people start talking and thinking about their individual profiles. Last but not least, they have the opportunity to work with their individual profile when they attend the OCAI workshops.

Administrators of the organization's assessment account are able to see the number of participants who did the assessment so far, but they're not able to see who they are. This is a hard guarantee.

During the assessment...

The progress of the assessment reflects current culture. Do people need reminders or is the assessment done within the first week?

One big engineering company with 200 participants did the assessment in two days. They had a strong results–oriented market culture. The majority joined within 48 hours.

Other organizations may need extra reminders. They could have an easy–going culture where you can get away with things easily. But it could also reflect resistance or a lack of communication/understanding about the reasons why the OCAI could be helpful.

Participation rate

The assessment can encounter very low or high participation and it may be tempting to jump to conclusions. There are so many reasons why people don't do the survey or on the contrary, why everybody is participating, that you cannot go by the numbers alone. You have to ask for the meaning.

For instance:

Low participation can be caused by mistrust. "I don't trust my boss and this organization. I'm worried about my privacy."

Another reason for low participation can be resistance – "I'm opposed to the changes. I like the status quo."

People could suffer survey attrition. They just had the biannual employee survey that usually ends up in a drawer and here's another one. It could be technical frustrations because some organizations have a firewall that makes the online survey slow. People could simply be too busy with an overload of projects. The timing isn't right. Sometimes people don't see the value or they don't believe that culture can be changed. They might feel indifferent – "Whatever. I'm looking forward to 6 o'clock and then I can go home."

So many reasons – and we cannot jump to conclusions. The same goes for high participation. It looks like everybody's engaged. But the scores could reveal all employees are dissatisfied about the status quo and they all grabbed the assessment to ventilate this feeling. High participation could express positive involvement – "Let's improve things," or discontent – "Let's express that it's terrible to work here."

Rules of thumb regarding participation

When do you have enough participants to provide a valid and reliable impression of the organization? Let's take a look at some rules of thumb regarding numbers.

Under 20 participants

If you have less than 20 participants, a group profile is great to give a quick overview. It provides a reference. But it's feasible to discuss individual profiles and to see all the differences. Individual differences may stir a meaningful dialogue about culture but can also be traced back to different personalities or positions.

Why is one team member experiencing hierarchy culture while the other thinks it's mostly market culture, for instance? The team discussion can stimulate mutual understanding and respect within the group, but also point to blind spots that the majority tends to forget...Under 20 people the collective OCAI team profile is useful, but also ask participants to bring their individual profiles to the meeting.

Under 50 participants

Let's imagine you have 50 participants from an organization of 100 employees. From a statistical point of view, their group profile gives an overview and is indicative for the organization as a whole, but it is not strictly representative. It provides a good impression and in most cases people recognize this collective profile and say "That looks like our culture."

In case of many participants, we work with collective profiles because it is not feasible to discuss individual profiles in a plenary session. However, you can divide your attendees in smaller groups to learn from and have a dialogue about the individual profiles.

50–100 participants

With 50 to 100 people of a larger population, the collective profile is indicative and tends to be representative. For instance, when we had 100 participants in our health care research, the outcome of the assessment was set. The profile remained the same even when the number of participants grew to over 1600. In market research this rule of thumb also applies. When they call 100 random people, they get an overview of the opinions of a whole country or market. When you reach over 100 participants, you're secure from a statistical point of view. In that case, work with the collective profile.

What is a "normal" participation rate? We see big differences among organizations. In one very large organization the participation rate was 25 percent, which wasn't very much. Because they were large, the outcome was statistically safe (600 participants) so they could work with their results in workshops.

In this case, the majority felt indifferent towards the organization as a whole; it was so big that they focused on their jobs. Their challenge was to engage people to care about the organization. On the other hand, some organizations reach a 65 to 90 percent participation rate. In small teams participation tends to be higher. People cannot hide in small groups if coworkers ask one another if they did the survey yet. People feel more obliged to participate by peer pressure.

Group and/or individual profiles?

When the survey is done and closed, the outcome consists of individual profiles for all participants and the collective, averaged profile for current and preferred culture of the organization as a whole, as well as separate profiles for the six culture aspects and any sub profiles (separate group profiles for departments, levels or professions).

One word about individual profiles: those are strictly personal. Participants of the online tool receive their personal profiles by email. But their bosses, coworkers or corporations never receive these individual profiles. If you want to work with personal profiles in your meeting, you have to ask individuals permission to bring their profiles to the workshop and share them with you.

When should we work with group profiles and when should we rely on individual profiles? Cameron & Quinn recommend to work with individual profiles. That's why all participants get their individual profile.

But working with all of them is sometimes not feasible. When you're working with a large organization, you can use the collective group profiles as a reference and later on, in the OCAI workshops, people can work with their individual profiles in small groups.

Summary

There are some things to think through before starting. The organization of the assessment and the subsequent change process is often done by a Change Group. Its composition is very important to credibility, trust and motivation for the change.

The organizers define the exact purpose, the concepts and target group to join the OCAI. We plead to invite all staff to do the assessment. Participation rates vary greatly between organizations and relevant information about the current culture in an organization may be revealed. This will be helpful when you enter the change process.

Chapter 9 How do you Communicate?

The importance of internal communication cannot be stressed enough. Remember the 7Cs from Chapter 4, the conditions for successful change? Here's 4C: continuous communication. Let's take a quick look at different communication levels, your internal communications plan and how to communicate. Lack of communication is an important reason why change fails and resistance develops. CEOs or managers decide to do an assessment to prepare organizational change, but they might forget to give enough attention to communication.

To change involves communication – all the time. This may be tiring when you are leading change. As a CEO, change consultant, HR manager or a member of the Change Group, you're accustomed to the subject. You know everything about it, you've read this book, you've discussed it and thought it over. But for the other staff it's different. They are busy doing their jobs – and they may not see why change is necessary. It's your task to keep communicating about the change and entice people to come along.

Invite people to do the assessment. Entice them to think about their preferred culture. Entice them to work with you in the OCAI workshops and to really get them engaged.

Our goal is not to pull the chariot of change as consultants or HR people. The goal is to have people take ownership and start to move themselves. That is why we need to communicate well. It's great that we understand the OCAI and culture change. But it's essential that the others understand the change.

Communication isn't the whole story, but it is a condition for successful change, remember 4C. More important than planning communication, is to simply do it: communicate. Continuous communication is not a one–time with the CEO inviting everybody to the survey and then to the workshops and finally publishing the results on the intranet. That will not do.

You need communication like a two–way interaction, exchanging information, continuously. Explain what you're doing and why you're doing it. Answer questions and stay open to the responses.

Listen to concerns and see what you can do about them. Keep communicating even though it may get tiring. The rule of thumb is you can never communicate too much in a change process.

Large organizations and communication planning

An internal communication plan can help facilitate the change in larger organizations. When you have a smaller team, it may be enough to interact with your people all the time. The communication plan is not meant as a paper exercise, but to become aware of different ways of thinking and different target groups and to help communicate. You're not done after sending the invitation to the assessment. You're not ready after one explanation. In large organizations, it may be wise to include the communication department in the Project Group for Change.

The plan defines the core messages you would like to communicate to these target groups. Target groups may be defined by their response to change. You may want to stimulate the change–early adopters and to comfort or secure the change–avoiders. Important general messages are why the assessment is necessary; that everyone is included and why we need to achieve this particular change.

Utilize various communication means, like emails, speech, bulletins, personal initiations, workshops, meetings; you can have messages on the place mats in the lunch canteen, etc.

Though written communication is a great reference during change, the most vital and effective communication is verbal and non–verbal in small workshops and one-on–ones. It provides the opportunity to connect and understand well, to talk in a way that leads to true consensus, meaning and decisions and ultimately, to do it. This interaction cannot be completely planned and controlled in a communication plan.

Two responses to change

When you use the OCAI tool people start to expect change. Change leads to a new, unknown situation and may cause anxiety, enthusiasm or reluctance, depending on the individual, current culture and former experiences with change.

You might see discomfort – people are no longer working in their comfort zone. "I have to change the way we do things around here but I'm used to my old habits." This can feel very uncomfortable and create tension. People may start guessing about the change and start to feel insecure.

On the other hand, change may also lead to curiosity and expectations and even excitement. That depends on your personality type and your earlier experiences with change. The people who are starting to pull the chariot of change are the people with a positive attitude who are open to new initiatives.

The passive majority in the chariot, or the people who resist, experience more tension, discomfort and insecurity. We have to focus on those groups to give them the information they need. Stimulate the change agents, explain to the majority and respond to the fears and objections of the resistors.

What we want to avoid are wild tales and gossip. Anxiety and fear, indifference or distrust are impediments to successful change. I have often seen distrust by workers toward the managing team. "What are the executives up to? I'm not sure but I'm feeling bad about it." This sentiment can spread easily. "Let's resist this."

On the other end of the spectrum, you'd better avoid too–highly–set expectations about the change, because this can damage an organization as well. If the expectations get high but you cannot live up to the promises, people will get disappointed – you might demotivate and discourage your change agents. A communication plan may help you stay aware and communicate rightly and timely to respond to these needs.

"We don't know yet"

Communicating continuously means that you have to share information all the time. In general, information reduces insecurity. The meta–message of communication is: "We respect you and that's why we want to tell you about it." Information in itself is a deed of respect.

Information may contain content like: "We don't know yet. We're still in a decision making process but we think it's so important that we will let you know." Some executives hold their fire and won't say anything until they are absolutely sure about something. But if people know there's change ahead and they experience three months of silence, they may get scared and wild tales and anxiety emerges. It's best to avoid that, not just because it's a waste of energy, but it may be hard to turn these sentiments back.

The best thing to do is to tell people you don't know yet what to do. It makes executives look like normal human beings and it can make change less scary. Persuade CEOs or managers who are reluctant to share information or their own "dunno's". It's better to communicate. No communication enhances distrust.

Be as open as you can be. Be honest. Be timely. Be a role model for those executives who feel scared themselves or who are not used to communicating all the time.

Communication layers

Communication has three crucial levels:
♦ Connect: listen and understand
♦ Talk: words
♦ Walk: behavior

Effective communication requires all three levels to be present. We must first connect, make "rapport" to be able to truly communicate. If we don't, our talk will not be heard or understood or appreciated. It means nothing and will be dismissed. If we do connect, we understand the other and can adjust our message to help them understand and change.

If we have truly connected, we are able to create meaning. We need talk to create consensus, to influence each other, to discuss the situation and to really agree on this particular change. This is the level where some change initiatives end. In some cultures people love to talk about things. They can talk for ever but will not reach the phase of action. They prefer talking above doing.

The talk–trance can be culture – a habit that is reinforced by copying, coaching and correcting. Some organizations are loaded with meetings based on the collective belief that things should be discussed thoroughly. Taking decisions without extensive talk is not appreciated. The preference to think and talk can be an individual thinking style as well (measured by personality tests like Birkman, etc). But sometimes, the talk–trance is a passive form of resistance to change. It is safer to talk about it than to do it. If it happens, I try to find out which reason applies to help them get through the talk–phase to the action.

Finally, we have to do what we agreed. We have to walk our talk to be credible. We have to actually change behaviors or else our meeting notes and assessment reports will end up in a drawer and everything stays the same. Behavior including non–verbal communication is the most powerful level of communication.

All three levels require great communication skills. To connect means to listen, observe, perceive and understand the other person. To talk means to adjust your language to the other person, to exchange and create meaning and use neutral language as well as respect. To walk means utilizing non–verbal communication wisely and doing what you've promised.

Connect

A big pitfall in communication is the often tacit assumption that "Everyone thinks like me." We live inside our own heads and we are used to our own ways of thinking. "It's obvious that we need this change. And it's obvious that we're going to use the OCAI tool."

We might see our own perspective as the one and only absolute truth, when we're busy, stressed out or focused on a goal. Focusing requires our minds to narrow down. It gives purpose and direction, at the cost of losing the broad view and open mindedness that we need to connect with others. It's not about us. Culture changes one person at a time. It's about all the others who have to change their views and behaviors. We can't order them to do so. We have to understand before we can be understood.

Executives can gain insight into this "common" pitfall when they compare their OCAI profile with their employees. One leader concluded: "I assumed that my whole team was with me and that we had the same focus, but we don't." For some, this is an eye opener. But all of us tend to forget this from time to time. Maybe we could all listen better so we learn how to communicate well.

Talk

After the assessment, the OCAI workshops are an important vehicle for communication and change. They are an intervention in itself. The message is: "We're going to change. We respect you enough to include you." People construct meaning together in the workshops and influence each other to change. Enhance trust by openness. Do what you're saying and tell what you do... This interaction is vital.

Walk

The most compelling communication device is human behavior. Executives, team leaders – anyone in a managing position – should BE the change they want to see in the organization. People will do what you do – not what you say. People will assess whether you walk your talk and decide if you're serious about it.

In spite of mission statements on the wall, pep talk from the CEO; or a new logo: change won't stick if leaders don't walk the new talk. Behavior is the most important means of communicating. Around 80 percent of our communication is nonverbal communication. Action speaks louder than words. You can do whatever you like with the communication department but if you don't get the role models of the organization to behave according to the new culture, you're not likely to guide successful change...

Summary

Communication isn't the whole story, but it is a condition for successful change, remember 4C. The rule of thumb is you can never communicate too much in a change process. On a spectrum, there are two responses to change: embrace or avoid it. Both attitudes need a different approach. A communication plan can help to define target groups and their needs, but should not end in a paper exercise.

True communication is done all day long by everyone, especially by leaders or change guides. It involves three levels: connect, walk and talk.

You have to communicate all the time – even when there's nothing to tell at the moment. Respect and secure the others by keeping them up to date – even if the message is: We don't know.

Understand the others before you can be understood. Talk and listen. Then do it. The best means of communication is behavior – because action speaks louder than words. Be open. Be honest. **Be the change.**

Chapter 10 How to organize
OCAI Workshops in your organization?

Let's explore a few topics around organizing the OCAI workshops after the assessment. What is the purpose of the OCAI workshops? Who is going to participate and how are you going to organize that? We examine the features of great group leaders. After this chapter with practicalities, we can get started on our OCAI workshop from Chapter 11 and share cases and insights... But first – we need to prepare the change workshops.

The OCAI is a great tool, but it's only a starting point for change. Nothing will change if you don't act on it... Change needs to be DONE. The biggest added value emerges when you do OCAI workshops and you stimulate a dialogue about the results.

Without consensus on current and preferred culture, nothing will change. You can't order the others to change, you have to include them and co–create the new culture together if you want sustainable change. You need the workshops to reach this consensus and to add the qualitative information like stories and anecdotes that illustrate your typical culture.

The workshops are the first vehicle for change, including all stakeholders in small teams, energizing and engaging people to truly change. The workshops carry intensive communication: go through the communication sequence of 1. connect, 2. talk and 3. walk so people will reach the phase of action and true change. You can start with a one– or a two–day workshop, depending on your objectives, participants and goals. But more time may be necessary to develop a feasible change program.

The purpose of OCAI Workshops

The OCAI Workshops serve as a vehicle for change. Purposes are:

◆ Introduce openness and collaboration in the workshops, as an intervention in itself
◆ Raise engagement and awareness and agency ("I can contribute!")
◆ Have people take ownership for their workplace culture, behaviors and change
◆ Get buy–in from the group – an open dialogue of doubts and second thoughts, finding solutions

◆ Team–building for the group so they will support each other in the change
◆ Influence old beliefs and behaviors...to change to new
◆ Create consensus and a better understanding of the current culture
◆ Create a better understanding of future challenges and goals; feel the Why of change
◆ Create consensus about the preferred culture that we need
◆ Understand and develop the preferred culture, specifically, from beliefs down to behaviors
◆ Co–create the new culture, designing plans and taking ownership for them

The workshop starts by creating a safe space that enables participants to speak their mind and feel equally respected during the workshop. Starting with the outcome of the assessment, the first goal is to reach **consensus on current culture**. We have to recognize it and agree that this is our starting point. It may be useful to understand individual differences. Working with a small (managing) team, it's possible to use the individual profiles as well. In this case the workshop serves as a **team–building** process, because in understanding their different perspectives or unexpected similarities, people get to know each other better. It is a great way to build a more value–conscious, stronger team to guide the change.

Next, we will customize our results to **better understand our current situation**. We specify the rather generalist culture type and discover which values, beliefs, typical behaviors and events make up our current culture. This is where we add the qualitative information that makes the difference for us, here we identify typical behaviors and details that matter to us. We make a list of things we like and dislike, we explore what is good already and should stay and what we would like to change.

Next, we're going to **assess the future** – "What are we headed for? What threats or opportunities are out there? What challenges do we expect?" In this important step we look outside and see what is happening in our market, in our environment. What is going on that we should anticipate?

Once you've got the picture, we reach **consensus on the preferred culture** that we need to be successful in the future we just painted. Another important and interesting step in the OCAI workshops: Our preferred culture from the assessment may be different than what we need to meet the challenges we discovered. Take a look at our preferred culture and wonder: "Will this culture type help us reach our goals and meet those challenges? Or should we adjust the preferred culture?"

Imagine – "Right now we're in market culture and employee retention is difficult because people feel they have to work too hard. We need our best employees but talent is leaving."

If this is our challenge, what preferred culture would we need? Maybe a little bit more of clan culture with a people orientation. When we agree, we're going to customize that further. We're going to see which specific values and behavior make up the culture that we need to retain our employees and attract new talents.

For instance, *"We value people but we also value results, so we'll create our own mix of market and clan culture. We're going to support our employees to achieve their targets and we'll give feedback based on results, but we'll be respectful to individuals. We give them time and support to improve performance if necessary. We'll give recognition and challenges to our talents so they will feel rewarded and inspired. We're going to adjust the performance appraisal system, introduce one–on–ones with managers and provide great training, etc."*

This customizing of results is very important to make culture and change tangible.

In the OCAI workshops, it's possible to **engage participants from all levels**. You can develop change programs and improve plans because you're collecting information and ideas from all levels. Thus you can tackle objections and find solutions before you start to change. This engagement and co–creating process in the workshops can unleash your organization's potential. It may take a little more time in advance but you will gain time in the long run.

The workshops may be an **intervention** in itself; an expression of the new culture that is inclusive with engaged employees. We're together **developing a plan to change** and we're building the bridge while we walk on it (like Quinn called it). We're doing this process together, so we can collectively as well as personally change behaviors, practice new habits and support each other to persist.

This involves everyone. Though our workshops may be led, initially, by an external consultant, we can't outsource this change or make the others change by mandate. We have to agree and really Do it, from CEO to the door man.

The workshop outline looks like this:

♦ Set the space and the "rules"
♦ Understand and agree on current culture
♦ Add qualitative information; esp. behaviors in current culture; rank behaviors (keep them or not)
♦ Assess the future and feel the Why of change
♦ Agree on the preferred culture that we need in this future
♦ If necessary, adjust the preferred culture
♦ Understand and elaborate the preferred culture by defining key behaviors

◆ Co–create a change plan of how to change from current to preferred
◆ Commit personally and collectively

One or two day workshop

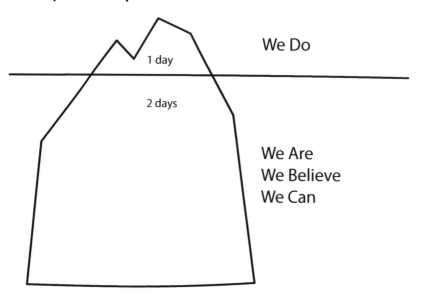

This book covers a schedule for an initial one– or a two–day workshop after the assessment, based on this outline. We will elaborate on the workshop in the next chapters. The one–day workshop focuses on behavior: the D level of the logical levels, "I do." You're going to define culture down to daily behavior. It can be done in one day if you work hard, depending on the group. The two–day workshop covers all levels from A to E, from identity to beliefs, to capabilities to behavior and to effect. In this workshop you can work with the two directions of change – outside–in and inside–out. You include the crucial level of beliefs, convictions, norms, values and assumptions.

This can be interesting for executives who have to become role models. Working with beliefs, they might encounter beliefs that they themselves have to work on to BE the change they want to see in the organization. Working with all levels, we enter the fascinating puzzle of finding leverage in the system: what is going to make the difference in changing this particular organization?

However, for some participants, this may be too complex. When you're working with the shop floor or with an operational, busy team the behavioral level is a good enough focus to start changing culture together. "What is our way of doing things around here?" You may relate to the values later on, but you're focusing on this visible level of behavior.

The workshop schedule is easily adjusted to your needs. It can be great to focus on culture for one or two days and get out with a change plan that everyone took ownership for. But sometimes it's not feasible and you have to work with the time you can get: one afternoon with small groups in a big conference room, or every first 2 hours of your weekly team meeting. Whatever the time schedule, make sure that you work with your results and adjust the workshop program to your needs.

Before we dive into the contents of the workshop, let's review what kind of leaders we need to guide them.

Group leaders: keep the safe space

The group leaders who are guiding the OCAI workshops could be outside consultants or inside executives or managers.

If you hire an external consultant, they are not hindered by hierarchy or taboos. They are paid for excellent people skills and to alert participants respectfully on their current culture and everything that happens during the workshop. They will speak their mind if necessary and may be the only ones who feel free enough to debate the CEO's ideas and bring in experience from different organizations and teams.

On the other hand, you could also work with internal leaders: executives and team leaders guide their own team. This may stimulate ownership. They are going to change their own workplace, co–create a new reality which can be very energizing. People may feel respected, inspired and accountable. They will give their best to make things work.

Again, your choice depends on your objectives and on the quality of management present in this particular organization. If they are mature, senior leaders with good people skills, it may be easier to work with internal leaders. But if the organization faces problems and management development still needs to be done, you might choose to work with external consultants.

In the workshop you want to reach consensus. You want people to really engage and participate and get ready for change. Moreover, you want them to co–create the change and the new culture and take ownership.

That's why you need to have a safe group where people are willing to participate and share ideas. You need a group leader who can skillfully guide this subtle process. A well–guided workshop yields a lot of insights and true will to change. Otherwise, people may not speak up or play a game like on a stage. They play the act of consent, while they don't. If this happens, you might discover later on that people don't really agree and therefore are returning to old habits. So, it is vital that if you take these workshops seriously as a vehicle for change, you need an excellent group guide...!

Confidentiality

If people don't know each other (like in an open organization–wide workshop), it's important that they introduce themselves and agree on some group rules. Use some exercises to break the ice and make people feel comfortable enough to share their ideas.

Agreeing on group rules before starting the actual workshop will help guarantee safety within the group. For instance, the information that is exchanged in the workshop is confidential until further notice. This helps assure people that they can speak their minds and express second thoughts and objections. We create a free space. It is confidential until we decide what we'll do with the outcome.

Mostly, the examples of current and preferred culture and the change plans that are developed are shared with the board afterwards, but without naming individuals. The outcome is a product of the group.

Respect

As you know, people have different views. That is obvious. But during fierce debates, people may forget it. It's sometimes difficult to respect different perspectives. To generate understanding and valuable ideas, participants must be able to express their views without getting responses like: "That is not true. You're completely wrong because ..."

It may be true, it may not be true, but in this participant's view it is true and that's why they are sharing. It's important to listen and try to understand the perspective from the sales department, the assembly line or the CEO who might have a completely different outlook. They are right in their own particular way.

It can be an art to combine these perspectives and see the big jigsaw puzzle – the picture of current culture as seen from different angles. The point is not to end up in a fierce debate about what is true or false. Respect for different views, being open minded and feeling rewarded for thinking out of the box, that is the mindset we seek in our workshop.

Safe Space

As a group leader, let your participants comment on the issues but not on individuals personally. In some company cultures it is a common practice to attack the person who is expressing a view.

Someone might say "I think our market culture is too competitive. It feels like it's never good enough or fast enough. I experience my boss as a hard driver." Respectfully responding would be: "Thank you for sharing your experience of the market culture in your department. Is this recognizable for the others?" But in some cultures, the practice is to attack them like: "I think your job may be too hard for you. You're always complaining." This is addressing the person instead of the issue.

Some groups use a lot of jokes to address individuals – getting away with "Hey, it was only a joke." But they have made their point and create a feeling of caution – or you'll be mocked.

If this happens in your group, it's important to intervene immediately. If you allow this behavior, the group becomes unsafe and people will stop expressing their thoughts. It is socially unsafe if you risk being mocked, laughed at, joked about, scaffolded, castigated. In such a disrespectful interaction, people are losing face.

The safety issue sometimes irritates managers (in my practice). They argue that no heads are being chopped off. So why would you not be safe? They feel that people should say what they mean anyway. But in a position where you can be ridiculed or punished for expressing ideas, people will hide and hoard information to protect themselves.

While to gain the added value from the workshops, we need them to share and collaborate, engage and get enthusiastic about the change. This is why you should be very alert as a group leader. You're facilitating the free space to have this dialogue, to guide the group so well that the best may come out of it. Respect and listening are key to a great OCAI workshop.

Another task is to **entice quiet people to speak up**. This is why we want small groups – in a group of 10 nobody can hide and keep their second thoughts to themselves while later on criticizing the process in the hallways. Of course we have extrovert people who will tell you what they think right away, but the introvert people are equally important. Please ask them to express their views. They may need a little bit more time to feel comfortable but make sure that everybody gets a say.

It's also important to **manage criticism**. We should be critical when we assess new ideas. How do we reach the preferred culture and what measures and interventions do we need? People come up with all kinds of ideas and you need to select the best ones. You need a critical mindset, but not upfront. First invite people to have a brainstorm and anything will do. Only after that, select the best ideas. We can criticize ideas after they've had some time to sink in.

Always respond to what is happening in the room. Hidden issues may come up during a workshop. Working on culture, people share their experiences and assumptions, expectations and some emotions. We've already discussed respect, feeling safe and caution for "jokes". Some people may be bothered with prejudice about other departments and others feel attacked. You may encounter a conflict or mistrust between leading managers and employees. Topics may be sensitive or taboo.

Simply respond immediately to anything that happens in the room. If you see people frown, sigh, lean back, get angry – deal with it **at that moment**. When you acknowledge what is happening in the room instead of pushing your Power-Point slides through and ignoring the signals, it makes people feel safe. When you respond timely, you give the signal: "I'm noticing you. I'm here to guide and I take you seriously."

Respond to nonverbal and verbal signals. Sometimes a conflict or an old prejudice needs to be solved before you can move on with culture. It might even mean that you have to stop your workshop and continue some other time. The scheme of the workshop is not a fixed, dogmatic thing. The most important thing is to work with the group and achieve openness and true consensus. That is not possible when people are playing games. Behaviors and beliefs from outside the safe space may interfere and need to be solved before you can proceed. You may need to build trust first, or consider other interventions necessary to create a safe space. The safe space is the condition to benefit from the workshop and truly energize and engage people.

Respond to nonverbal behavior

One of the most important features for group leaders is being responsive to verbal and nonverbal communication. For instance, respond to someone who's frowning and invite them to express their second thoughts – this is a very subtle process. We're all trained to respond to words, but we're not all skilled in perceiving and responding to nonverbal communication. Because nonverbal signals can be ambiguous, we have to share our observation and ask what it means. *"I see you frown. Is there something you'd like to share about this proposal...? Could we improve it?"*

Nonverbal signals cover the whole range of human behavior. Being silent and only answering to direct questions (this is the observation) because you're afraid your

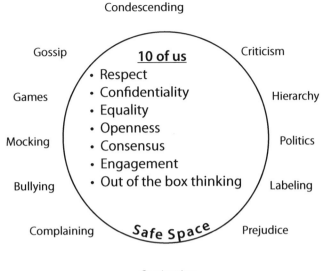

boss won't like critical thinking to improve plans (this is your meaning, interpretation). Or, being silent and hiding, because you don't see how the workshop can be useful and you're texting on your mobile (below the table). It could be leaning back (just being tired, in this case) or leaning forward (interested but anxious).

It could be finishing first with all questions and exercises, to either show off ("I'm good") or out of engagement ("I care deeply about our workplace culture, let's improve it"). When the leader responds to nonverbal signals, they enhance the feeling of safety. It signals to participants: You're being seen and acknowledged.

Respect others and be neutral

Group leaders must be able to create a respectful and safe atmosphere where expressing different opinions is encouraged and everyone really participates. Group leaders should be neutral guiders of change, aware of their own biases. Everyone has a right to speak their mind.

Remember the three Cs at the interaction level – we copy, we coach, we correct each other. This process doesn't make it easy to deviate, to disagree, to think out of the box, with all your coworkers watching – or your boss. The group leader facilitates this process and gives the signal "This is okay. We need people to think out of the box and think differently."

Group leaders must have the will and the skill to serve this process. It's not about their ego. It's not about pushing the change program you have in mind. It's about serving and facilitating this subtle process very well so everybody gets heard. Participants must be respected, acknowledged and enticed to express themselves, because this is the way to reach **true consensus** and this is your first building block to sustainable change.

Of course, people can stage a nice play for you. Some are great actors and you can never be 100% sure if they have the will to change. However, guarding a safe space makes it more likely to find the true meaning of the workshop: are we in for real change, or are we playing games?

Group leaders need to be **results–oriented**. It's great when everyone can express their views, but we have a timeframe – at the end of the day we get tired and we need to be done. Group leaders should be able to focus and to cut through lengthy discussions that aren't helpful – though sometimes you need deep dialogue to achieve consensus... Watch the competing values at work here... It takes intuition and experience to know the difference, probably, and assertiveness to cut these discussions off.

Small, active groups

To achieve true consensus, to have a dialogue about change and to take ownership for it – those goals can't be achieved in a hall with hundreds of people. Therefore, 10 people is a great group size for interactive workshops; 15 people is an absolute maximum. You have to divide a large population in smaller groups. This is necessary because you want active participation: it's a work–shop. Change starts in supportive, small teams.

In large groups, people tend to lean back. They can hide by sitting at the back end of the room but they can also hide by not speaking their minds. Also, the bigger the group gets, the scarier it gets to say something. In a smaller group, there's more time for interaction, more time for serious dialogue to reach consensus and people hopefully feel safe enough to speak their mind.

Practical choices

Now that we are fully aware of the importance of the workshops as a vehicle for change and the conditions, let's organize them! The Change Guiding group usually has to make some practical choices to organize OCAI workshops. When you're working with one team, this may be straightforward. Invite your participants and get to work with your results. But in the case of an organization–wide OCAI change process, you have to organize a lot more.

You can have workshops:

◆ top–down
◆ bottom–up
◆ crisscross

The outcome may be different. Top–down or bottom–up, people are working with their own teams and managers. In this case, people can be more specific and create their particular team culture to the level of (new) behaviors and agree to support each other with changing routines. Their culture may differ from the overall company culture in details, fine tuned to meet their tasks, as long as the main values of all teams are aligned and they agree on company–wide collaboration.

Crisscross workshops can create a fascinating exchange of ideas from all levels: helping people to understand the others, breaking down silos, ending "Us versus Them" and inspire people to collaborate as one organization. The outcome is an overall organizational culture, but not as specifically defined to behaviors as is possible in workshops with your own boss and coworkers who share your daily routines.

Depending on the main purpose of your change effort, choose the best way to organize the workshops, or, make a combination of the options.

Top–down

Top–down OCAI workshops are conducted by level. The board of directors or top executive team starts with their OCAI workshop. Once they're done, they can pass on their perspective of future challenges and opportunities and their strategy. The board sets the boundaries and could say: "These are our top three challenges that we need to overcome."

You can pass that information on to the next level. They don't have to scan the complete future but will get these three challenges or goals. With this information, it's easier for those who don't have the (top) view to create a preferred culture that aligns with the organization's strategy. You go down to the next level and you have an OCAI workshop with the executives at this level. If you teach them how to do it, those leaders can have OCAI workshops with their teams and employees.

An advantage may be that they take ownership because they're all going to guide change in their teams. They are accountable and make sure that the change within their department/team is successful. But you have to assess the maturity and competencies of management, before you roll–out this approach. Sometimes, the top–down workshops are better guided by an outside group leader, as we have discussed.

It's very useful when managers work with their specific team or department culture. The marketing team has a different outcome than the sales team, the financial department or the assembly line. Every team has the freedom to customize the results to meet their needs in their own workplace with their people. But they will develop within the boundaries of the overall organization–wide culture.

When the last team is done, it's important to gather all results and compare them. You can see deviations in the details – which may be very functional for different departments – but it's also important to check if the overall values are still shared.

Based on these outcomes, the board may need to adjust some of their assumptions, goals or strategy. They receive important information from the other teams. It is often useful to have a plenary session afterwards, on a company day or so, to share all results, emphasize similarities and reinforce the overall organizational culture.

Working top–down has great added value when everyone is included and gets engaged to really change behaviors in their workplace. But once you've reached the bottom of the organization, you need to connect again to the top. The plenary day will serve as a grand finale of the workshops. But the change is not over by then. It is only beginning. Continuous adjustments, reinforcing the change and communicating about it, new interventions and plans will remain necessary. Having done the workshops with everyone, you have built a shared reference and a structure to keep supporting the change: in your teams, day–to–day, based on building new routines together.

Bottom–up

Another possibility is to work bottom–up. These workshops go by level, but instead of starting at the top, you start at the bottom of the organization Invite all employees of the assembly line, all your help desk people etc. and start working on current and preferred culture. This creates another effect.

When the outcomes of these workshops reach the top, they may surprise the board with extra information from all levels. The top gains great insight in how culture and the upcoming change are perceived and they get valuable proposals for the change.

Not many top executive teams are willing to try this approach. It seems uncontrollable. And indeed, a possible disadvantage is that outcomes may not be aligned with the strategy and that employees' expectations weren't managed. In that case, dismissing their proposals could cause demotivation, disappointment and even distrust.

This bottom–up process should be carefully managed and is only possible in smaller organizations with an open–minded board of executives who are courageous enough to let go – and be surprised. If it works, tremendous potential is unleashed and employees are truly empowered and are taking ownership to be the change and be their organization. I haven't guided such a change process just yet – but I've heard other consultants who got this opportunity once. So far, these boards still seem rare...

Crisscross

The third option is to organize the OCAI workshops crisscross, organization–wide. You mix people from all levels. Top executives work together with team leaders and other employees on change programs. These workshops stimulate interaction and exchange information and ideas from all parts of the organization.

It may feel like doing a jigsaw puzzle – you're collecting pieces from all corners. Learning from each other, gaining understanding, getting inspired, the participants work on creating an overall organizational culture and overcoming prejudices, silos and "us versus them" feelings.

Mandatory or voluntarily?

Should the workshops be mandatory? If you're rolling out top–down, the OCAI workshops happen to be mandatory because every executive, manager or team leader works with their team.

Another option is to invite a random selection of participants because it's not feasible to invite everyone. This may be tricky because people may feel excluded. Communicate extremely well about this, if you decide on random selections for workshop participation. The goals of such a workshop will be limited because we need everyone engaged to change their habits... A random selection could shed some first light on questions and add stories and examples, but cannot change the others.

Another option is to invite everyone to subscribe to the workshops voluntarily. People who are interested, can sign up for these open crisscross workshops. You could still start with the board of directors and the project group for change. Mostly, they prefer their own workshop before organizing open company–wide workshops.

These open workshops are likely to attract the early adopters; people who like change, who are curious or excited. But you may appeal to employees who are dissatisfied and like to complain. It can go both ways. An advantage of this approach is that subscribers to the workshops will be engaged, whether with a positive or negative motivation. They're not indifferent. They join voluntarily and that gives a different energy to start with.

Overall culture in open workshops

When you are working with subscribers to open workshops, you're co–creating organization–wide culture. The overall culture is not fine tuned to meet the needs of specific departments but is based on collectively shared values (that we reached consensus on) and pieces of information from all over the organization. You may achieve a cohesive overall culture and an improved change program that benefits from these information pieces.

This picture of culture is shared with everyone afterward, but the people who didn't attend will not feel as committed. The subscribers who voluntarily attended the OCAI workshops might become change agents because they may take ownership for the change ideas they came up with. You need them to persuade the others who didn't attend at first, pulling the chariot of change, becoming role models for the upcoming change.

Team culture in mandatory workshops

The mandatory workshop that every leader does with their team has a different outcome. If necessary, a group coach or external consultant can guide these sessions. It is important again to establish trust, openness and safety. But in a team that operates well, there's a good basis for the OCAI workshop.

People will decide on their own team culture, with the overall company culture on the background. These team workshops give a chance to differ in useful details and to arouse peer support. Actually, if you want change to stick, it is essential to have team sessions because daily coworkers need to support each other in the new behaviors.

This time, the accounting team can agree on specific accounting behaviors, like: "We move from hierarchy to market culture: getting things done. We will help coworkers skip unnecessary details and leave these outdated forms "A and B" out to speed up. Every team member will set targets and support one coworker (John with Peter, Kim with Sylvia) to improve results and make the deadlines, etc..."

Organizational culture

*Teams have their specific culture but all share the core values,
beliefs and key behaviors of the overall organizational culture.*

See, how specific you can get? Accounting differs from marketing, but the basic values are common. They are moving to a results–oriented focus.

These specifics are a condition for building new routines! They make clear "How we do things around here". "We always check form C. We never use form A and B anymore. We always use weekly targets. We never drop goals without consulting our direct coworker."

Because we're inclined to get tired and give up, our direct coworkers will help us, so we organize peer support in this small team. We can look each other in the eyes and promise to help. We have witnesses. Our team leader sees to it. It's a topic in every team meeting. And so on... This way, teams with a human size (up to 15) can create successful, lasting change.

There are several ways to organize workshops and what's best depends on your objective – what you value most – but also on the current culture. For instance, if there is a lot of fear in an organization and you conduct open workshops, people may be afraid to speak up because leaders are watching. But this could also be true for working with your own team.

If departments suffer from strong prejudices, you may not begin with organization–wide workshops because this might hamper open communication, people might get defensive and feel like "Us and Them".

However, sometimes these silos are an excellent reason to start with organization–wide workshops to break the ice and get to know the other departments better (and hey, they weren't so bad!). From experience and/or intuition, decide what fits your objectives and the current culture best, now that you've seen the options and their (dis)advantages.

Final practical choices

Having organized the workshops, there are a few, final things to decide:

Individual or collective profiles

Before you start the workshop, decide whether the participants are going to work with their individual profiles or use the collective profile. That depends on the number of participants in the organization, the people in the room and your purpose.

In a managing team or board of directors, you can use the collective profile but also ask participants to bring their personal profile. But when you're working in an open subscription workshop with people from all parts of the organization, the details of individual profiles don't add that much value because they don't work together and you're developing an overall organizational culture.

Six profiles or one?

Check the six separate aspects of culture to see if they are congruent or not. Sometimes it's just adding complexity when you show the separate profiles for these six aspects. But if you see interesting results, you can incorporate those profiles in your workshops and work on these separate culture aspects as well.

Summary

The OCAI outcome is the starting point for change. The OCAI workshops serve as the first vehicle for change because people start a dialogue about their results and create consensus on current and, eventually, preferred culture.

The ultimate aim is to have them take ownership and develop their personal and collective change by identifying key behaviors that will make the difference in the new culture. These new behaviors will be practiced, supported by peers, until they have become habits: The new way we do things around here.

But before that, you need to think about and organize the workshops. We need group leaders with great people skills to set a safe space for free exchange in the workshops and to help people speak up.

We need small groups that enhance dialogue and true consensus, as well as everyone's engagement. We have to decide whether we prefer top–down or bottom–up mandatory workshops to elaborate on specific team culture, or open crisscross workshops to work on overall organizational culture.

Ready? Let's see how an OCAI workshop goes...

Chapter 11 Do you understand your Current Culture?

We're now going to start our OCAI workshop. That is exciting! We will present the outcome of the assessment and start the dialogue. The first part is a short repetition of the Competing Values Framework and an overview of our profiles. Next, we're going to work on understanding our current culture and creating the will and skill to change to the preferred culture. Our showcase is the Care Center for Disabled people, "CCD".

We are in the workshop room. We have discussed the rules and we created a safe space. People know each other and feel comfortable, hopefully even excited to get started...

Workshop Rules

◆ Information is confidential until further notice
◆ People have different views. Right/wrong is often not applicable.
◆ Comment on issues, don't criticize individuals
◆ Respect and listening are key

The first thing we discuss with the participants is how the assessment went. What information came up during the assessment? Were people complaining in the hallways or did they have inspired conversations like "Things are going to change." What did your participants think of it?

Sometimes this may not be relevant. "We had to send three reminders but that was because this calamity occurred." But sometimes it is relevant and participants can tell you that these calamities are a regular thing and may be part of a chaotic culture.

Or, another example: "We needed reminders because we have so many surveys. The CEO probably wants to keep us quiet – he throws another assessment down the line and we don't take it seriously." It might tell you something about their culture. The workshop starts with a short repetition of the Competing Values Framework because some time has passed between doing the assessment and the actual workshop. So we repeat the culture types for our group – as quickly or extensively as necessary to be able to work with them as a shared reference.

Next, we can check their expectations of the current and preferred culture profile. Before showing the results, you get all kinds of stories and assumptions and expectations. Most of the time, people predict the outcome before they see and recognize the actual profile.

This is all kind of warming–up to start working with current culture: to understand it and add qualitative information to customize our typical way of doing things around here. To show you an example, let me present the case of the Care Center for Disabled people, "CCD". Let's look at their outcome and attend their OCAI workshop.

Case: Care Center for the Disabled

CCD, the Care Center for Disabled people, had a staff of 300 people. Their management team consisted of 18 executives and experts. They were very committed to patients and mutual solidarity. They were in a rough market and downsizing had become necessary. New competitors were entering their region and they had tough financial targets; things were going downhill.

CCD decided to use the OCAI tool to start the change. 80 percent of their staff did the assessment in three weeks. That's a high participation rate. They were committed to one another and to saving the organization. People talked about it a lot – "What did you get? What about my scores?" Downsizing scared them, so there were some wild tales going round.

The managing teams had to appease staff that things would work out in the end. Managers explained why it was so important that they use the OCAI as a starting point for their change. Downsizing was one thing, but what they needed for a sustainable future was a different way of "doing business" to stay out of hazards next time.

After the assessment, the managing team engaged in a workshop. They wanted to get familiar with the results first before discussing the outcome with the organization because people were already scared.

I asked them what they expected of the results. They expected to have a dominant clan culture because they recognized its strong people–focus. They expected the preferred culture to be clan culture as well, but they added: "We know we cannot go on with clan culture this way.

We face extreme difficulties and we have real challenges ahead. There is a lot of competition entering our market, there are new government regulations that we have to meet and our financial reserves are almost gone. We do need to make more money and that's a big challenge ahead."

Let's take a look at their profile. The black graph is the current culture and the dashed graph shows the preferred culture. What stands out when you look at this particular profile? They had a very dominant clan culture at the time. Also, there is little difference between current and preferred culture. This is interesting to see, especially when you think of what the management team had just told me – "We need to make a big change."

Let's take a look at their culture profile in numbers. They have more than 40 points of clan culture currently, 26 points of adhocracy culture and more than 20 points hierarchy culture. What they have the least of is the results–oriented market culture that scores around 13 points.

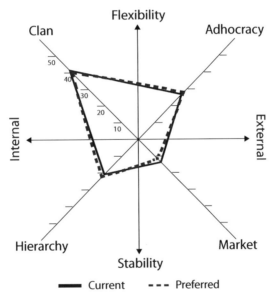

The managing team was right – they had a very dominant clan culture. Adhocracy culture came second. They valued flexibility and professional freedom. The two culture types are in the upper part of the Competing Values Framework. They like to do things in their own way and as flexible as possible. They meet their clients' demands, even if that means going beyond the extra mile.

Current culture and preferred culture were very much alike. They didn't want to change, really. "We do have a lot of people–oriented clan culture. Maybe we could have one point less of it…?" They'd like to have a bit more adhocracy culture and maybe they could agree on a bit more hierarchy culture. What they valued least of all is market culture – not only in current culture profile but also in the preferred situation. Market culture diminishes even further with two points.

Their culture profile was very congruent. All six aspects of culture scored highest on clan and adhocracy was second on all six culture aspects. Their profile aligned well with the health care sector as a whole. All other care institutions scored highest on clan culture. This seems to be a very good fit for this professional field.

Last but not least, the culture profile shows their phase of development. Some pioneers started the care center for disabled people – a few parents launched this organization because they wanted the best possible care for their disabled children. Because they were so dedicated to their patients/children, the organization grew rapidly because they attracted others who cared for disabled people. They grew to a staff of 300 and moved from the yellow adhocracy culture to the green clan culture.

Now, it wasn't simply a matter of developing to the next phase and maturing into hierarchy culture, because they needed to better organize work in procedures, structure, and clarity. They also needed to change because of outside challenges – the threats from competitors and government.

New government regulations were introduced. Health care institutions didn't receive government funding like before, so they had to make more money. Moreover, there were new competitors entering their market in this specific region. CCD needed more structure, rationality and businesslike performance – hierarchy and market culture – because they needed to survive. People didn't want change but they had to change, whether they liked it or not.

Since current clan culture was very strong, it could take more effort to change because people hung on to it for 40 points out of 100. Their biggest challenge was that market culture, which they absolutely needed to survive, was not desired at all. The participants even wanted less targets, less hard work, less rational, businesslike performance. The diagonals in the Competing Values Framework represent a huge polarity. How to swap your friendly people–focus for a rational, competitive results–orientation?

The culture profile gave insight and recognition in the blink of an eye. The managing team said "That's us," and they were a bit shocked that preferred culture was so close to current, even more than they'd expected. They were sure now that people did not want to change. This was a great starting point for change...

The team's individual profiles

The managing team started with their individual profiles because they had to develop the strategy for the care center. It was important that they as a team would

Overview Current Culture Profile

- Do you recognize the profile?
- What is the dominant culture type?
- How is the gap with preferred culture?
- Is the profile congruent?
- What does this mean to us?

understand each other. Their individual differences were based on character, people's position and their tasks. This was a rather large team of 18 people: managers and experts on the disabled.

Differences because of character: one member liked to keep things under control, so she preferred hierarchy culture for the future. She thought the flexibility of clan and adhocracy culture was too much. That was partly based on her personality trait; conscientiousness.

Differences due to their position: the CEO had a slightly different culture profile because he had a more results–oriented financial perspective and preferred a little more market culture. It was an eye–opener for him to see different culture profiles.

He assumed: "Everybody thinks like me." But now, he realized: "The other team members are with me but they are not the same. They don't share my view that we should fight for results and that our challenge is this huge." That gave him insight. He should lead his team, but not right away into market culture, if he wanted their buy–in.

Other team members got insights as well. Some people said: "I thought I was very results–oriented but what I really value is the personal relationship with my coworkers." The discussion about the individual profiles brought many insights. The CCD–team agreed on their current culture. "We have our little differences but we all agree that clan culture is dominant." The next step was to define what exactly was their clan culture.

Current Culture: Consensus

• Understand individual diferences
• Reach consensus: is this our culture?

Customize Current Culture

Doing this step creates awareness and insights into current work habits and culture. A collective willingness to change could emerge. People sometimes want to skip the step – "We don't have much time. Let's start working on the future." However, it's important that you first customize the results of your current culture. Going quickly and saying "Clan culture is fine" is not enough because you need insight and agreement on where you are – including behaviors. These are the details that matter.

We have to understand the subtleties of our current whereabouts to discover what details could make a difference, how to change and what not to do, knowing us. These specific stories and examples don't come from the Competing Values Framework. They can be mapped in the framework, but they are specific for your organization.

ABCDE

We're looking for examples of the current culture. Remember the ABCDE scheme – if you have enough time. Start with the A – "We Are" – this is the organization's identity. Think of your mission and vision. Think big values and concepts – core beliefs. Some examples: "We are helpful." Or: "I do therefore I am."

B – "We believe" – discuss with your group what is important and what is not. When is our work adequate? Who is successful and why? What beliefs back that up? What are our collective assumptions? What beliefs are visible in our workplace? For instance: "Money matters more than clients." Or: "If a coworker asks your support, you must always help." Or: "Never give unpleasant feedback, always keep it nice and cozy." The list of beliefs is endless, but only a few collective beliefs will be key to the culture and to the change.

The next step is C: make a list of the organization's competencies, capabilities, resources, your unique selling points – what is it that we CAN do? "We're good at delivering in time," etc. "We never say no, so you will get any extra service."

D: how do we behave? What do we do? What events and anecdotes are typical for us? What happens in our workplace? Find a lot of examples. This is the way we DO things around here. This is where we must change habits…or nothing will change at all. Find the key behaviors that define us.

Last, but not least, is E: the effects and environment. When we look around, what kind of environment have we created? What results do we generate? ABCDE is very systematically defining your current culture. You have the broad concept of clan culture and you're going to fill in the details. This is an extensive process but it yields insights and awareness of your current culture. Especially the 2B's will be useful when you develop your change program: Beliefs and Behaviors.

ABCDE Levels of Current Culture

- A: We Are - Our vision and Mission
- B: Beliefs - What is important? What do we omit? When is work adequate? Who is succesfull and why?
- C: Competencies - Our competencies, resources and unique selling points are…?
- D: Do - How do we behave? What events are typical for us?
- E: Effects - What can be seen in our environment? What effects do we cause?

CCD used a quick tour through ABCDE

Their identity – level A – "We are warm and caring; like a mother or a warm bath." Remember, how they were founded a few decades ago by some parents…? It was still part of their identity, though all team members were hired as professionals.

B – their core belief was "Clients matter most." They are disabled and they need the best. Solidarity is key. If you don't share this belief you don't fit in here.

C – what are our competencies and capabilities? "We can deliver the best possible care. We have an expert team of therapists and our buildings look like home. We really make it cozy and we are the best care providers because we do it from our heart."

At level D, what do they do? They give extra attention. They go the extra mile for their clients. Anything is possible. When somebody is feeling depressed, a caretaker will sit with that person until they feel better. They will do anything for you – bring you an extra cup of tea, even if they don't have time. You will see people chat, take time for clients and colleagues.

E – Their environment, their buildings are cozy like a home. Everybody feels comfortable and safe. But there's another effect – caretakers get very tired because they bring that extra cup of tea but they don't have time. There are other clients – it's slightly chaotic. Sitting with a client means my coworkers have to look after other patients. Coworkers are burdened but personally, giving extra attention feels good – making a difference for this client.

Last but not least, we don't like our administrative tasks and since we have little time, we will procrastinate and then skip them. Our files are not complete. So this is our culture. It's warm but also a bit chaotic and not really businesslike. Results are not on our mind at all. This is how you define a current culture. You go from ABCD down to E. If you think it's too comprehensive for your participants to work with ABCDE, you could focus on behaviors only, level D. **Behaviors are key** – if they don't change, nothing really changes. You could use this schedule and find out: "Clan culture – it means and doesn't mean …" Work your way through all four culture types.

What does it mean for us, that we have this much clan culture?

The CCD defined their current clan culture. "Our clan culture means … we go all the way for our clients. What doesn't it mean? Clan culture does not mean that we take care of our coworkers enough, because if I sit with that client who needs a talk, my colleagues have to do more. I know that they are tired." This is another way of defining your current culture.

You can do the same for every culture type. Adhocracy culture – what does it mean and what does it not mean? Hierarchy culture, market culture …

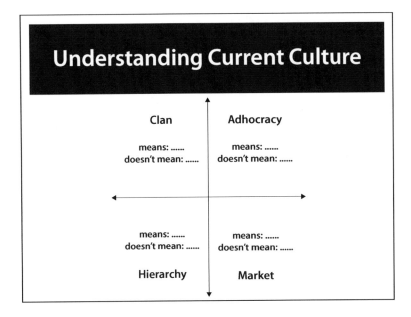

In the CCD example, clan culture means listening to employees and clients. Always care, take time for people, but it also means lots of meetings and deliberations. It does not mean that they chat all day; it does not mean that coworkers are close friends who meet in their spare time. Their adhocracy culture means that you can improvise whenever you feel like it. You can change routines because you'd like to try something new. It does not mean keeping track of changes and new ideas. So innovations only spread when we talk about it.

Market culture – it means that they dislike targets. We don't like money and goals. It's got nothing to do with us. It's not why we work here. It feels like the opposite of taking the best possible care of disabled people.

Hierarchy culture means governance, procedures, safety and quality manuals. They have to be present but we don't like them. That's why we're behind in administration all the time.

Finding examples of current culture

In your workshop, you can ask people to do this in little groups – two or three persons – to inspire each other to come up with a lot of examples. Sometimes people do this individually and then get back in the group to discuss the results.

Sometimes it's difficult. Some people are not used to thinking of human behavior. "I cannot come up with examples." Simply start in the other direction – ask for their irritations. This could provide the best entrance to their memory.

"What is really annoying you at work? What should change immediately?" Irritations are easily remembered. "What is wrong here? What do we miss? It is a shame that … this should not happen again."

Make a list of incidents, behaviors, examples. Then analyze: if this is happening, what does it mean? What do we believe apparently? Is this an example of adhocracy? Hierarchy? Market? Clan? Entice people to come up with examples and categorize them in the right culture types. Then they will start thinking about their culture. Take as much time as the group needs and address the issues that need to be dealt with first.

The process itself is current culture

The process – anything that happens in the workshop – is an expression of current culture. Maybe they like to work in an organized way: an expression of their hierarchy culture. Is it the CEO or the team leader who speaks first all the time? What happens if you ask one of the others to give their view?

If current culture entails more or less counterproductive habits, you should deal with those first. Intervene if there are sick jokes or personal attacks. Ask a lot of questions if the leader speaks and the others remain silent. Share your observations with the group to make them more aware of current culture. It's your job as a workshop leader to help them "see" their culture. Ask them "why".

"Why are there so little examples of irritations while the profile shows a huge gap with preferred culture..? You seem to be dissatisfied?" "Why does no one speak up? What do you need to share 10 points that should be improved?" "I have heard person A contribute many ideas. Why are the others silent? Is this an example of current culture? What does it mean?"

Sometimes people need to be enticed to open up, even when there are no major distrust or safety issues. You could have them write down examples and throw all the papers in a basket, discussing them one by one without knowing who contributed the example. You could have them share examples in groups of three and ask them to share one example that was not their own in the plenary group.

This may take possible shyness away and may help everyone to open up.

Do anything that is necessary to get this group feeling safe, sharing their ideas and feeling equal, for the moment, in this workshop. It is great if people leave their formal positions at the doorstep and contribute equally.

Current Culture: Irritations?

- What is wrong here?
- What do we miss?
- What should change now?

Current culture as an image

The ABCDE scheme and the forms – what it means and what it does not mean – represent an analytical way of understanding current culture. Some groups may benefit from a "right side brain" approach. Ask them for metaphors, or have people make a drawing of the current culture or even create a "group tableau" together, taking positions and postures in the space of the room.

Current Culture: Diving for the Iceberg

- If this happens, what does it mean?
- What do we believe or assume, apparently?
- Current collective beliefs are...

An image can reveal other aspects of culture and might communicate its core. Images are easily remembered. Ask the group to draw or act their current culture as a personality type. If your current culture walks into the room right now, what does he or she look like? Is it an old woman or a young man? Are they relaxed or uptight? These metaphors often entail instant recognition, reveal core features that might otherwise have stayed tacit because they go beyond analytical thinking. This way of understanding current culture may make people more aware of it.

In the case of the care center for disabled people, they shared an anecdote. "We really care for disabled people. One of our clients only calmed down in a warm bath so we built him a bath instead of the showers. It was great to see how this client thrived on taking baths."

Summary

The workshop is held with a small group where everyone is enticed to contribute equally. We have made sure that our participants feel comfortable. We offer a quick recap of the Competing Values Framework and present their OCAI Profile. Then a respectful dialogue about the overall outcome may begin.

We spend as much time as necessary on understanding and reaching consensus about the current culture. We need to understand the details and the typical appearances of this current culture – we need specific examples, precise incidents, typical events, shared meanings, collective criteria and beliefs.

We start digging for the iceberg, we try to grasp what is taken for granted, the behaviors no–one will normally notice, the decisions no one will question because they are simply "the way we do things around here". We give our participants new glasses to help them see a new perspective: "Yes, this is our current culture!"

Meanwhile, the process IS the current culture. Share your observations with the group to make them more aware. Help them overcome obstacles to a safe space and productive group process.

Chapter 12 What Preferred Culture do you need?

Next, we're going to explore the future and reassess the preferred culture in this workshop. We will adjust the preferred culture profile if necessary and define it further. Like we did with current culture, we're going to understand what behaviors exactly make up the culture type that is necessary for a successful future.

Exploring the future is always an interesting and important part of your OCAI workshop. We need to have an idea of our future opportunities and challenges to decide what would be the best culture fit. Which culture type would support the strategy best? What should we focus on? What are the five most important trends that we are facing in the next years? Our five most important goals? What is important for us as an organization or a team?

Let's think about the demands we face from the market or our clients or the other departments – whatever the purpose of your culture assessment, this is where you check what is going on outside your team or organization.

Exploring the future

♦ What opportunities and threats do we see in the future /or after the merger /or after we have launched our new product /etc.?
♦ What do we expect to happen?
♦ What are critical success factors? Do we need to find new target groups, new markets? Do we have to innovate more? Is the biggest problem attrition and do we need to find motivation? What is it that we need to be successful?
♦ What are our strengths and weaknesses? Do we have the right people? Is there enough motivation? Is our workplace ready for Generation Y?
♦ How do we want to work and want to be?

The future can be a very inspiring topic although you don't want to spend the whole day debating it – unless you're working with the board and they're not aligned on their strategy yet. In that case they have to do their "homework" first or they can't decide on preferred culture. They may even need to come up with a new strategy.

It sometimes happens that a top executive team doesn't have true consensus about their strategy. Imagine the different messages and priorities they subconsciously communicate to employees when they're not aligned... No wonder that change or improvement is hard to come by and they decided they needed culture change.

If the true priorities are fuzzy, activities are headed in different directions, wasting scarce resources and getting people confused and frustrated. A clear, consensus strategy is vital to successful change. So, if necessary, spend time on the future with the board or top executives. Don't proceed until the strategic goals are clear.

But if you're working with another team, you could keep this short and present them "According to the managing team, the five most important trends for the future are …" and work with this reference. How much time you spend on the future depends on your participants. It's important that everybody understands this context because your preferred culture needs to fit these (expected) circumstances.

CCD's challenges

Let's go back to the care center for disabled people to get an example of this part of the OCAI workshop. One of their biggest challenges was downsizing because they had to cut costs. They said: "This is what we fear most and what will happen for sure in the next six months."

"Another development is that our clients, but especially their family members, are very demanding. We provide excellent care but they want even more. Nowadays disabled people are not put in a chair behind a window to watch the world go by; they actively participate in society. Care takers focus on what they can still do and find them little jobs to experience as much quality of life as possible. We have to be prepared to keep up with these expectations."

"We are facing strong competition as well. In the beginning, we were the only organization in this region providing excellent care. Lately, numerous competitors have entered the region. There's no government funding anymore but clients pay through their health care insurance.

Insurance companies are powerful players in the health care market. We all have to cut costs to meet their demands. We also have new rules for good governance and accountability that we need to adjust to. We used to be the first and the best, safely funded by government. The new situation is really a threat."

Knowing all this, you have to reassess preferred culture. People do the assessment but may not take all these challenges into account when they complete the survey. Some people wish for a fairy tale, where everything is perfect and they can have it all at the same time. Stay in a cozy clan culture AND be financially safe without having to change. But will that work in reality?

In the case of the CCD people, current and preferred culture was very much alike, in spite of all these challenges. They didn't want change – but they had to change. They made a list of future trends, weaknesses and strengths, opportunities and threats, and looked at their preferred culture profile, wondering: "Will this preferred culture profile get us there?" The CCD participants imagined a good fairy – wishing everything could stay the same.

Welcome to reality: we have some constraints and boundaries and we have just defined them by listing these future trends. Let's take a look at which culture we need to survive and achieve our goals. People have to reach consensus about their preferred culture in the workshop. Of course, the preferred culture profile from the assessment can be sufficient to be successful in this expected future. But groups may decide that they want to adjust their preferred profile once they get more awareness of their probable future. You're allowed to do so because the preferred culture doesn't exist yet. Based on your future insights, this is the moment to adjust the profile. But it must be done by consensus.

Adjusting the Preferred Profile

How do you adjust a culture profile in the workshop? Ask your group to list the ranking of necessary culture types. What is the culture type that you need first to achieve your goals? To implement your organization's strategy, what is the dominant culture you need? What is second? Rank the importance of the culture types.

Once this is done, continue to imagine your preferred culture as a pie. What pieces do you need to slice? Do you need 25 points of each culture type? Or would a dominant culture of 45 guarantee a successful future? The CCD managing team agreed immediately that they needed an adjustment. Competition, downsizing and demanding customers asked for a different focus. There was no discussion about that.

"Downsizing – we need more hierarchy culture to get that done. We need more efficiency, we need better procedures, a clear structure, less chaos; if we want to survive. The trend of demanding clients – we need market culture to emphasize an external focus. What is our competition offering to our market, what is going on, what do people want nowadays? We have to look outwards and get results. We also need adhocracy culture because we need to innovate. We have to find the latest therapies and develop competitive care, comfort and services for disabled people."

Though they agreed easily on these statements, the actual adjustment was difficult. From the assessment, their current culture was 39 points clan, 27 adhocracy, 22 hierarchy and 12 points market culture.

But from their future exploration, market culture emerged as their first priority. "We wanted less, but in fact we need more market culture. Secondly, we have to innovate – adhocracy culture. Thirdly, we need hierarchy culture to help us work efficiently. Clan culture will be last – this is who we are but we need to change to survive." They had a huge discussion. It was difficult and painful because they were so attached to their clan culture. But using logic, they realized they needed a fresh focus on market culture.

Another challenge was reaching consensus not only on the ranking of culture types but on the size of the pie parts. How much market culture do you need? During the assessment they wanted to diminish market culture because they felt care is not a job but a calling. Now, market culture turned out to be their lifeline. How many points would you give to market culture out of 100? They decided to settle for 35 points, which is a fairly high score on market culture in a care organization, to emphasize the new, necessary focus.

They decided innovative adhocracy culture should be second, though one could argue that they badly needed hierarchy culture to stir efficiency. But they weren't ready for another culture type they found difficult. They wanted to emphasize the external focus after "working cozy with their clients and each other". It was time to

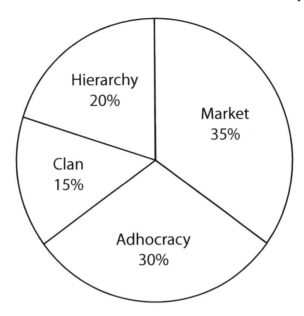

look outside, improve and achieve sound financial results. It was a radical change and the managing team found it hard to decide. This team was very comfortable and open to each other. Those are great conditions to reach consensus. But even they found it hard. They agreed, still chewing on the consequences, but they had to sell it to the organization. That was an even bigger challenge.

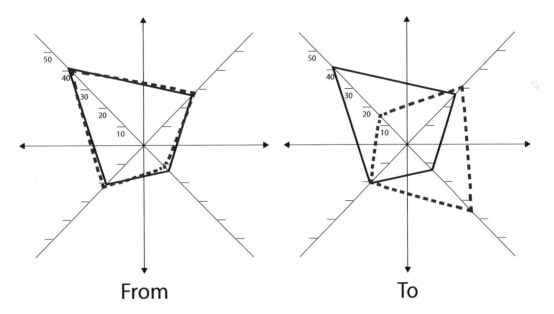

This is a radical example of what can happen during an OCAI workshop when people adjust their future and decide to change their direction. Most groups probably won't be as radical, but prepare for real discussions in this part of the workshop.

The future that hasn't happened yet gives room for different thinking styles and views and often stirs discussions. Lack of alignment around strategy may show – that needs to be solved first in a managing team. If they don't fully agree, the people in the organization are likely to be confused, pursue their own agendas and not implement changes. During each dialogue or debate, we see the current culture at work. Address relevant issues at once, when they take place. As discussed earlier, this helps participants perceive their culture.

Perceive Points of Current Culture:

♦ Who does the talking?
♦ Who decides?
♦ Who is leaning back?
♦ Is it allowed to disagree?
♦ Do we respect other opinions?
♦ How do we treat differences?
♦ How do we go about reaching consensus?

Glimpses of Preferred Culture:

Do we see behaviors that may feel awkward now, but that could be great examples of the preferred culture? Isn't this exactly what we need to do more in the future? Notice these behaviors and showcase them. Stimulate those behaviors. This is the way to the future...

Translating Preferred Culture into Behaviors

After a lot of discussion, the CCD team adjusted the profile and they were now ready to define their preferred culture. First, they had a dialogue about the meaning of their new culture mix. The Care Center wanted to decrease clan culture because they had too much of a people orientation. They used the schedule: what does clan culture mean in the preferred culture and what does it not mean? This question helps to find new meanings and behaviors and operationalize preferred culture from values down to daily habits.

"The new clan culture means that we care for current clients and employees within budget boundaries. It does not mean that we care less. You're admitted if you fit into our admission policy. We care for people within healthy boundaries that secure our future."

They needed a huge increase in market culture. What does that mean?

"It means that we are aware of our financial framework. It does not mean that we care for money only and that we pursue results at any cost. We want more market culture under the condition that a healthy results–orientation helps us provide sustainable care. It means we will focus on getting things done and sticking to planning and time frames."

What will this new culture look like – when it has come true?

"Clients are admitted on clear criteria. Our meetings start on time, our files are complete – we're no longer behind on administrative tasks. Our customer service is regularly assessed. We have shorter coffee breaks – but in return we can leave on time instead of working long hours and complaining about the workload. These are some indicators that we have reached the new culture."

Note that these are sensory perceivable indicators. We can check and see complete files, clock times and customer survey results. This image is a result of their new behaviors and helps working toward their new, more results–oriented and sustainable future.

Next, they started to further define culture by specific behaviors. "If we look into the future, after the downsizing, what does it look like when you're working here? What do we do differently? Because nothing will change if we don't change behaviors. We will see new habits."

You can define your preferred culture using the levels ABCDE. If that's too much work, start with the behavioral level at D – what will we do? Found these new behaviors on a few key beliefs – and you'll get important details to change culture.

Preferred Culture: Do

- What do we do?
- What behaviors and events take place?
- Examples must be specific and sensory palpable:
  hear, see, do...

CCD was working on the "do" level – what do we do in the preferred culture? In small groups, they started to focus on market culture. They came up with several examples. Market culture means that we're going to be on time for meetings. Currently we're always late, but we should be more results–oriented.

We should check our admission policy because we currently admit all clients. We should focus on target groups because there are so many disabilities… We need a businesslike return on investment and focus. We're not going to build baths because an individual client prefers it. That is what a family would do, but we are a professional organization. We want to give our best but we also have to make a living.

We have to make appointments with each other. For instance, if my door is closed it means I'm working and I need to concentrate. Currently, doors are always open and people walk in to chat – distracting you as well. We're going to catch up with our administrative tasks. We will complete files at the end of the day as a routine.

What will we do more of?

In Cameron & Quinn's book is an easy to use scheme. You can ask your workshop participants to complete this: "What will we do more of in the preferred culture?" And: "What should we sustain? What should we stop doing? What should we start doing?"

The CCD answer was: "We will do more planning, administration, appointments, time management, measuring – we measure money, time and results. We think twice before we do anything. We tend to be a little too spontaneous. We go in all directions but the new rule is that we stop and think: Is this wise? Do we have the time and money? Will it yield sufficient results? We check with our new criteria of time, money and results."

What will we keep doing?

People are doing things and you want to keep those good things: "**We continue** to care for clients – that is so important – and we give the best possible care, but within the budget. This time we have some boundaries. We're in reality."

What will we do less of?

"We will do less chatting. We like to talk – sometimes even gossip a bit. But there's so much work to do that we must chat less. We must say 'yes' not so often. Here's the rule again – think twice. Whenever I say 'yes' I have to stop and check. It may be difficult, but it's necessary."

What is it that we should stop doing?

"It's admitting everyone, no matter what. We will tighten our admission policy. We have to define target groups. We have to exclude some disabilities to provide better care." This schedule is very simple and participants often like to complete it – what would we do more of, do less of, what we will continue to do and what to stop doing all together.

Balance Opposites

The admission policy seemed to represent the core of CCD's new culture. Caring for people and giving yourself away if necessary...is as a calling. Now is there something as businesslike as an admission policy?

In the Competing Values Framework you need to balance competing values and switch between them when necessary, in order to be successful. So, how could CCD balance care with businesslike boundaries? How to integrate a people orientation with a results focus?

CCD wanted to care for everybody, but they needed to survive and thus focus on results. In this diagonal between clan culture and market was the contradiction they needed to balance. "We give the best of care but set some boundaries – businesslike – and that is our new market culture." That was their challenge.

Reframe to new Meanings

They also had to find a different meaning for "providing the best possible care". The old meaning was something like "We give everything away. We're like family. We care for you, all the time." This belief founded their family–like behaviors.

They had to find a different meaning for caring for people that aligned with market culture, or they wouldn't be able to make the switch. "Caring for people includes responsible care for current clients and employees. So if you admit everyone, you will not be profitable in the long run and you will thus not care enough. Boundless caring means that you exhaust your resources. Sustainable care for people means care within boundaries. You need to think like a business and work according to admission criteria and criteria for time, money and results. Good care for people is realistic, so you will endure for the long term."

This process of finding a new, inspiring meaning is called "reframing". You take one situation, in this case caring for people, and you give it a new frame as if it were a painting. The different frame changes the meaning; the colors look different.

"Caring for people means that we care in the long term, so employees will still have a job and clients receive the best possible care within realistic boundaries so they can count on continuity. That is really caring for people; giving security and a sustainable home."

The managing team reached consensus and they were aligned on this new strategy. Their challenge was to convince the caretakers who had been working with disabled people for years in that limitless way of "anything is possible."

Depart from Current Culture

Because they had such a strong clan culture, it was important to depart from the people–oriented values. This is why the reframing was important – they were "selling" the market culture approach from a clan culture point of view. "Because we care for people, we respect budget boundaries so we can exist in the long run. We provide the best possible sustainable care and employment."

Thus, they redefined budgets and a more businesslike approach in a positive way, tying it to care for people in the long run – hierarchy culture values. It's important to start the change from the current culture. We can't start anywhere else: this is where we are. Departing from clan culture, valuing what we collectively share (people), we move to an approach that embraces market culture values (results). The way this is presented can make a huge difference in either resistance, acceptance, or even better: engagement. (More about that later on).

If you don't acknowledge the current starting point, like denying the importance of people values and starting with business targets right away, you're likely to end up in the infamous category of failed change programs. Of course people will resist or sabotage if you're not open to their values. Why would they be open to your approach – if you're not open to what they value? Especially if the new values are the opposite of their current beliefs. We need to build a bridge first. We need to understand before we can be understood.

Understand current culture: what is it that people value in this organization? What are their drivers? Depart here, acknowledging what is good about current culture, showing what could improve and reframing the meaning of alternatives. Results may not have been appreciated before, but now they are tied to sustainable care for people, everything feels different. So, why not try it...?

Develop and dream Preferred Culture

This part of the workshop can be very exciting, with a lot of brainstorming, creativity and new visions. You can use any exercise that you find useful. You could paint or act your preferred culture as a person. You can break out in small groups and have brainstorms or a "world cafe setting" about the favorite preferred culture.

Make up anecdotes like a novelist or metaphors that illustrate this preferred culture. Don't only use the left brain, analytical, critical thinking; your right brain creates and stores images, metaphors and stories that are easy to remember and that will guide you through your busy daily business to reach your preferred culture.

Consider this exercise: Imagine one magic night, the new culture would be realized all of a sudden. You don't know about this nightly magic spell – you come to work in the morning ignorant. How would you recognize the new culture? What would happen, what would you see?

Make real images. "See the 8 digits on the organization's bank statement. Show the award for best client care. See people smile when they answer the phone. See how the team's administrative files are complete. Watch coworkers finish their to–do list. Hear the pace of dynamic, energetic footsteps in the hallways. Hear the building buzz with activity. Etc..."

Make real stories. They entail instant recognition, communicate the core and will be remembered. A great story or image or vision/goal will guide behavior more easily than an ABCDE–scheme. It will be present in the back of your mind and remind you what to do and why that matters.

The more common practice to elaborate on preferred culture is the analytical way. You can use the ABCDE schedule. Customizing and finding the specific details of your preferred culture will use the
A – "we are" – how do we see ourselves in the future? What is our identity?
B –what is important? What do we assume about employees, executives, customers, market competition, about work – what do we believe? What are our criteria? What is good and what is bad?
C – what competencies do we have? What resources? What unique features?

D – what and how exactly do we do things in the future? What events take place? Describe typical events that would take place in your preferred culture. Try to come up with specific examples at a tangible level. In the future, we're going to see, hear, feel, say... Envision this future as if it were already there.

E, what is the effect? What does the environment look like? What is our position in the market? What are the results? What does it look like on a material level, in our offices, on our banking account?

Customize Preferred Culture:

- A - We ARE. Our mission and vision....
  A metaphor or image is....
- B - We Believe. We value... What is important? When is work good enough? Who is successful? Why? Our criteria for good/bad/ugly are...
- C - We CAN. Our competencies... our unique selling points are... Our resources?
- D - We DO... typical behavior, incidents, events, habits, anecdotes and stories?
- E - We effect? This leads to... Our environment looks like... Our building...?

Questions to help customize ABCDE

We Are
How do we see ourselves? What is our vision and mission? What image, keyword or metaphor applies to our organization?

We Believe
What is important? What values come first? What are norms for behavior? What ranking of values applies? What are criteria for: performance/good work, leadership, promotion, budget approval, projects?

Questions to help customize ABCDE continued

We Can
What are our competencies? What resources have we got? What are unique selling points and strengths?

We Do
What do we do? What events happen? Specific! Sensory!

We Effect
What tangible results do we effect? What does our building, parking lot, office show? What market position have we got? What image, performance, social presence?

Be Specific!

Whatever approach you choose, make sure that it leads to specific behavioral, sensory descriptions of the new culture. As specific as: This is what we will do differently in the new culture. "We should communicate more" is too vague, for instance.

Work on images of inspiring lunch meetings or company–wide coffee breaks. Work on resolutions like: "We don't email coworkers who work in the same building. We phone or meet in person." "We discuss all schedules in a plenary Monday morning meeting." "The CEO sends out our business results every Friday afternoon," etc. Be specific. Who does what by when and how and why? When you become specific, you will find objections and enter discussions. It is easy to agree on broad concepts and abstract values. Many people value "communication" or "honesty". If you leave it at that, people will leave the workshop thinking they reached consensus. But what do these values mean in everyday business life? What are the exact criteria? When are communication and honesty adequate? Do we tell others to improve their competencies every time we meet, out of honesty? Do we publish individual wages on the Intranet? Do we share all strategic considerations with all staff?

Wait a minute... in the new culture we will... and here come the specifics, the criteria, the details that will make the difference. When you achieve true consensus on details, you can be sure that everyone understands the new culture and that all trade–offs and objections have been lifted or resolved. Only then can people turn words into action, take ownership and be accountable for the new culture they agreed on.

Summary

This part of the OCAI workshop can be fun and tough because you spend time in the future – with no facts to check on – just yet. Explore the future and wonder what culture you need to be successful. Make your preferred culture come alive and real and create a great vision.

Spend as much time as necessary on reaching consensus on the necessary preferred culture for a successful future. Make up all the details and the typical appearances of your new culture. It is yours!

If necessary, adjust the preferred profile from the assessment. Elaborate on every level – identity, beliefs, capabilities, behavior, effect and results. Find the details that will make a difference and engage your group in the OCAI workshop.

Be specific. Translate the new culture into behaviors. Balance opposites, departing from and respecting the values of current culture. Create new meanings. Develop and dream the new culture, using a magic wand. Reach consensus on what exactly to start doing, what to sustain and what to stop doing. Solve objections and obstacles. Make it sensory palpable. This is what we will DO.

Chapter 13 How to Change from where we Are to where we want to Be?

Now that we have a clear picture of our current and preferred culture, including behaviors, we know WHAT we want to change. We have reached consensus and strengthened our collective will to change. We know why we need change. We know why now (instead of next year). We know what we need to change.

But HOW will we get there? This is the key to successful change. People often ask for a recipe. "Tell me what steps to take, describe what we must do to evolve from clan to market culture." But there are only general guidelines for this road from where you Are to where you want to Be.

Every team and organization has to do the work of finding their particular key to change. Knowing their specifics, every solution is customized. This is where you need all your participants, their combined perspectives, intelligence and creativity to find out what will make a difference in this system.

An organizational system is complex and comprehensive with emergent side–effects. Put another way, it is an exciting and interesting combination of personal beliefs and behaviors and collective beliefs and behaviors – emerging in daily inter-actions where people copy, coach and correct. This dynamic is influenced by outside, "non–people" factors as structures, procedures, budgets, office buildings, resources, market conditions, competitors, customers, governments etc.

The power of 10

A motivated team of 10 people can change "the way we do things around here". If they are open to question their beliefs and change some comfortable habits and mutually support each other to practice these new, changed behaviors. An organiza-tion of 100 can do so, too. They simply need a little more time.

An organization of 1,000 employees faces a greater challenge. They might need more time but also more will, skill, persistence and creativity to change collectively. The good news is that 1,000 people collaborate in smaller teams and can still apply techniques like copy, coach and correct and peer support. They might need some extra effort to coordinate these multiple teams and their organization wide procedures.

But they can still engage in successful change – as long as they check their 7C's regularly and operate in small teams! Small teams mean that people are visible for each other. People have the brain capacity to know 10 others, give them attention and support and build trust. In groups of 20, 50, 100 or 1000, this is not possible. Already in groups of 20, not everyone is visible and some will "hide" or lean back. In groups of 10, people are able to see each other in the eye, notice participation or maybe reluctance – and engage in finding solutions to proceed.

If you are aiming for true change, work with this power of 10. You might organize plenary sessions for information, but don't do workshops in large groups or they might end up in a stage play, with some actors and some people behaving as the audience – maybe criticizing the change without contributing.

The systemic puzzle might be more complex with larger numbers of employees. But the process is the same. It comes down to human behavior in the workplace: what we collectively believe and do in our daily work lives and how we stimulate or hamper each other to contribute to our shared goals.

In the last part of the OCAI workshop, we're going to engage in this exciting puzzle. We wonder what will give our particular organizational system leverage. What will work if everyone starts doing it? How can we achieve a new culture?

Together, we develop a plan for change that will never be "done". Simply because culture change is constant evolution and we can't plan and design exactly how things will go, what meanings will prevail, how people will feel and what behavioral patterns might emerge.

We're building the bridge while we walk on it. But if your workshops were truly engaging, you may trust this process and walk that bridge safely. So far, we have reached consensus and a deeper understanding of the current and preferred culture. We have done the first six steps of the 7–Step Guide of Culture Change:

Step 1 Assessment Current + Preferred Culture

This is where we decide to start working with culture, using the Organizational Culture Assessment Instrument (OCAI) based on the Competing Values Framework.

Step 2 Diagnose the Quantified Culture Profiles

Time to see the outcome of the assessment in one glimpse.

Step 3 Understand and Add Qualitative Information

The OCAI workshop starts! Participants start discussing their outcome and add qualitative information to better understand their current culture.

Step 4 Raise Awareness, Consensus and Engagement

Participants are enticed to engage and take ownership for their culture.

Step 5 Future Scan, see the Why, the Vision and Strategy

They explore the future, building even more change readiness (whether the platform is burning or not... here they find the answer to Why change is necessary now).

Step 6 Understand and Customize Preferred Culture

To achieve the preferred culture, we have to become personal as well. What will I change as of tomorrow? What preferred culture do we need to thrive in this future? The next step is to come up with a plan on how to achieve this preferred culture – what do you need to change in the way we do things around here? We will take a look at the necessary actions, the obstacles you may find – and the solutions to move forward. It's time for magical step 7:

Step 7 Co–create: How to Change Plan... and DO it

Collectively, customize a plan of How to change – for everyone personally as well as a group, prepare for obstacles and mutual support and then: Just do it!

Step 7 can be an exciting journey:

♦ Find out which details/behaviors can make a difference: the puzzle!
♦ To actually DO the new behaviors (and stop talking about it)

♦ To stick with the new behaviors and turn them into habits (persistence).

Viral Change: Behaviors in a Network–ocracy

Before we turn to the puzzle of which behaviors would make the change in the Care Center for Disabled people, let's take a brief look at the concept of Viral Change. Nothing changes until you do something differently.

Departing from this idea, Leandro Herrero wrote the excellent book "Viral Change" (I absolutely recommend reading this). It focuses on behavior change: Viral Change means "contagious" behaviors that spread easily through the organizational system.

Though Herrero acknowledges the importance of beliefs and culture, he stresses the importance of making these concepts operational and visible in behaviors.

From a behaviorist point of view, Herrero explains that:

♦ All behaviors that occur are rewarded; they have an advantage or you wouldn't do it
♦ Behaviors stem from multiple causes but are maintained by the context: they are or are not reinforced (rewarded)
♦ Behaviors are specific: they are an observable action by an actor with a clear meaning (no interpretations are necessary).
♦ Behaviors can have various rewards (check for the reward – what makes it worthwhile?)
♦ Behaviors can disappear when you take the reward away or when you add punishment
♦ Behaviors can occur when you add a reward or take the punishment away

So, simply stated: What you reinforce is what you get. This is an interesting, practical view to look at behaviors when we're doing the puzzle of how to change which behaviors in our OCAI–workshop. We define the preferred culture down to new day–to–day behaviors: what to do and what not to do. Which behaviors are flexible and which are non–negotiable for the new culture? Moreover, how will they spread through the organizational system?

Non–linear Network–ocracy

We have already discussed that people copy, coach and correct one another. We utilize this mechanism to enhance new behaviors in a group of people. Finding opinion leaders or "positive energizers" (see Chapter 21) who'd like to pull this chariot of change will help new habits to spread. Adding the right rewards will help. But how will we reach a tipping point?

Finding leverage becomes easier when we see the organizational system as a network. Delete all images of the organization as a pyramid or a chart with the ever–powerful CEO on top. The CEO gives orders. The organization cascades them down in a linear way, level by level.

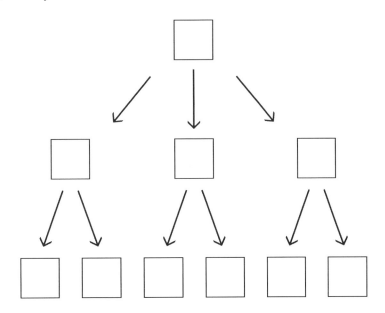

Big change initiatives were necessary to create big change into this cascade where energy and information were diminished with each level. Big words to reach the broad base of the organizational machinery. Cause and effect. Newtonian physics. "What goes up, must come down." Great pain will bring about large gain.

Now, imagine the organization as a web with many nodes. A dynamic hub with multiple interactions. A brain with countless neurological pathways and information and energy flowing in all directions. There's no top or bottom. Cause and effect are hard to discern. Complexity and comprehensiveness prevail. Everything is tied together, influencing each other. Yet, simple behaviors can spread easily and in a non–linear way. Small actions can produce huge outcomes. If many networking nodes copy a few small, easy behaviors, the network system at large will respond differently.

The nodes multiply and reinforce energy and information. Quantum physics might apply. The same idea emerging from two different directions in the system and

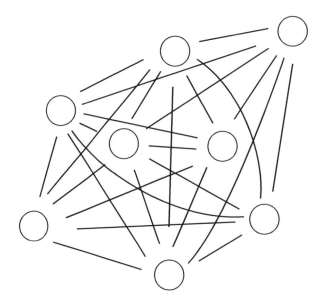

reinforcing. Some ideas go extinct without pain. Finding new gain without pain. Habits reinforcing each other, spreading easily and in a non–linear way through the organizational system.

Get the picture? Long story short: we'd like to find easy, copyable behaviors that we can do (even though we're busy, tired, etc.) and spread them through the system with a little help from our change agents or energizers (see Chapter 21).

The magic questions during this puzzle part of the OCAI–workshop are:

♦ Which behaviors will make a difference if everyone did them...?
♦ How can we help them spread? Or better: Who can spread those behaviors in the organization?

How to change? What to do?

Let's go back to the case of CCD. They knew, more or less, what their new culture must look like. Now they started their puzzle of how to change...? What to do to achieve this culture? The care center made a list of possible changes, like:

♦ They were going to revise their admission policy with clear criteria.
♦ They wanted to catch up on the arrears in administration and files. Everything should be up to date.
♦ They wanted to encourage "think time" because they tended to be "hyperactive". They tended to do things before thinking; always said Yes. They proposed a rule:

"If somebody asks you something, train yourself to first think: No, unless …" This is not because they wanted to reject all requests and proposals, but simply to encourage "think twice" as a practice for everybody.

Doing this with a group can work very well. It could feel like a game, an exercise in critical thinking. "No" as your standard response buys you time to assess if this request should be done immediately.

Does it match your criteria and priorities? Caretakers are trained to be active and respond quickly. But now they needed to think more businesslike. The new habit was to stop, think and make a conscious choice: Yes or No.

♦ They needed a training time management.
♦ They wanted to measure customer satisfaction and client's needs.
♦ Meetings start on time and closed doors are respected. We don't want people disturbing each other or jumping into meetings 15 minutes late asking "What did I miss?". We respect each others' time and concentration.
♦ It's essential to reframe the meaning of "care" with our team leaders. We care for current clients and staff. Because we care for them, we cannot admit everyone to this center. Professional, sustainable care in the long run means letting go of boundless family–like care and introducing realistic boundaries of time and money while still providing high–quality care. People are important but we also need to stay in business.

What is holding us back?

Next to the possible actions, we assess if there are any blockages that we need to solve first. What is holding us back? If this preferred culture with new behaviors is so important and we all agree, why aren't we already doing it? There must be a blockage. On which level are there any obstacles?

Thinking about the ABCDE levels, you could have a blockage on the B level in beliefs and basic assumptions, or there could be an obstacle at the C level – your capabilities. Identifying the level of an obstacle may help discover what you need to do to solve it. The solution to a problem is always on a higher level.

Imagine that the CCD employees agree on more awareness of time and money limitations. They say: "I'm going to wear my watch and not sit with a client for too long. Let's act more like caring professionals instead of family members."

However, team members continue to spend too much time with certain clients.

They agreed, but they're not doing as they promised. Maybe the blockage is on the B level because they didn't change their beliefs. They rationally know that they need to be more results–oriented, but they find it hard to do so. They still feel that a depressed client deserves all of their attention. Because they didn't change this belief, they will not consistently change their behavior and we cannot rely on them. They will skip administrative tasks to give the extra care the client needs according to this deep belief. We have to find a way to help them change this particular belief or nothing will consistently change in their behavior.

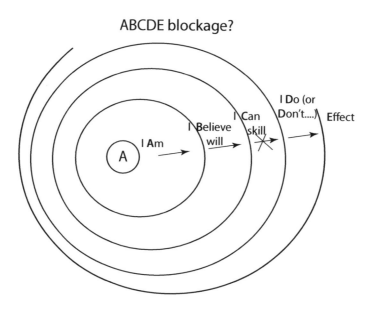

ABCDE blockage?

The care center identified a belief that held them back: "We must care for everyone like a Mom. We still have some second thoughts about market culture, achieving results and competing like a business. We feel like a family in our care for people. This is an important belief that we share but it may be one of the major obstacles to change."

Belief is at a high level of the ABCDE scheme and changing it can be a challenge, especially in a larger group. "If we change this belief that we must care for all disabled people, we slightly change our identity as an organization. That's not easy. It might cause some of our coworkers to leave because they don't feel comfortable. We've been working this way for almost 20 years. Is it worthwhile?" The managing team decided that this was a core belief that held them back. Changing it would take effort, but was necessary.

What else do we need?

They decided that they needed time management skills. They needed to know how to make business plans and work with budgets. Those were all at the competencies level, the C level, and could be easily solved by taking courses.

What should we honor to get support?

"We should honor our relationships with clients and among staff. We care for people. We're going to decrease clan culture and increase the business–like market culture, but nevertheless we honor relationships."

What little things can we start or stop with?

"We'll start working on a new admission policy. We agree on clear criteria within our financial framework and it will be clear to all staff who we're taking in and who doesn't fit according to our admission policy. Also, it's very important to be on time. Being on time for meetings means that you respect other people's time and that you care for people. This is what we start with right away."

What's the biggest leverage for our change?

"Focus on the budget and time management will help us change, though we still value relationships and we care for clients. It may feel harsh when you keep track of time and act like a professional while working with clients, but we'll stay in business in the long run when we focus on time and money. Reframing the meaning of true care will be vital to change our behavior and stick with it."

Start small...

Sometimes you can really work hard on something big – but it doesn't have to be big. This stems from our tacit assumption that we live in a linear world and change in large organizations needs big initiatives. However, science reveals how systems may operate in a non–linear way. Small things can cause huge effects. Question your tacit assumptions when you're working as a change consultant or agent. Do you believe in this change? Or are you merely following a method and hoping the best of it...?

People are busy and may have become weary of big change projects. They might even activate negative associations and memories. "Watching the CEO speak on a big screen all around the world, reading the change program on the Intranet, having New Change posters and logo's, but nothing changed. It cost a lot of money."

So, why not start small? Remember Herrero's Viral Change. I often try to find small, easy to copy behaviors that people can turn into habits even though they are busy. Keep it simple, small and easy. We can create long to–do lists and set up official and large change teams, scheduling meetings and producing paperwork – but that stirs talking instead of doing. How can we walk our talk even though we're busy?

Is there one behavior that would make a difference if everyone would do it? Imagine you can cast a spell and install this new habit overnight. What would happen?

Don't tell yourself that your new little habit won't change this whole organizational system. You can make a difference! While you do this you might inspire and reinforce the others to do it, too.

Remember the powerful interaction pattern between people of copying, coaching and correcting. Remember the tipping point. Inspire the others, find leverage, spread the habit among more people, see the difference, strengthen your motivation and enter a positive spiral of small changes – fueled by this belief that change is possible and every individual does make a difference in the system.

It can be worthwhile to spend some time thinking of a little thing that you can change that will have a major effect, a multiplier effect – the leverage to magic, the tipping point to real change. It becomes visible and thus very motivating for people to join the change.

◆ Which behaviors will make a difference if everyone did them...?
◆ Who can help those behaviors spread?

The care center decided it would be vital to glimpse at your watch and keep track of time, as a metaphor of the new, sustainable care within healthy boundaries. The watch would symbolize things like: be on time, time is money, think twice ("Is this wise?" and "Do you have time to do this?"). The essential nodes in the web to help this attitude and behaviors spread, would be their team leaders.

Can you create urgency?

"Why would we do it now?" This is a rightful question. "Why not work with culture next year? Let's first solve the financial issues." It's important that we feel this urgency. "We should have the OCAI workshops right now because they help us change our financial situation because we change the meaning of care, we question out–dated beliefs and agree on new, essential behaviors." The managing team of the care center felt: "We must change now. If we do, we won't go into bankruptcy and have to say goodbye to our clients."

Priorities. What first?

After exploring your actions, obstacles and solutions, you need to set priorities because you can't effectively focus on everything at the same time. CCD wanted to take four actions in the next year:

1. One year from now, our staff shares this idea of realistic care. It is acceptable to watch time and money and define good care as sustainable care.
2. One year from now we have a new admission policy that is clear and acceptable to everybody.
3. One year from now, our customer survey is done.
4. We have no more arrears in administration; client files are complete.

Indicators of change

Next they decided to keep track of change. Everything that is measured gets important. Budget is measurable – how much do we spend? But you can also measure the time spent on meetings, the number of meetings or how many people are working overtime in a week.

Choose a few things that are relevant and easy to measure. Everyone is busy enough – so keep this simple and quick – but do measure! A few indicators will help emphasize the biggest changes that are important to stimulate the new culture. Check the appraisal system when it comes to measuring indicators of change. If employees are not acknowledged for the new behaviors, let alone rewarded by formally including them in their annual job evaluation, the new habits may feel redundant, like a bonus or optional, instead of vital to the change.

Including new, specific behaviors in the appraisal system sends a strong signal: this is vital to our culture. This is a must–do. It enhances accountability. "It's not a favor when I try to do the new behaviors. It's part of my job as a professional in this new culture. It's great that I get peer support and back–up by my team leader. I am allowed some time to practice. But in the end, it is part of the job and I'm supposed to do it."

This is an example of a measure outside the individual that stimulates behavior change. An employee can be convinced and find inner motivation to change habits.

But the E–level, the environment outside the individual mind, is very powerful. Here we find peer support and coaching leaders but also new procedures that enforce new behaviors, actual results (time and money indicators) and other measurements like the appraisal system.

How does the care center know that they have achieved this change?

1. They have a new admission policy that is being used.
2. Their customer survey is done.
3. Their files are complete.
4. The new meaning and belief of realistic care is expressed in new behaviors by all staff.

It means keeping track of time, effort and money. It becomes visible in a smaller number of employees working overtime, if everyone sticks to their schedule and doesn't sit with clients for hours. It means that meetings start on time and you can't get in if you're late. It means that the total hours of meetings are reduced (and meeting time is measured). The belief is visible in behavior, which will be proved by the meeting records, work time records, absenteeism, etc.

BE–lief

This particular managing team truly adopted the vision "We are the change." This famous quotation from Gandhi – "Be the change you want to see in the world" – inspired them to walk their talk and be role models of the new culture. They showed extraordinary leadership in change (more in Chapter 20).

"We are the change. If we can't agree or we have any doubts, we should talk and try to solve it." They understood they could only lead this change if they were fully congruent. They had to believe in the new culture themselves. They needed to change personally. They needed to wear a watch and keep track of time and budgets.

Everything you believe is ultimately expressed in behavior. If a manager doesn't trust his or her employees, this belief will be visible in behavior. The manager will check files and working hours and ask employees what they did and why. Even if the manager claims to trust the team and withholds from checking files, the distrust will be visible in subtle nonverbal signals like frowning, tone of voice, etc, that will be detected by employees.

When people are not consciously aware, automatic responses control their behavior and non–verbal communication. It's an efficient short cut of the mind. It runs automated programs so the conscious mind is free to think about other topics. These beliefs and responses are conclusions you have drawn from earlier experiences.

When people are distressed or in a hurry for instance, these beliefs surface by e.g. frowning, bickering or shouting – in automatic mode people are not controlling their facial expression, posture or voice. They express beliefs they would normally hide or suppress, like: "My opinion is more important than others." Or, "I'm worthless." Or, "Others are dangerous, never trust them." Or, "Change is impossible."

If you think this is exaggerated and these beliefs don't count in the workplace, please think again. Most dysfunctional or unpleasant behaviors derive from automated responses based on tacit beliefs and assumptions we hold about the world, reality, work, other human beings and ourselves.

An example: I claim that I really care about people. You might find this is only lip service because when I'm busy, I simply run past a client who is obviously and anxiously lost in our building. I'm on automatic mode and my belief is guiding my behavior.

Deep down inside, this could be phrased like: "I'm more important than others and I want to get things done. I care about achieving results." I want to catch up with my deadlines and I ignore the lost person – I'm not helping out and putting people first. Being the change you want to see in your workplace supposes that you really believe in this change because your nonverbal signals and behaviors will tell the others if you are for real...Make sure to read more about this in Chapter 21 on Change Leadership!

The care center for disabled people needed workshops for all of their staff and support from opinion leaders because they faced a major change in their belief systems. This was touching the core of their organization. The workshops facilitated a serious dialogue about the new meanings – what is good, sustainable care? We care for people in the long run. They needed to reframe their old belief.

Stories are important to sell the change because stories, images and metaphors will easily be remembered. The managing team wondered "How can we make this change more clear? Because we still need too many words to explain."

This is the metaphor they used:

"Imagine we draw a party and we have supplies for 20 people. If we admit everyone, it means that we will get hungry eventually. If we dig in our supplies we can provide for 35 guests, but then we're running out of drinks and food.

How to change beliefs?

The behaviorist approach is important and I always try to find typical behaviors to do in the new culture and to reinforce those through copy–coach–correct, finding leverage in the system by engaging positive energizers and other change agents. Sometimes, as we have seen, core beliefs or meanings must be changed because they block true, sustainable change.

The OCAI–workshop in itself is a way to influence and change collective beliefs and meanings by respectful dialogue, acknowledging what is good, bending what could be improved and altering meaning by reframing in a safe group. You can't change other's beliefs, but collaborating this way can entice every individual to start thinking differently. This can be powerful!

However, sometimes this is not enough. People might hold personal beliefs that hamper new behaviors. In that case, one–on–one coaching is necessary. This can be done by team leaders, outside coaches or other professionals. There are numerous exercises from disciplines like Neuro Linguistic Programming (NLP) designed to alter beliefs.

A method that addresses the powerful, habitual subconscious mind (that stores beliefs and stirs automatic actions and responses) is Psych–K. This can be more efficient than talking with the conscious mind that will understand and verbalize but eventually does not control beliefs, non–verbal communication and sustainable behaviors. That's the realm of the subconscious mind.

Sometimes this type of one–on–one intervention for key individuals in the system is necessary to get the change going. Key individuals are those nodes in the network who are very visible (leaders for instance) and who can make a difference by being the change. Others are prone to copy their behaviors.

The exercises to change beliefs are not explained here because they must be executed by a trained professional. If beliefs are blocking your change, please find a coach, NLP or Psych–K practitioner to facilitate this belief change process! These key one–on–ones may make the difference for the organizational system as a whole and be well worth their time and money spent. You'll find an example of beliefs in Chapter 14.

This theme is from the fairy tale of the ant and the cricket. The cricket is living in the moment and not thinking ahead and guarding our winter supplies. The ant works through the summer to be safe in the winter.

So we cannot admit everyone. We'd love to share, but it means that current clients and staff will lose everything in the end. Care, attention and quality means sharing wisely and making provisions in time before the winter.

This may feel a bit harsh and against laws of hospitality, but here's the thing: We are not the only house in the street. There's a village of care centers out there and we share clients with them. We're not leaving anybody in the cold. Clients can go to another place; we have good competitors that will take care of them."

The care center went through a very heavy process. They had a major obstacle on the high B–level: their belief that they must care for everyone all the time. Staff got very emotional. The higher the level you're trying to change, the more emotions are associated with it. Some people quit their jobs. They couldn't live with the new rules. The majority developed to make the change: after the first shock, it made sense.

Eventually, they were able to alter their core belief and attach a new meaning to their work as care takers. They saw themselves as professionals. They were not family members to clients, but doing a great, meaningful job and contributing to society. But it was a very heavy process for an organization facing a downsizing.

Change from two sides

Note also that they used change from two sides. The inside–out part was from changing beliefs to changing behavior. This process started in the workshops. The dialogues helped to see the necessity of the more results–oriented new behaviors and to agree on a new collectively, shared meaning. "Our care is good, sustainable, professional care."

The team leaders worked with their teams on accepting this new meaning. The metaphor about admitting everybody to your house, helped employees to change their minds. They wanted to provide sustainable quality care.

Some people left eventually. This took a lot of time: talking and feeling, mourning over past times. Moving from denial to resistance to exploration ("maybe this could work out") to acceptance. Like in the Change Cycle (based on the ideas of Elisabeth Kübler–Ross):

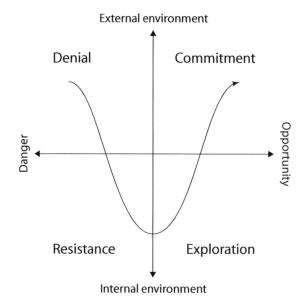

Because of their people–oriented culture they knew the importance of true buy–in, instead of pushing the new rules and forcing people to obey. That wouldn't work because they had always valued consensus and participation.

Though they were in a hurry, running out of time and money, they aligned with current culture; departing from the familiar way they did things around here. Employees felt appreciated, because they were acknowledged in their feelings and asked for collaboration. They shared a fate; together they would survive.

There was also change from outside–in. People can have great intentions and try to execute new behaviors but it's easy to go back to old habits. Most of the time we need something to help us persevere. The care center changed their admission policy and that was support from outside–in. Team budgets were frozen and they published meeting times and overtime working hours.

Team leaders stimulated staff to be on time and to think and act more like care professionals. Most team leaders provided a different environment for employees because they embodied the change. This was a powerful signal, telling everyone it was serious this time. New behaviors by leaders provided an outside stimulus for employees to change, too. Because the managing team so believed in the change, they were very trustworthy in bringing the message. The managing team was very close, collaborating as a true team, which helped them execute this major change. They supported each other to display the new behaviors themselves and stick with it.

Being open, they won the hearts and minds of employees. They were genuine and credible, because they shared their own pain. "It is hard for all of us, but if we don't

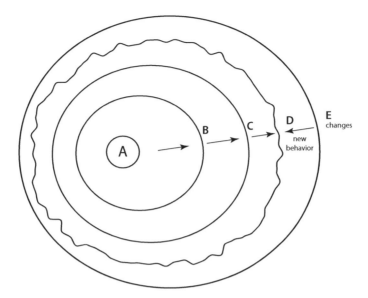

change, we will go out of business. I find this awkward too, but I have to prioritize..."

They also shared the gains, publishing decreasing number of expensive overtime hours and emphasizing long–term advantages like sustainable care thanks to planning, timely breaks and more efficient work.

Leaders practiced new behaviors to create a different experience. Action speaks louder than words – and small things can have great impact. Leaders create the outside context for their team members.

The same counts for coworkers around me. When everyone does it, my outside context changes, enticing me to change, too. I'd like to belong to the team and start copying the new behaviors. I'd like to be appreciated and I respond to my team leader's compliments for the new behaviors.

This is how peer support (copy–coach–correct) in a small team (remember the Power of 10) creates a different Environment (level E) and helps people to practice and stick with the change and turn the new behaviors into habits.

Leaders help change behaviors. An example:

If you are too late for a meeting you can't get in anymore, in this new, professional care culture. You are 10 minutes late and the door is closed but you know your team leader likes your input. You try: "Come on, John, you know me. Sorry, I had a problem with a client but I'm here now!"

2 Directions of Change on the ABCDE Levels

A – Reframe your story or metaphor: find new meaning
B – Change or lift limiting beliefs by one–on–one talks, the OCAI–workshop or team meetings
Give people coaching, NLP, Psych–K, Provocative coaching or Theater Playback
C – Offer people skills training
Practice new skills with coworkers (peer support or practice sessions)
Hire new staff with the right skills (and copy those)
Provide (other) resources that stimulate the new skills and behaviors

DO it, Do it, Do it (beware of just talking about it)

E – Leaders and coworkers behave differently (creating a new context)
New behaviors are rewarded in the appraisal system
Indicators of change are measured: meeting time, budget, working overtime, etc.
New structure reinforces new behaviors
Other office lay–out reinforces new behaviors/more communication/less meetings etc.

This is a challenge for John because he has to say "No". – We're not used to that... Our old culture fostered Yes – a cozy, friendly clan culture where people felt comfortable and avoided confrontations. If John gives in, we might not achieve the preferred culture in the end because all these little actions make up our culture. If he gives in once, you're going to try again next time. The others in the meeting room witnessed and will try it too, next time.

They might tell their coworkers and people will start coming late again, starting a non–linear reverse spiral... John might end up waiting 10 minutes before the others arrive to meetings. This way, we will not reach the critical mass we need as a tipping point to change.

John has to say "No" when you are late and not let you join the meeting. This will teach you and the others to be on time. It is an unpleasant experience. But if John explains it friendly, you may not take it personally. We have to respect the new rules – or nothing will change.

This is an example of a very small action that has large effects. John shows consistent leadership and motivation to persist – to keep doing it even when it's hard and people plead to go back to the old ways... "Please let me in. We used to do it. Just once ..." You must be motivated and persist. This is the will and skill of change, especially for leaders as role models, whether they like it or not. More about this later on, in Chapter 21.

Recap: Change tips

When you have finished your puzzle of How to Change, there is some general advice on change that we've seen before, remember:

◆ Find a small, quick win that is visible to everybody. Start small, with copyable behaviors that are reinforced.
◆ Obtain support from the opinion leaders. If you have organized it well, the most important opinion leaders are also in your project group for change, so you're working with them. But if you're not, find out who they are and obtain their support. Use the leverage in your Network–ocracy and use Viral Change.
◆ Make your targets smartie (S.M.A.R.T.I.E), so they are specific, measurable, acceptable, realistic with a time deadline, and above all, Inspiring and Energizing. If you make your goals specific, you have a much higher chance of actually achieving them. You measure everything that you want to achieve. Find some indicators that will tell you that you're on the right track because everything that gets attention will grow. If everybody starts measuring the time they spend on meetings or the budget that they are using with their clients, everybody knows that this is really important. While measuring these indicators – everybody is training themselves in market culture.
◆ Communication is incredibly important because we are exchanging meaning and building respect and relationships. What does it all mean? Should we worry? What's next? Who do you value because you bother to inform them? If you find that the accomplishments so far aren't good enough, simply focus on the progress

and say "We're not there yet, but if we keep doing this we'll achieve our preferred culture." The focus on the process might help people stay motivated and not discouraged because they haven't achieved preferred culture yet. New habits, a new culture, may take some time...

◆ See it through... Practice Progress, not Perfection. See below:

One last thing. You can stop here, thinking you are done. Engage everyone in workshops. Understand current and preferred culture down to the level of typical behaviors. Feel the urgency to change. Identify and solve obstacles. Agree on new key behaviors that will make a difference. Leave optimistically. And go back to your old habits.

We're accustomed to talk and think a lot. But don't just read this, DO it...! If we leave out 4C, 5C, 6C and 7C, we have wasted time and money on this culture assessment and workshops. We have raised expectations but went back to business as usual, damaging faith in change processes, in management and in the organization.

We should continuously communicate (4C) but above all consistently copy, coach and correct (5C). We lead the way to create critical mass (6C). We must carry on, though we get tired or bored (7C) in the messy middle, longing for a happy ending...

I have seen too many change processes that stopped here. Having commitment from top management (1C), working on clarity about current and preferred culture (2C) and truly engaging to get consensus and commitment from all staff in the workshops (3C).

From that point on, those organizations took over for rightful reasons of budget and the will to take ownership for their own change. They thanked the consultant who left, feeling excited about their will and skill, their potential...

But they were like normal people. They were busy. They had too many goals and too little hours in a day. It was hard to focus. Most of them were serious about change but their customers needed attention, their boss walked in, the profits went down, this emergency occurred...

One way or the other, they found it hard to sustain the momentum, to communicate, to copy–coach–correct, to be as alert and focused on behavior as you need to be. They were lacking true change leadership and did not reach a critical mass, let alone they could persevere because they hardly practiced new behaviors in their busy working days. You are never done. Change is the new normal. Once the workshops are over, true change begins in everyday life. Here is the proof of the pudding: in the eating. This is why you need to organize your outside–in change measures very well.

See to your managers and leaders; teach them how to role–model change and respond to old behaviors, thus reinforcing the desired new habits. Support your change agents. Organize true peer support. Utilize each other. It's perfectly human to find it hard, every now and then to give up – like when you're on a diet or want to quit smoking.

Make it work! Arrange reminders, refreshers, new momentum. Stimulate and anchor new behaviors in systems (appraisals) etc. If you give up now, the damage is much worse than a few workshop days spent in vain. You give up the belief that change is possible at all. If you do, your organization might be doomed in this speedy 21st century.

Summary

Spend as much time as necessary on reaching consensus about your plan of change and all its details. Use the Power of 10, identify obstacles on different levels, find solutions, come up with some smart actions within a good timeframe and then persist. This is the exciting HOW–puzzle. What will make a difference in your organizational system...?

Engage everyone in small teams. Encourage them to change their ways of thinking and encourage new behaviors.

Develop change inside–out and outside–in. Agree on small actions that can have a huge impact on achieving your preferred culture. Use system leverage and help change go "viral". Check on behaviors and how to reinforce them.

Use the network–ocracy. Find small, copyable behaviors that spread easily. Don't hesitate to apply one–on–ones to change core beliefs for key individuals. Actions by leaders create a different context for staff, stimulating them to change habits.

Select priorities – you can't do it all at once! Keep change feasible and motivating. Find the details that make the difference and stick with them.

Now that we've finished the workshop, we're not done yet! We'll explore different behaviors and dark sides of the culture types in Chapter 15 and show examples of interventions and persistence in Chapter 16.

Also, attend some more OCAI–workshops in the cases we present. These will help you gain more insight into organizational culture and change. We've got change leadership and positive change in Chapter 21.

Last but not least, explore the vision of organizational future in Chapter 23... Ready for more views, insights and examples? Let's go to the next chapter and attend another workshop in the Rehab case.

Chapter 14 Case at the Rehab. Is Choosing Losing?

In this chapter we do another OCAI–workshop, this time with a Rehabilitation Center. This case gives you more ideas on typical behaviors and beliefs, but we also show how to start influencing beliefs in the workshop and how to design new beliefs – that you'd like to be true.

This group also analyzes the rewards for typical behaviors (why do these behaviors occur?) and decides to respond differently, thus taking the reward out of them. We'll see how hard it can be to minimize your strategic goals – but how powerful if you do!

Last but not least, we will use the CVF to narrow down their preferred priorities: What is most important now? Simple questions help discover the Value/Criteria hierarchy and make a unique blend of Competing Values.

The Rehabilitation Center exists more than 100 years, aiming to help people who suffer from physical disabilities and who are recovering from illnesses and accidents. Their main location is in a city but they have six other locations in smaller towns as well. With a staff of 700 and an annual patient population of 7,000, they are rather large.

There are many developments in health care that call for change. We see an aging population and an increase of wealth–related diseases. In the field of care, there are many technological developments that enhance specialization, e.g. robotics. When it comes to competition, more and more care homes are offering physical rehab programs as well.

Patients prefer short programs close by their homes. Government agencies provide less and less public funding while the quality demands for care stay high. At the same time, there's an upcoming shortage in the labor market for specialized nurses and caretakers.

The Rehab Center just smoothed their structure to get more efficient. Now it's time to look at their culture and become future proof. The first workshop is for executives: the Board of Directors and the medical heads and managers of the six locations attend, including some staff managers from HR and Finance. About 23 people recognize their current culture immediately from the assessment.

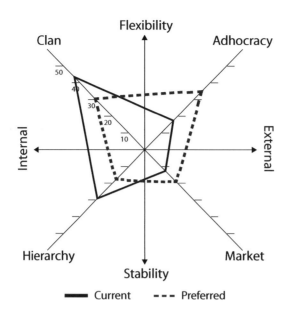

Current ——— **Preferred** ----

A dominant people–oriented clan culture (over 42 points) backed up by over 28 points hierarchy culture. Their current focus is internally while the developments described above call for an external focus – as they all agree instantly.

Current Behaviors and Beliefs

We start with gaining a deeper understanding of their current culture and finding the particular behaviors that make up their typical Rehab culture. In small groups, the participants come up with a list of current culture:

◆ We are loyal to each other and we care
◆ We meet with colleagues after work, in our spare time.
◆ We don't make choices (we want to do everything)
◆ We want to do everything very well.
◆ We don't give feedback to a person directly (but we talk about them to others)
◆ We are waiting for information, we don't actively go get it
◆ We resist decisions by not executing them (though we agreed or understood the decision)
◆ We question decisions that are taken by the right authority. Participative decision making goes too far, leading to endless debate.
◆ We are self–centered, safeguarding our personal comfort zone. The next circle of commitment is our direct team and only sometimes we look at the interests of the organization. Example: If school times change and I have to pick up my child earlier, the team has to cover me and the organization has to alter my schedule. Employees expect this but don't take control by making other arrangements at

home. "The organization is looking after us".

- ◆ Leaders are like a father figure and have a parenting style. Empathy and attention.
- ◆ We still share stories from way back (we are a 100 years old!)
- ◆ We are loaded with meetings. We talk, talk, talk – but we don't always take action.
- ◆ If we disagree, it is quickly labeled as a conflict.
- ◆ We communicate in the hallways, preferably.

While we discuss this list in the plenary session, the participants start like this: "People do... They..." But who is displaying these behaviors? How are you, as executives, part of the current culture? Is this something that "people" do or is it something that WE all do, from time to time?

The group admits that the behaviors should be labeled as something that WE all tend to do... This is an important insight. It takes the "us and them" out of the discussion and closes the classical gap between managers and employees. It shows that we are all human, and we tend to do certain things and keep old interaction patterns alive by the way we respond. Note also that the current culture list could be further specified. "We are loyal" could be elaborated into specific behaviors, like: "We replace a colleague and do their chores when they ask for help."

Current Collective Beliefs

Next to the current behaviors, that are mostly rooted in clan culture, the group makes a list of collective underlying beliefs:

- ◆ It has to be cozy and nice around here
- ◆ Conflicts are to be avoided, they're wrong
- ◆ You may not disagree
- ◆ New things are scary and risky
- ◆ Everything should stay the same
- ◆ The organization should take care of us
- ◆ Health Care is a caring clan (It is NOT a business)
- ◆ Choosing is losing – everything is important!

It is interesting to see how these beliefs support the current behaviors.

"It has to be cozy and conflicts are wrong, we're not supposed to disagree." They don't give direct feedback and keep things "nice" on the surface, but they don't execute decisions they don't agree with. "Everything should stay the same" keeps them in their comfort zones, away from doing new things and taking action on decisions. They re-tell old stories. "We always used to do it like this..." "The organization should take care of us" keeps them waiting for information and passive, expecting coaching and solutions from leaders and within their comfort zones. Note that these beliefs are largely limiting beliefs that are able to block change. They must be addressed to proceed.

Influencing Beliefs

Identifying and altering beliefs can be done in separate one–on–one sessions with a coach or in small workshops with a group of close colleagues who are comfortable enough to open up.

Behavior exists because it is rewarded. To find the advantage of beliefs and behavior, keep asking why – until you find the ultimate reason. This ultimate advantage could be obtained in an alternative way – this is where you may find the solution. This way, you can safeguard important values or advantages while replacing limiting beliefs with alternative, empowering beliefs and behaviors. Let's take a look at an example how that can be done, to give you an idea. If you want to apply such techniques, consider an NLP course to learn more.

Why?

Why do we want to keep it cozy?
Because that is comfortable
Because we like each other

Why should you never disagree?
Because it leads to conflicts (always?)

Why should you avoid conflicts?
Because conflicts cause hassle and discomfort
Because people might get hurt
Because we like each other and we want to keep our relationships well

The reward is comfort: belonging to a group of like–minded people.

Now challenge these beliefs:

Is it possible to always fully agree about everything with all the others?
No...

What do you do if you don't fully agree with someone?
I don't directly say so (but don't keep the appointment)
I talk about it to others

Does that behavior provide the reward?

Is that comfortable?
Uh– yes, at first. But eventually, they ask me why I didn't do it...and then I have to say it anyway. It doesn't feel straight to talk to others. I feel powerless, tiptoeing around issues. It can be a hassle, really.

Keep the reward and tie it to new, alternative behaviors

How could you keep the comfort of belonging to a group of like–minded people and avoid the hassle of tiptoeing around issues and gossip?
By agreeing to disagree – sometimes – in a respectful way. We may disagree or give feedback about the content – but not about persons. We accept people, but not all of their behaviors or decisions. But you still belong to our group.

This is a short example of a possible intervention on the Beliefs–level. If a close team truly agrees on this resolution, they can make a plan on how they will do this. Do they need a skills training on decision making or giving feedback? (the C–level of Competencies). How will they support and reinforce the new behavior in the team? (the D–level, we Do). What will happen as an effect? Should they take measures on the Environment–level? For instance: they institutionalize disagreement by appointing a different "devil's advocate" in each formal meeting who must disagree on purpose.

This could help all participants to the meeting change their think style and check if they really agree with a decision, help them get used to respectfully disagreeing on the content but keeping personal relationships well, working out a solution.

Strategic Plan: Focus, Short and Simple?

Let's go back to the Rehab workshop. They nod and agree: This is our current basis of collective beliefs and behaviors! It gives quite some insight to see those beliefs on the flip. This is what we really feel...

Looking at their future challenges, they must change. They can't have everything stay the same with the world outside changing: less government funding, scarcity in specialized staff, increasing specialization and technological developments in the Rehab field, demanding patients who want short programs close by. They need a shift to the right–hand quadrants of the Competing Values Framework and work on their external focus, they agree immediately.

The Board has developed an extensive strategic plan for the coming five years. It contains topics like:

♦ Customer and market orientation:
♦ 3% growth, offering new services and treatments, provide great quality and reliability, accomplishing the best Rehab results.
♦ Research and development: more research and scientific publications, including funding to do so. Innovation is necessary.
♦ Achieving cost efficiency and higher productivity (with many details on how to do this).
♦ Investment in human resource development.

These topics are worked out in a detailed plan of many, many actions.

However, the present executives find it hard to reproduce their strategic spear points by heart for the next five years. What are the most important goals to achieve? Do you know, if you don't check the strategic plan? They hesitate.

The human brain can keep approximately 3–7 items in active memory. As a rule of thumb: 5 things at the same time, like the fingers of one hand. Though this is a simplification, it helps to bring goal setting down to realistic proportions.

Their strategic plan may be too extensive and too comprehensive. You can't do everything at the same time – it will be a little of everything and that means a dispersion of energy plus getting very tired. If you want to move, you need to take the first step in a particular direction.

More is Less

By the way, this is not the first time that executives of an organization can't tell me their strategy and most important goals by heart, in a few sentences. Let alone employees. Professionals are trained in creating detailed, well–formulated packs of paper.

But what matters ultimately is not the length or comprehensiveness of the strategic plans, but whether they are implemented or not. Do they make it from thinking to talking to... doing? That depends on many factors, one of them being the staff's engagement and alignment with current culture, but an important key is: More is less.

Is it simple and short? Can we memorize it? Visualize it? Is it inspirational? Can you tell your mother in five minutes what you're doing and why? Can you boil it down to a few points?

In their current strategic five year plan, all culture types are present. They want everything and this is understandable. However, if you have a square of 4 equally important things, the square is not likely to move.

It is solid and massive and a lot of everything while a strong focus on one culture type gives direction to a change. A triangle profile points you in a certain direction, enticing you to move. It provides clarity. So, if you want to move, you need to take the first step. Towards...Adhocracy culture? Or market culture? If they want to shift to the right, external focus, what will be their first direction?

We get a fierce debate and a great dialogue. They don't want to choose. They think it is too exaggerated. They see their collective beliefs in action: Choosing is losing – everything is important! And: We want to do everything well.

The Board, especially, hangs on to their detailed, well–balanced strategy. This is simply an exercise. This is exactly why I ask them to take a stand and chose now between either adhocracy or market culture. What will be the first step?

Of course, you need them all. But they need to become aware how "everything" might create "neither meat nor fish" as the Dutch saying goes. It is a square culture profile that doesn't stand out in one direction and is likely to get stuck. So I make them chose. They need to establish consensus of what the most important focus should be for the next period of time.

If you're standing still on two feet and you want to move, which foot are you stepping on first? To the left, to the right, in front of you or backwards? Every first step has a direction.

Hierarchy of Values and Criteria

So, what is more important? Cost efficiency or research, development and innovation? Should you focus on new treatments and robotics or on a 3% growth of annual patients? Is human resource development and feedback skills training more necessary than higher productivity?

The line of questioning to discover your ranking is:

◆ Would you swap (efficiency) for (innovation)? (=yes/no)
◆ If you would have to give up (innovation) to achieve (efficiency), would you do so? (=yes/no)

The brackets can contain any value or criterion you like.

By asking these questions, you can determine your ranking of values and criteria. The CVF is a framework of Competing Values. We'd like to have them all at the same time, but, hey – welcome to reality. This ranking or "Hierarchy of Values and Criteria" is important to know. If a group finds true consensus on their ranking, they stand strong when they are tried by reality. The same counts for individuals. First, they have to decide on this ranking. Later on, we can find nuances and combine the best of both worlds by answering the questions that the Competing Values Framework poses:

◆ How can we foster innovation while keeping the costs acceptable (to this specific extent)?
◆ Or: how can we control costs while we focus on these specific innovations?
◆ How can we help employees speak their mind while enhancing productivity (without endless meetings and debate)?
◆ How do we develop new treatments while we're busy achieving a 3% growth rate?

The line of questioning from the CVF is:

◆ How can we achieve [topic] while we keep [topic]?
◆ How can we achieve [topic] without [topic, criteria, behaviors to be avoided]? Or, reversely:
◆ How can we avoid [topic] while we focus on [topic you want to achieve, stimulate, do more of]?

Answering these questions can be very powerful and inspirational. This line of thinking may stimulate creative thinking and finding solutions to choose well – while still keeping some of the old advantages, values or habits. This way, you can depart from current culture, without completely denying it, and slowly bend it towards the preferred culture.

Random example:

You can achieve better performance (Market culture) while you keep a people–orientation (Clan culture). All leaders will emphasize and score performance on their appraisal forms, but they will do so in their "old" people–oriented way: they set the targets with participation of the employee, coach them to achieve the targets, then evaluate and score.

Employees get three chances to make the targets, only after they don't make those three times, they are kindly helped to find another job. This may seem like you're still not choosing, but you are. You put targets and performance first in your criteria ranking. But you achieve those in a friendly, fair way, helping people, but they are second. Eventually, their results decide whether people can stay or not. Though it looks a bit harsh and not nuanced, the ranking–questions–and–answers look like this:

♦ Would you swap people for results? No.
♦ If you have to give up people to achieve results, would you do so? Yes.

Ergo, results are 1, people are 2. Now, determine the nuances and criteria–how–to...

♦ How can we achieve results while we keep people?
♦ How can we achieve results without whipping people with targets, scaring them (so they don't perform at all) and stirring resistance or enhancing burnouts? Or, reversely:
♦ How can we avoid resistance, burnouts, fear and losing friendliness while we focus on performance and results?

For the answers, see the example above: we coach them to focus on results and targets. Achieve market culture in a clan culture way... Depart from current clan and eventually achieve preferred market culture.

Back to the Rehab: Preferred Culture

The Rehab executives choose adhocracy culture as their main focus. If they enhance entrepreneurship and ownership, if they feel accountable for their own job (not wait for the boss), if they have the flexibility to do work their own way, if they become creative, open to learn, daring to disagree, looking for new treatments and innovations, trying new things, giving and receiving feedback... they will get there!

Other–focused

"External" is a keyword, they see. External focus could mean: looking outside of the organization, to the market, patients, research, government, competition. But it could also mean: looking outside of yourself. They'd like to add this meaning and use external as "other–focused".

Some suggest they should all question themselves with anything they do: "How would this be for my coworkers, my team, the other department, the patient, the organization?" An answer could be: "My behavior could be disappointing and frustrating for the other, who believes that I agree – while I don't."

Answering this question, will help all employees and executives gain an external focus at all times – avoiding undesirable behavior like waiting for the boss, agreeing on the surface, but not truly speaking your mind, guarding your own comfort.

And the next "mature" thought could be: "Because I am people–oriented and value my coworkers, I will be straight to keep our relationship well and comfortable in the long run. I will deal with the short discomfort of saying No and explain it well. We might gain a better understanding and the trust that if someone says Yes, you can count on it."

Practice to disagree

Uncomfortable as it is, this dialogue is about the focus and spear points of the strategic plan. The chairman of the Board feels personally attacked and starts to defend his plan. The others respectfully disagree but find it hard – they're not used to challenging him or his plans.

I tell them to go on: this is the new behavior! Practice it now... "We agree to disagree, we dare to disagree." They all know how to do it, they have to simply practice this more often.

I help the chairman to not take it personally. They are not attacking him as a person. They value him – he's been their anchor for over 25 years. But he is like a strong father figure, while these modern professionals, highly–educated, committed and mature executives are ready to do their jobs. They have valuable ideas as well. They must be aligned with his strategic focus to implement it consistently.

This is not about the chairman. This is about a team of professionals taking ownership for the strategy, aligning on the focus, reaching consensus and clarity on the next collective step. This is evolving into a mature leadership team. They're excited and uncomfortable at the same time... Learning new behaviors on the spot, during the workshop, practicing with disagreeing, speaking their minds and learning.

Preferred Culture

Next, they move on to elaborate on their preferred culture. They start to get some idea from the previous discussion. They make lists of new behaviors in small groups and present the outcomes in the plenary session. Eventually, they come up with this summary of the most important things:

Clan culture

New behavior:
Check according to the criterion "Other–focused"
Give and accept honest feedback

We keep:
Loyalty and participation
Empathy and attention
Small teams with a coaching leader

Less of:
Regular meetings
Consensus – this is not always possible!
Avoiding conflict
Re–telling old stories
Gossip and talking–about–others

Stop doing this:
Paternalism, keeping the others small
Re–disputing decisions

Adhocracy culture

New behavior:
Check with the keyword "External"
Take risks within boundaries
Experiment and innovate
Take and give space, take ownership
Dare to disagree
Learning is giving and getting feedback
Try something new
Stimulate innovation in projects

Hierarchy culture

Less of:
Regular meetings
Relying on the boss (they must solve it)
Waiting
Finger–pointing
"Everything" – we start making choices

Market culture

New behavior:
Set priorities and stick with them
Set goals and give feedback on professional behavior
We make rational choices ("Choosing is professional")

Their dominant clan culture currently keeps people comfortable in small groups while their current hierarchy culture reinforces a dependent attitude ("My boss must sign for permission, I wait and see"). Their main challenge is to stimulate an attitude of ownership and mature professionalism. Ownership is the label to describe an empowering, professional mindset like: owning the problems of the entire organization or team, feeling responsible and doing something about issues. Instead of: wait–and–see, just talking about it, complaining, finger pointing, hiding, justifying and "it's not my job". Ownership could be part of any healthy, effective culture type. Their main focus is to combine this empowering mindset with an emphasis on adhocracy culture interventions.

Now they know "What" they want, they have to find out "How" this can be done most effectively. The How depends on many factors, but the daily behavior of the leaders is always a crucial factor – it creates the context or Environment–level (E) for employees. It helps employees change from outside–in (next to inside–out, if you engage your team in their own workshop and help them reach insights). Leaders have to coach and correct their teams all the time, being as alert as you would be when training a puppy. Thus giving signals: "This behavior is okay, this is not". Next to intervening and interacting, leaders should embody the new behavior and make it easy for their teams to copy them.

Take rewards away

The executives take a look at what they must stop doing, unlearn or decrease. Stopping is best done by discouraging these undesired behaviors and taking the reward away.

♦ Discourage paternalism as a leader by not giving your employees a solution. Ask them: "How would you solve this? What else can you do? What have you tried already?"
♦ Discourage gossip by intervening immediately. "Have you told this person what you've just told me? I think you'd better tell them." Giving them the signal that you do not respond to gossip.
♦ Discourage endless discussions by stopping them. "This is an authorized decision. It's no use discussing it anymore. We have to accept it and we've got work to do."
♦ Discourage too many meetings by assessing necessity. Is it need to know or nice to know? Is this about sharing information (can be done by reading documents as well) or opinion forming (a good reason for a discussion) or decision making (a good reason to meet).

Add rewards to new behaviors

The Rehab leaders can increase the new, desired behavior by adding rewards.

♦ Publicly appreciate someone who took ownership and who arranged something (even though it wasn't how you would have done it yourself) by complimenting them in a team meeting. Describe the desired behavior: "This is the new Rehab culture: not waiting for permission, but taking action when something needs to be fixed immediately."
♦ Check on frowns and other non–verbal communication and ask: What's your opinion? Do you disagree? Appreciate people who disagree and try to bring hidden conflicts to the table.
♦ Stimulate debate – before the authorized decision is taken. Afterwards, reinforce acceptance of the decision.

Take obstacles away

What obstacles against the new behavior do exist in our systems, procedures and structure? Do you need interventions that are non–behavioristic?

♦ Broaden the budget range within which people can take decisions without their boss's signature.
♦ Put the topic "discussion" on every meeting's agenda – as a gentle reminder to

discuss subjects.

- Abrogate certain "standard" meetings, enticing people to call for a meeting only when this is necessary to take a formal decision.
- Install a formal "devil's advocate" role in each meeting that circulates to different staff members each meeting.
- Investigate if changes in the organization's structure can stimulate a valuable difference in behaviors...
- Do people need a skills training to learn how to give proper feedback? This could be an important intervention in the Rehab system as well. During such a training, they can influence beliefs about feedback, the value of disagreeing and comfortably collaborating. How about: "True coworkers give each other honest feedback to improve their work."

Be the change

The leaders will apply the new behaviors themselves, as executives. They could check in what ways they depend on the Board as an executive...? How could they take more ownership themselves? How would they give and take space in their location or department? I give them reflection questions to take home. For now, they decide to do five things (Not more! Choose! More is less! Focus!):

- Check if your behavior or decision is "other–focused". "What does this mean for the other department?"
- Check if your behavior or decision is "external". "Would this help our patients? How would this look on the market?"
- Check if your behavior or decision is innovative or enhances learning in any way (by complimenting employees who openly disagree, for instance).
- Beware of more than five priorities or topics. "To choose, is to be focused and professional!"
- Ask for feedback daily and appreciate it.

It is helpful to describe the new criteria out loud and help others apply them. Describe the new, appreciated behaviors in your team meetings or otherwise in public, to help employees see the new culture. "This is the new Rehab culture: asking what the other department prefers and actively asking them for feedback."

Develop new beliefs

They are motivated to start practicing the new behaviors. An additional exercise is to find the key underlying beliefs of the new culture. If you could design them, what would they be? Of course, you can't design and apply beliefs into an organizational system just like that. But thinking of new beliefs enhances awareness and can lead to new mottos to guide behavior in different situations where people could have doubts.

◆ We are caring professionals
◆ We dare to disagree
◆ We welcome feedback as a chance to learn
◆ We are professionals and thus open to change and improvement
◆ We take action to solve, improve and achieve: "Just do it"
◆ Choosing means a deliberate, professional focus to give our best

Imagine those beliefs were widely held. Imagine you had adopted them. How does it make you feel? Mostly, such beliefs stir a response. People immediately recognize a Yes or a No within. In a group, you can see whether the proposed belief touches on something, or not. People nod or frown or stay neutral (bored?).

Beliefs can be very subtle. Sometimes you have to search for the right phrases.

Empowering beliefs are always:

◆ Positively stated. They describe what is, not the opposite. "We welcome feedback" instead of "We are not afraid of criticism". Otherwise, your subconscious mind might stick to the image of criticism and fear – and will not be helpful.
◆ In the present tense. As if this belief has already come true. "We welcome feedback" – not "will welcome" because in that case, feedback stays out of reach in the future.
◆ In the I–form. It's within my control to do so! Beliefs should not depend on the actions of others. For the sake of culture workshops, I use the We–form. But this could cause hiding. "We welcome feedback" feels different than "I welcome feedback". "As a team, we welcome feedback, but, hey, I don't always have to do so..."

Of course, it takes a motivated leadership team to apply these new beliefs, to experiment with them, to check: What would happen if I applied this belief right now...? And then try the new behavior...

If you want to really "believe" these new beliefs, consider using the method of Psych–K. Psych–K facilitators can be found worldwide (see reference). This helps integrate new beliefs into your system by using the subconscious mind. This is change inside–out: You change a belief and automatically start doing things differently.

In a team, it is stimulating if everyone acts as if these beliefs were true. It can be motivating and inspiring to repeat them and show the associated behaviors. Leaders can support each other as a team and start doing these new behaviors. By doing new things, you change outside–in: You might change your beliefs – just because you do things differently.

Summary

We have seen how limiting beliefs can be challenged. Find the belief and ask why it is true. Ask why until you find the reward and try to achieve this reward with other behaviors... Don't worry if you can't apply these techniques. Find yourself a proper NLP, trainer's course or management development program and you'll practice this.

In this case we have also showed how to find the ranking of criteria, or, hierarchy of values. This is important to achieve true alignment in a team and find out what matters most. It helps gain sincere consensus and balance opposites from the Competing Values Framework.

We have also seen how they puzzled to take the rewards away from undesired, old behaviors, while adding rewards and advantages to the new habits of the preferred culture. Hope this provides inspiration for your change process...!

Chapter 15 What are Effective and Dark Sides of Culture?

Now that you've joined some workshops, you probably start to get the idea. You have to find specific behaviors to solve the change puzzle and discover what would make a difference in your particular organizational system. The culture types are rather generalist: rough outlines of an archetype. In the workshop you find your specific expression of that culture type. "What is typically our adhocracy culture?" You add qualitative information to the quantitative profiles, which helps to understand your current culture. "Aha, this is what we typically do…"

Each culture type is neutral in itself. It isn't good or bad, but it could be a good or bad fit with your market, employees and product or service. A culture type has an effective side but also a dark side: when there's too much of one feature, it can turn into a disadvantage, shifting to the other extreme. Let's explore some examples.

Effective adhocracy examples

Let's start with some effective expressions of adhocracy culture. Adhocracy culture is an entrepreneurial culture: innovative, visionary and change–minded.

Adhocracy culture has many expressions. Compare A and B:

In organization A, they love to share new ideas and start experiments but they're not good at implementation and evaluation. The ideas pop up easily– they're creative and they love the learning part of adhocracy culture, but they don't foster the entrepreneurial part. In organization A, they're not putting ideas into sustainable action.

In organization B, ideas and pilots are welcomed, so people can try, make mistakes and learn but they are devoted to implementing ideas into business. They learn from action and they have a stronger focus on the entrepreneurial part of adhocracy culture. Organizations A and B both have a high score on adhocracy culture as their dominant culture type but they differ in their specific focus. This may be more or less effective. A is creative and thinks "out of the box" but B is making money from improvements. They differ in the details of their adhocracy culture.

More effective examples:

1. Mistakes don't exist – learning does

Effective adhocracy culture could be a learning organization based on a deep–grounded belief that "mistakes don't exist". Mistakes simply provide information. People are learning from this feedback ("This way doesn't work – okay") and it is socially safe to make mistakes because it means that you're pushing your boundaries to learn. You don't lose face: you don't get a bad performance appraisal. Failures provide factual information and you simply move on to the next option.

2. Free space on Friday

Another effective adhocracy culture fosters inspiring brainstorm teams to gather new ideas, working with temporary project teams to solve issues or improve things and having a "free space" to experiment every Friday. Employees get four "free" hours to innovate, reflect, talk to each other, read or study. It's a free space of developing and innovation. This free space for innovation has clear boundaries. Some organizations have a certain percentage of work time or budget that people can use to experiment and see what emerges.

3. What rules – not How–to

Another aspect you may find in an effective adhocracy culture is a lack of detailed prescriptions. They are not telling you what to do and how to do it: they are just giving you rough lines – some boundaries. It's up to you how you accomplish your goals as long as you achieve them. Detailed prescriptions and 'how to' regulations tend to hamper creativity and innovation. If you give some space in one way or the other, you foster innovation in an effective adhocracy culture.

Dark side of adhocracy

Let's take a look at the dark side. What exactly is the dark side of a culture type? If you have too much of a particular feature, it turns into the opposite and becomes counterproductive.

The Dutchman Hans Wopereis describes counterproductive organizational cultures. Unfortunately, his book is only in Dutch (Title: "Het licht en de korenmaat"). But we all recognize them instantly... Some examples of adhocracy culture that turn to its dark side:

1. Solitary Geniuses

In one organization, they collectively believed that "It's OK to do it my way". Their culture had elements of nurturing and admiring the "autistic genius" – "I do it my way. I'm experimenting. Don't disturb me." This corresponds with a so–called withdrawn culture. Everybody is in their own cubicle or office, doing their own things. They're not sharing. The "withdrawn culture" is one of the organizational pathologies that Wopereis describes.

2. Too many Entrepreneurs

Too much of an adhocracy culture can also lead to chaos. No one has an overview. It's out of control: people are innovating and responding to the market, they are outgoing with an external focus. With a building full of entrepreneurs at work, it's easy to waste resources and turn chaotic. They try to communicate, they are not solitary innovators. But they have so many initiatives that it's hard to keep track of everything. Ideas are turned into projects and pilots at high volumes and a high pace. Focus is a word we don't appreciate. It's like a bunch of frogs jumping in all directions – how do you get them in a cart? How can you go anywhere with the whole group? Individuals keep finding ways out.

3. Too soon, too much

Another dark side of adhocracy culture is jumping into each and every hype: being too responsive to external demands. If you sense a need for a new smart phone app or an innovative health care service, you act immediately and go for it, but this may not always lead to good results. Looking outside at the expense of looking inside, knowing your strengths and weaknesses, may lead to imbalance. Such responsiveness in turn may lead to exhaustion of people as well as other resources.

Doing before thinking, valuing the future above the present (and certainly above the past), responding to incidents and seizing opportunities everywhere, changing rather than sticking with something, innovating solo instead of slowing down through collaboration: these characteristics can be overestimated on the dark side of adhocracy culture. Adhocracy culture can become chaotic, dynamic, restless, individualistic and ad hoc – as opposed to collective, aligned working together based on an inspiring vision or strategy that gives direction.

Adhocracy culture

Effective

- Innovate, Experiment & Learn
- Entrepreneurial; take action
- Create and align with others
- "Mistakes don't exist"
- New projects
- What rules, not How–to
- Respect for Professionals

Ineffective

- Withdrawn culture
- Autistic Genius: I do it my way
- Hyperactive – exhaustion
- Doing before thinking
- Starting things but not see it through
- Chaotic, wasting resources

Effective clan examples

Let's take a look at clan culture. This is a people–oriented culture: It fosters participation and HR and development of employees. It's a culture of "doing things together" where people are important.

Clan culture has many expressions. Compare A and B:

Organization A fosters an agreeable work climate and people are exchanging tasks – "Can you do this for me and I'll help you with that?" This kind of behavior is rewarded – the team leaders praise people for this.

But they become dependent on each other and on managers. They don't take solitary action – ever. Their belief under the waterline: "Leaders must solve problems". And: "As an employee, I need support from my coworkers." Employees are allowed to complain – that is all they can do in their typical, paternalistic expression of clan culture. They also have subgroups – "Us and Them." They're talking about other groups instead of addressing each other. The subgroups are affirming prejudice and type casting, making it harder to see things for what they really are. But apart from this, people score their work culture as agreeable, having a warm relationship with direct coworkers.

Organization B has clan culture as well. People know each other well and feel responsible for getting things done together. They solve issues and take action. Here is more focus on the participation aspect of clan culture, next to developing yourself.

You can ask a coworker for help and learn from them, but you're responsible to get your own job done. If you need additional skills training, negotiate this with your manager. You can't expect the team leaders to read your mind and know what you need. The culture is friendly, informal and inclusive. The only thing you'd like to change is the time you're tied up in meetings. "Do we need to discuss everything in the team?" Though your manager frowned, wondering if you don't value participation, he accepted your solution to distinguish topics by "nice to know" or "need to know".

B represents a more mature expression of clan culture but they can both have the same scores on the clan culture type. This is why you have to find the examples in your OCAI–workshop! Understand what exactly is typical behavior for our culture. Some other examples are:

1. Self–organizing teams

An effective expression of clan culture can be to know one's colleagues well and work comfortably in a friendly atmosphere. You might see self–organizing teams in a clan culture that take democratic decisions. They reach consensus in teams and organize themselves, divide tasks, arrange time schedules and collaborate.

2. Care for people

Effective clan culture may lead to a lot of attention for your customers or your patients, coming from the people orientation. Service with a smile and your clients feel it – so they come back for more.

Clan culture may foster coaching and training for the staff so employee retention and satisfaction are good, keeping your organization's skills up to date. It may create commitment and the work council is cooperative because staff feels appreciated while their education is taken seriously.

Dark side of clan

However, there's a dark side to clan culture as well.

1. Disease to Please

Too much clan culture could develop into a "disease to please". People like to keep it cozy together. They love harmony, based on the shared belief that colleagues should be friends – or the collective belief that conflicts are dangerous. Harmony on the surface can hide dissatisfaction and complaints. People will not tell you directly, but you hear them gossip or complain in the hallways.

I've seen the 'disease to please' regularly in strong clan cultures. They tend to become too cozy. People don't give each other feedback or, if they do, take criticism very personally so next time, you will not do it again...

It's not about pleasing your boss but everyone, to keep it nice. "We should keep it nice" can be a deep–rooted belief. Or: "It's a threat to your career to disagree." Or: "If I don't bother you with feedback, you will leave me alone as well." That is comfortable.

2. Group Think

You may even see "group think" – people are not open to alternatives anymore and they start to think alike. There is no one who dares to disagree and play the devil's advocate and say "Shouldn't we check alternatives? What if …" If you want to keep it cozy, you might not check the alternatives and avoid conflicts. You may be afraid that it might damage your relationships. It is not done to disagree and might be regarded as a personal attack.

3. Helplessness

People gossip about others to ventilate their feelings. Doing so, they develop bonds with the ones they're gossiping or complaining to. It feels safe to share feelings in a subgroup like this – but it also confirms your powerlessness. You're not changing the situation by addressing the right person or coming up with solutions. You complain about and confirm the problem, leaving yourself in a victim's position and emphasizing helplessness.

4. Culture of Complaints

A culture of complaints seldom means openly complaining. It happens in one–on–ones with coworkers and people take no action upon their conclusions. Here's another organizational pathology described by the Dutch researcher Wopereis. I have seen it often in the health care sector in the Netherlands. Complaining in the hallways; spreading negative energy but not taking action. Nurses, caretakers or therapists don't tell their managers so he's not able to take action either – because he doesn't know how people feel.

5. Paternalism

People can also become very dependent on the group or their leader. Too much of clan culture and strong, sometimes authoritative leaders like father figures could lead to paternalism. You're waiting for your boss to fix problems because you cannot take action.

The opposite of empowerment and participation occurs when this feature is emphasized too much. Leaders fill this void of action and paternalism evolves. Leaders and employees might not be happy with this interaction pattern, but it is not always easy to reverse it because "we're used to it".

The moment an authoritative leader lets go (thanks to executive coaching or so), their employees may complain: "Hey, he sticks the problems with us! It's his task to solve this!" And the leader says: "Told you so. It doesn't work with them. I have to take charge."

6. Chat culture

Another "dark" expression of clan culture is a lot of chatter and long coffee breaks. People are so happy together that they might even let the phone ring or let clients wait because they're not finished with their stories yet. I have seen anxious patients in health care who had to wait longer because the nurses were still discussing their weekends.

7. Us and Them

And how about those cliques that sometimes arise in organizations? Including you and you, but excluding others? Gossiping about the others, being judgmental about the shop floor or the sales guys, reinforcing organizational silos?

The moment we bond in mutual agreement about the others, complaining or gossiping, we exclude them and label them. The losers, the hippies, the top dogs, the power puppies. We start to see them through these labels and create a self–fulfilling prophecy. We will find evidence for our convictions. We will see what we expect. "Told you so! The sales guys have big mouths but no brains." Us and Them are a fact.

A people–oriented culture can take all directions. Clan culture can be great within clans, but terrible when you're seen as the outsider. Some clan cultures develop strong subgroups, including some but excluding others. It is accounting against marketing. It's the surgeons against the managers.

These functional exclusions may be straightforward, but some lines are personal. And they create social hazard, eventually leading to lack of trust. It is clear whether I belong to the surgeons. But when I'm a team member just like you, why didn't they tell me...?

People can include or exclude others, based on unclear criteria, using gossip and political moves to create an "Us" versus "Them" or, even worse, "You". Especially when particular individuals are excluded, you have a strong signal for a dark side that will harm individuals as well as the organization.

Clan culture

Effective

- ◆ Participate, Engage
- ◆ Loyal to each other
- ◆ Care for People
- ◆ Self–organizing Teams
- ◆ Development, Education
- ◆ Coaching
- ◆ Friendly, supportive, comfortable

Ineffective

- ◆ Culture of Complaints
- ◆ Chat culture
- ◆ Disease to Please
- ◆ Group Think
- ◆ Paternalism
- ◆ Helplessness
- ◆ Us versus Them

Effective hierarchy examples

Hierarchy culture is based on clarity, efficiency, uniformity and control. They love smooth coordination. An effective hierarchy culture could have set up a system for quick error detection and quality control. Everyone knows what to do, what the quality standards are and how it needs to be done. They value reliability and efficiency. They have their factory neatly designed, all of their logistic processes fine tuned, and take pride in timeliness, quality and control. There are no surprises, just incidents that they tackle with the right procedures. In an effective hierarchy culture, the overview is great. You will admire a well–oiled machine, no confusion or ambiguity, but everything designed, calculated, controlled and coordinated. "Certainty is better than complexity."

Hierarchy culture has many expressions. Compare A and B:

In organization A they always follow the procedure. It's important to get the right signature to get permission to do something. They like to be on time for meetings and they communicate with formal reports – to be conscientious and precise.

There are not informal chats in the hallway and you can imagine that this takes a lot of time. They go slow. You can't act until you formally know something. They produce a lot of paper. They become good in thinking, reflection and research, they're skilled in discussion and debate. But what do they accomplish? They are precise and do things the right way, once they get to the stage of taking action. But do they do the right things...?

You could also have a hierarchy culture like organization B. They are certified and well organized. They have a quality control process, they're keeping files and they monitor progress; but they do it efficiently so they are great in evaluating outcomes and adjusting their processes based on this feedback.

Organization B fosters the same values as A, but they have a more mature expression of the same hierarchy culture type. It's good to be precise, but being precise is never more important than a timely output. So, if need be, they will send you the detailed report later on, but first take action to ensure a smoothly operating process.

Dark side of hierarchy

What is the dark side of hierarchy culture? The label "hierarchy" itself often raises negative associations, due to Kafka and powerful, incomprehensible bureaucracies... But effective hierarchy culture is a nice, efficient, clear process culture. However...

1. Power culture

Hierarchy culture can turn into a power culture. The organizational chart, the processes and your position become more important than the goal of the organization as a whole. This can happen in any culture type, but hierarchy is sensitive to such power culture because positions in the formal structure are important and thus give

Criteria, or Ranking of Values in your Culture

You can easily test your criteria by asking:

♦ What's more important than..?
♦ If...happens, would you trade X... for Y...?
"If you can make money, would you trade conscientiousness for timeliness?"

Mature cultures are likely to use refined, circumstantial criteria instead of one shared belief that is always applied, like a dogma.

"Always be precise and thorough" is a dogma.

"Be precise and thorough – unless the production might hamper/only if there's enough time/but action comes first/so you can report afterwards" are examples of moderated criteria and values that direct behavior in more or less clear norms. They have balanced the competing values to construct "this is the way we do things around here".

status to its occupants. "If I have to sign your plans, I have power over you. It is position power that I like to keep." Clan, adhocracy and market culture types are susceptible to power play as well, but the sources of power tend to be mitigated. It's not solely position power. It could be my people skills as a boss and how my team adores me (Clan), my numbers and results this month (Market) or my great new idea (Adhocracy) that give me power.

I have to do something and keep doing it – to keep this power. In dark side hierarchy cultures, all I have to do is just sit there. I am the boss with position power. Power cultures show a whole range of different behaviors. From bullying out in the open to various political games that are secretive. I have seen the dark side of hierarchy cultures mostly in government organizations combined with a strong political focus. It can be counterproductive because the ones in power can jeopardize anything, including a complete change process that they initiated – until they changed their minds. The position power that allows fast decision making and clarity can become a disadvantage when attributed to a leader who damages morale by turning back decisions or projects that affect a majority in an organization.

Power play eventually leads to management by fear because it's not safe to be honest. You're not sure what your boss or others are thinking and you cannot rely on people who are obsessed with their own interests and who play games.

You can harm yourself (your position, your career) if you speak your mind or disagree or criticize or come up with an alternative. Gatherings look like a meeting, but they are a play on stage because there are no real issues being discussed – that's what you do in the hallway with your allies. People who are afraid or uncertain will hoard information. It's a natural reaction to feeling socially unsafe. People defend their own territory – "This is my budget, this is my department, this is my ego. The more staff I have – the more budget I have – the more projects I do – the safer I am."

Simply hoard information. You say "yes" in a meeting but you don't do it and you never intended to – just play the game. You divide and conquer. You set up people against each other. You say "Sales is doing this …" and you tell Sales "Do you know what marketing is planning?!" People attaching themselves too much to their position might turn to its dark side. It has nothing to do with the transparency of effective hierarchy culture but is caused by too much formality and position status.

2. Culture of Complaints

A power culture yields a culture of complaints because it's too scary to open up. Hear the secret complaints in the hallways, gossip, divide and conquer, but don't take action. Actually, nobody takes action because it's a minefield out there so you better stay safe and secure in your office. Hide and hope that no one sees you. Just complain and bond with your allies...

3. Slow down

Eventually, a dark side of hierarchy culture may lead to slowing down and turning the organization into a very inefficient workplace. I'm waiting for a signature by my boss, so I feel helpless. And safe – because if he gives permission, I'm not accountable. If we hide and hoard, we slow down.

Hierarchy culture

Effective

◆ Clarity & Security
◆ Quality, Realiability, Timeliness
◆ Efficiency

- Control & Coordination
- "Everything is controlled"
- "No surprises, but incidents that will be handled."
- Clear decisions
- "Processes are vital but timely, reliable outcomes count."

Ineffective

- Culture of Complaints
- Power culture;
- Hiding, Hoarding, Helplessness
- Us versus Them
- Bully or secretly Divide and Conquer
- Play games
- Play your part on stage
- Wrong decisions by one signature from the power position
- Slow decisions – waiting for signatures
- No decisions – hiding
- Procedure is more important than the product/outcome

Effective market examples

Welcome to results–oriented market culture that likes to get things done. They have a strong customer focus and they are competitive – looking at what is happening in their market. An effective market culture fosters high performance teams or customer care teams to smoothly deliver services and support. In an effective market culture, people may work hard, but could also play hard; incentives make it an inspiration to work hard and celebrate your results. It can be fun to improve all the time.

Departments may unite and give their best to beat an outside competitor. It's exciting to focus on top achievements. It can also be fun to experience a playful competition with other departments or coworkers. "Let's see who can come up with the best plan...! Who wins?" We can be honest at times, giving feedback about improvements, but at least you know what we mean. No secretive gossip, but straightforward comments to improve performance. These are some effective examples of market culture.

Market culture can have different expressions. Compare A and B:

In organization A, it's fun to see if you win the debate in meetings; it's great if you outperform the other unit and it's important to negotiate well and keep strategic information to yourself.

Organization B has a high score on market culture, but it's different. They like to perform and you earn respect winning big clients and having a big mouth sometimes. On the other hand, it is a code that they share strategic information because they share a collective purpose as an organization.

You'll be sorry if you didn't share information with relevant departments or colleagues and your boss finds out. Share or regret it: the board is a close, winning team and they role model this attitude to the organization. You need to excel – and try to be the best – but not at any cost. The organization as a whole is key. Competition can be fun, up to a point. Eventually, we're in this together to crush our competitors.

They both have market culture but they have a slightly different focus on the typical market culture values.

Dark side of market

Let's take a look at the dark side. What can happen if there's too much market culture in a negative way?

1. Performance Grail

You could have an exaggerated performance culture where production is everything; it's the Holy Grail. But the employee of the month ends up with burnout. People are reduced to their output – they're not people anymore, they're production factors to be used – they are valuable if they perform or they are useless.

Performance as a Grail could trigger a short–term focus. Win the battle, but lose the war. Pennywise and pound foolish. Cut costs and cut in long–term profits... Work too hard and end up with a burnout. See people as replaceable production units.

2. Internal Competition and Power culture...

Sometimes counterproductive competition occurs. Departments competing against each other can be challenging in a good sense. Comparing who has the best figures for last month can be fun; stimulating each other to do better.

But if overemphasized, the competition becomes more important than the collective purpose as an organization. Each department becomes more important than the organization. It resembles a power culture with power play between departments, including the whole range of behaviors like hoarding information, bullying, gossiping, intimidating, dividing and competing. Who has the biggest department, turnover and profit gets more important than collaborating to build an excellent company serving your customers.

Market culture

Effective

◆ Getting things done
◆ Results orientation
◆ Competitive
◆ Confident
◆ Customer focus
◆ High Performance
◆ External focus; responsive
◆ "We are the best – and that's fun."
◆ "Who wins...?"
◆ Extrovert: I tell it like it is...Clarity.

Ineffective

◆ Performance Grail; exhaustion or short term results
◆ Internal Competition
◆ Power culture;
◆ Hiding, Hoarding,
◆ Blaming, Gaming
◆ Bully or secretly Divide and Conquer
◆ "My scores are more important than yours"

How to transform the Dark Side...?

This discussion of dark sides gives an impression of common behaviors in the workplace that signal that an organization is not at its most effective and is ready for change...! What is most important is: how do you get away from this dark side? If you are on the dark side, check on your opposite in the framework for inspiration. The biggest opposites are in the diagonals of the framework. If you have too much

Flexibility and freedom to act

Internal focus and integration

External focus and differentiation

Stability and control

Clan
disease to please
dare to disagree
I empower to change
I've got power
Hierarchy

Adhocracy
I do it my way
let's do it your way
we are people
I am my results
Market

of adhocracy culture and your workplace is turning into an innovative chaos with everybody doing their own thing, find inspiration in the smooth version of hierarchy culture which is the most opposite, at the diagonal axis. If you have too much of a "dark" Market culture and people are reduced to their output, check on clan culture and see how you can incorporate some people–oriented features into your culture.

Work with your opposite

If you have too much "dark" adhocracy culture, then your current mantra could be "I do it my way." What can you learn from hierarchy culture? Rephrase the mantra with their values: "Let's do it your way." Hierarchy follows not "your way" – but common procedures. Practice this. Evaluate behaviors and decisions with this new guideline in mind. Support each other in your team. Discuss behaviors. Who is acting according to this new mantra? What is holding you back? What new perspective does it yield? What advantages...?

If you have too much "dark" hierarchy culture, you might hold a collective belief: "I've got power and power is safe." You could shift to one of the beliefs in adhocracy culture: "I've got power to change." You're not fixed on static position power, but you empower yourself and others to change – as a sign of true personal power. If you feel strong enough to share your power – you can make a shift to adhocracy.

Imagine you're on the dark side of clan culture with a "disease to please." There's harmony on the surface. You might work on a market culture feature and that is:

"Dare to disagree and compete". In market culture, it is okay to debate or come up with alternatives and to compete. In clan culture that is not too comfortable. You might want to introduce a guideline that allows people to disagree. Don't look at similarities between people, but see how they differ and acknowledge and utilize differences.

If you have too much of a "dark" Market culture, one of the beliefs could be: "I am my results. I am useless until I produce some output." You could shift that assumption towards "I am much more than my results; I'm a human being, not a resource. How can I collaborate with you?"

Provocative, opposite change

The beliefs of the opposite culture type can help you gain a new perspective. See if you can make them a collective guideline – for inspiration. However, the most effective way to change a culture is not to jump to the opposite right away. Mostly, it is effective to depart from the current culture first (acknowledge its advantages and comfort) and then slowly bend towards the preferred culture. However, for some individuals, teams or organizations, the opposite view and provocative inspiration work well. Cross the diagonal line and learn from your extreme opposite, call it "provocative change". Adopt the associated mantra as a guideline and start practicing the behaviors. What would you do if this were true...?

"If I am a human being – worthy in myself – I don't have to prove myself with outrageous performance all the time. It suddenly becomes possible to build my relationship with colleagues and have an interesting conversation – that doesn't only take scarce time on a busy day. It also provides a feeling of belonging and yields new ideas and we can all tackle our targets with renewed energy..."

You can find inspiration from your absolute, diagonal opposite. And if it's not inspiration, call it medicine. You dislike it – but you know it will help you cure your imbalance. See the core beliefs from the "other side" like an exercise. What if your organization would adopt them overnight? See how the opposite can enhance creativity to move away from the dark side to a more effective culture type.

Summary

The big concepts of culture types are generalist and they are meant to be neutral – there is no good or bad. But too much of their features will turn into the dark, ineffective side. We have seen some examples of clan, adhocracy, hierarchy and market culture dark sides, loosely based on Hans Wopereis who described counterproductive organizational cultures.

You can transform the "dark side" into an effective culture type again by finding inspiration from your absolute opposite. If you're in dark clan, see what the core beliefs of true market culture can do for you...

Each culture type has numerous expressions that make up your specific situation. You need to dress up the quantitative scores of your culture assessment with qualitative information, examples and stories. The devil and the divine are in these details and they differ in each organization. You need to know those details to discover what difference will make the difference when you change.

Chapter 16 How to Develop Interventions and Persistence?

Let's take a look at some interventions and persistence. How do you use the levels ABCDE to develop interventions and secure change outside–in and inside–out? Remember, we need 2B's to balance our new culture: beliefs and behaviors.

How to apply small, copyable behaviors that spread through the Network–ocracy until you reach a tipping point? What beliefs could support these behaviors? Last but not least, how do you keep doing the change – instead of giving up?

What versus How?

After the culture assessment, organizations have a profile for current and preferred culture with, mostly, a gap between them. A shift in focus or a change is necessary. The preferred profiles show the WHAT you want (the first 6 steps of the 7–Step Guide) – but it doesn't tell you HOW to do it: that is magical step 7.

As we discussed before (see Chapter 13), interventions must be customized to fit your specific situation. There is no recipe, no 10 must–do steps to achieve preferred culture. You have to do the work: examine your particular organizational system and see what could work and what wouldn't. The How is tailored – and maybe that is for the better. It entices people to engage – to agree on collective behaviors that must be changed to achieve different outcomes.

You can't apply a magic trick or outsource this job to a consultant. You must do it yourself. You must do it together as a team or organization. If you don't DO things, nothing happens. If you keep doing what you always did, how can you expect a different culture? There's a point when you must stop thinking, talking and writing plans and start doing it. This is a common pitfall for organizations who are used to talking and thinking, like "darker" Clan or hierarchy cultures. Changing culture means action.

Some organizations have a habit of applying different tools and consultants to their problems. Tick the right boxes, follow the recipes, do the assessments, gain the insights, analyze, reflect, discuss and report. Research, design, control. Then lean back, wait for results and push the method, the tool and the consultant aside, deciding they weren't any good after all. Maybe they weren't. But if people don't take ownership, if they don't engage and start doing things differently, then nothing will change.

Culture change is an area where design is not possible, let alone control. It is developing, evolution, building the bridge while you walk on it. Yes, that can be quite a culture shock to hierarchy cultures for instance... Culture change is "hands on", or like the Nike slogan: "Just do it".

I invite you to enjoy the fascinating puzzle that your organizational system is. Find out how to make it tick. Be as creative as you can and customize specific interventions that will work in your situation. Discover how you're going to make the change sustainable and successful. Meanwhile, get inspired by some general examples and guidelines on culture interventions in this chapter and the cases in this book.

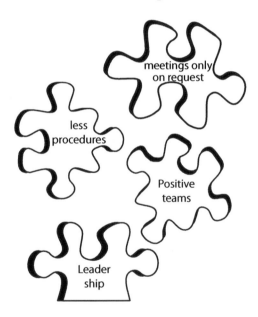

Recap – Change Do's

When developing interventions, remember the general advice on change we discussed before:

♦ People should feel urgency to change now or they won't move. It must be important and urgent.
♦ Arrange for some quick wins – small successes that are visible and measurable will enhance morale and motivation. Keep it small! Robert Quinn states (in the book "Lift") that small success will start a positive spiral that goes up.

- One small success makes people look for another success and get optimistic. They change their perspective and they are encouraged to go on with the change. Small actions spread easily – even when you're busy. You get critical mass and reach the tipping point. Remember; small is beautiful and change is non–linear. One butterfly can cause a storm. One positive new behavior can turn into a powerful habit that changes the system...
- Guarantee measurable indicators. Anything that gets measured will get attention. It's a signal that you really value this, otherwise you wouldn't measure it. Keep track of small things to support the change. Make sure to incorporate indicators of new behaviors in the appraisal system so they will be evaluated during everyone's periodic performance review.
- Support each other, utilize the advantages of group learning – "It's not just me, the others are doing it and we're in this together."
- Display positive leadership. Give a compliment a day and it will keep discouragement away – and read chapter 21 for more positivism.
- Change the management roles – adapting your leadership style to emphasize a certain culture type.

Two Directions of Change

Develop interventions that cover the two directions of change – inside–out and outside–in. Use the ABCDE scheme or simply use 2B: Let inner intentions and new beliefs be backed up by outside measures that support people to DO it. Make new behaviors comfortable by influencing meaning and supportive beliefs.

Inside out, from beliefs to behavior: The OCAI workshop is the first intervention to help people discover, question and maybe even change some beliefs. Executives and other role models can be assigned a coach to work on relevant beliefs that may inhibit them to show the new behavior. We change the way we think. Then we can change what we actually do in everyday life. Like a surgeon said:

"When I re–discovered my need to cure people and why I took the doctor's oath – I re–gained my belief that I am here for the patient. (Instead of the conviction that the patient is here for me – they are lucky to have me – like all surgeons were thinking and I somehow got used to this arrogant idea)."

Add interventions outside–in, from context to behavior. Support people from the outside to show the new behavior.

The new hospital procedure allows patients to chose their surgeon and request an extra explanatory consult. Some surgeons found this nonsense at first, but the new procedure forced them to display new behavior. By spending more time with a patient before the actual operation, they got valuable information and a calmer patient who trusted the surgeon. The surgeons started to value the extra time and were better servicing their patients.

Determine the Level of Obstacles

When using the ABCDE levels with interventions, obstacles to change must be solved on a higher logical level. Remember: A – I am, identity, B – beliefs, C – capabilities, D– what I do, and E – effect and environment. If you see that people are not doing the new behaviors (level D), check where the obstacle is – is it at the higher C level? Is it their capabilities? Maybe they should have another skills training to learn the new required competencies, like being customer friendly on the phone.

Maybe the obstacle is even higher, at the level B – and people share the belief that customers are nagging – they want endless after–sales service but they're too lazy to read the manual. Work with your people again – and find solutions for customer service and making the manual easier. Maybe it is just one employee, at the level A, who's not the right person for this kind of job – he's an introvert, reflective kind of person and every time a phone rings it disrupts his thinking. The ABCDE scheme will help you identify and solve obstacles that may occur.

Find leverage in the system

See which small, copyable behaviors can make a difference if everyone did them. Then determine who the change agents are; the people who are open to change and those well–linked people who work at nodes in the organizational web. They can help the new behaviors spread so you get leverage and reach a tipping point (See chapter 21). Engage the leaders in a management development program to help them gain new insights and skills on positive change leadership (See chapter 19) and support each other to form a collective leadership team.

Make change mandatory

We'd love to entice everyone to engage voluntarily and change as one happy family. But eventually, it comes down to discipline and doing what you said, or, sometimes, complying with the majority. Even when you're enthusiastic, change can be a challenge, let alone if you're not convinced but the others are. Whatever the circumstances, eventually the majority must do it. People must actually change behaviors or nothing will change.

Government and public organizations with professionals tend to rely on change on a voluntary basis. People have lifetime employment and know they can't be fired. This enhances staying comfortable in their own way of doing things. It sometimes takes the incentive out of performance and out of change. Why would they?

They can agree but not do it. Or they start the discussion once more, like professionals like to do in a culture of debate. They can sell their debates like true commitment and the will to really reflect on the change proposals, taking it seriously as professionals. This could be true. But such professional, engaged debates could also be a way of resistance and sabotage.

When you've had open–minded workshops and you have given everyone an open ear and they had their say, followed by participative decision making, you get to the point where people have to do as agreed. There is a point where you have to stop talking and start doing. There's a point where we need discipline. "Welcome to reality: you can't have everything your way at once."

People who are not delivering what they promised, can be coached by their peers or leaders. Of course, we all need time to practice. We are entitled to have second thoughts again and address them again – up to a point. We might need to change some beliefs. We might need to try harder. But eventually, we need to do it. To take this voluntary basis away ("I might change once I feel ready for it"), I recommend anchoring the culture change, and thus the new behaviors, into the performance appraisals. This is an official signal: We really mean it. We're doing things in a new way. We are appreciated and rewarded for doing so. It's not voluntarily, doing the new behaviors when you feel like it.

The organization is measuring and recording new behaviors – they are evaluated in our annual performance review. Peers and leaders will score employees according to the new behaviors. Employees rate themselves. They can take ownership and ask for more coaching or training to succeed in the new ways. But these new behaviors must be incorporated into appraisal systems. Otherwise, some lifetime employed professionals keep on discussing the necessity or, some employees will get away with playing a role, but not really doing it. It may sound harsh – but we need to get out of our comfort zones to learn new habits. Appraisal forms can help us do so. We engaged in the culture change for a reason; change is mandatory when all is said and done.

Stronger adhocracy culture

Cameron & Quinn listed some examples of culture interventions in their book, "Diagnosing and Changing Organizational Culture". Let's take a look at some examples of specific culture interventions. Adhocracy culture is a very entrepreneurial, innovative, visionary culture and it likes change. How to stimulate adhocracy culture?

♦ The manager roles are innovator and broker, so one of the culture interventions is to make sure that the leaders will apply these manager roles. Give them training and/or coaching. The coaching part could be necessary to help them overcome limiting beliefs that are still based on "control". Adhocracy cultures demand some letting–go by managers.

♦ Implement brainstorm teams, project teams or the "Friday experiment." One of my clients offered employees a free space on Friday: two hours that they could do whatever they liked – consulting coworkers, reflection, experimenting – anything at all. This was the time to be creative and try things out.

♦ Free space for innovations within certain boundaries of budget and time. Organize this is in any way that suits the organization.

♦ No detailed prescriptions but rough lines. Innovation is killed if you're not only telling employees what to do, but how to do it and when exactly... If you leave that out and give people some rough lines you stimulate creativity and people start looking for ways to make it work – "I want you to sell more products …. You have four weeks to improve. Tell me what you did and learned afterwards."

♦ Invite creative thinkers from other fields. It can be great to invite an artist to your board meeting and have them picture or express whatever you are discussing. Ask a musician to play the mood that they perceive in your organization. Ask teams to paint the image of the new product, the future, the other department. Find the hidden treasure in those expressions, make stronger what is good, diminish what is not.

♦ Cross fields of professions – invite other people because they think outside of your box. It can be a great way to enhance innovation. Challenge all your assumptions. Have mechanics talk with nurses – find similarities and differences. Learn from them. Share customers between a bank and a kindergarten.

♦ Give somebody the jester's role. He or she is allowed to walk into any office, nothing is secret from them and they can make jokes and give feedback without "punishment". This person could best be outside the organization like an artist with another perspective giving true feedback.

♦ Have managers work on the shop–floor once a month to get new ideas from this experience. Swap jobs for a day, once in a while, to give this experience to everyone.

♦ Organize a world cafe session where people discuss and solve challenges based on this format: one challenge per table. The challenge–owner stays at the table, the others visit all tables and spend 15 minutes contributing their creativity to the table–holder who must solve the challenge.

♦ Create an out–of–the–box vision just for fun. Take one hour and challenge all your assumptions. "We're going to create a different vision. It doesn't have to be serious but just to get this innovative thinking going."

♦ Encourage but also measure and reward innovative behavior. You have to customize this for your organization – it's not always easy to measure innovation. "How many new ideas did you come up with last month?" "What have you learned from whom last month?" Acknowledge mistakes as stepping stones to learning. Mistakes are feedback that what you were doing wasn't working – that's new information. If you "reframe" the meaning of mistakes as learning, people are encouraged to share their learning and the others can learn from that as well. The one who makes the most mistakes could be "employee of the month".

♦ Effective leadership – people can only learn in a safe place. When your colleagues are competitive or the boss is bullying, people won't share doubts or mistakes. Information hoarding hampers learning. In order to be innovative, it must be safe. We must all share our doubts, our experiments, our learning events. When there is not an open, safe group culture there will never be innovation, no matter how many artists you invite to your board meeting, how many project groups, etc. Safety is first because without safety we will not be learning.

♦ Read the book "The Learning Organization" by Peter Senge.

♦ Check on appraisal and performance criteria. Are employees rewarded for the right things? In adhocracy culture these would be creativity, growth, entrepreneurship and innovation. "What have you learned?"

Stronger clan culture

How do you foster clan culture? Clan culture is the people–oriented, participative culture that likes HR development, training, coaching people and collaborating.

♦ Enhance the manager roles of the facilitator and the mentor.

♦ Implement self–organizing teams that take democratic decisions. They can organize their activities, their schedules and so on.

♦ Give coaching, training and education. Keep your workforce up to date.

♦ Use 360–degree feedback. This can be scary and very confrontational, but done respectfully, people can learn a lot. A great intervention in a clan culture that tends to the "disease to please" is to take an organization–wide training – how do you give feedback in a pleasant way and how do you receive feedback without taking it personally? (Feedback should not be on the A level of identity – but on the behavioral level: what can you DO better).

♦ Act on the biannual, obligatory employee survey. Are your employees still satisfied at work? Make some small changes. Focus the managers on how to give compliments and daily attention, because people often don't feel acknowledged at work. "Hey guys, how are you doing today?" can be enough. Managers tend to forget this because they are so busy.

♦ Empower employees in a way that suits them. Build cross–functional teamwork – people from all places in the organization work together. Create an internal university – the "company academy."

♦ Improve relationships between support and line operations because next to the classic gap between managers and employees, here's another one... The people in the factory have a different perspective than the people in marketing and sales. Maybe the HR department is not appreciated by the managers because HR always blocks solutions: "You cannot hire people who ..." while line managers think "I just need my production secured." These different perspectives don't foster collaboration. Find ways to improve these relationships. The key consists of people getting to know each other better, understanding and respecting their differences. This can be done in training but also in a project team or by having lunches together.

♦ One big organization asked employees to share their life stories with an unknown colleague during a workshop. This had a great effect: it tightened relations at work. What people don't know, they don't like. Sharing stories, important decisions or troubled periods from your personal life will make the workplace feel warmer. This example is gruesome to some, inspiring to others. Pick your tailored approach to improve relationships and stimulate clan culture.

♦ Check on appraisal and performance criteria. Are employees rewarded for the right things? In clan culture these would be participation, commitment and development.

Stronger hierarchy culture

Hierarchy culture cares about clarity, efficiency, uniformity and control. How to enhance hierarchy culture?

♦ Ensure that the leaders know and apply the management roles of the coordinator and the monitor.

♦ Redesign processes that will cut delivery time in half. Think of Lean Six Sigma; one of the methods that builds hierarchy culture with its emphasis on logistics, efficient processes and business process redesign.

♦ Focus on error detection and quality control. Running a project around these topics draws the attention to these values of hierarchy culture.

♦ Improve the information flow. Take a look at how people share information, why it takes so long, where are the obstacles and how to solve them? Check on the criteria: what is need to know, what is nice to know? Are meetings held to exchange information, to take decisions, to bond with each other or to explore topics? Who is attending and why? Are people sharing enough – or do they lack information from other departments that would help?

♦ Freeze some budgets and first make a better plan to spend this money. Hierarchy culture fosters efficiency. See what people come up with to keep their budgets – or even find savings. This might enhance creativity as well.

♦ Make team leaders responsible for their own budgets to reinforce organization and monitoring of processes.

♦ Check on possible savings, that is a typical hierarchy thing to do – "Where can we cut costs?" It draws attention to an important hierarchy culture value.

♦ Check on appraisal and performance criteria. Are employees rewarded for the right things? In hierarchy culture these would be efficiency, reliability, conformity to regulations and procedures.

Stronger market culture

Market culture likes to get things done. It's very results–oriented. It has a strong customer focus and it's very competitive. How to reinforce this culture type?

♦ Take a look at the manager roles – the director and the producer – do the leading managers need support to fulfill these roles?

♦ Start up customer care teams and find out what could be improved, what customers want, are they served well, do they have more needs?

♦ Redesign processes from a customer point of view. Organizations find it natural to have marketing, sales, finance, HR, the factory or the services department. But the customer doesn't care that marketing is late or finance has a problem with billing; the customer wants their product delivered in time in a friendly way. From their perspective, what does your service or product look like?

♦ Engage in social media to stay in touch with your markets; prospects, customers, employees, suppliers, competitors, new hires, stakeholders in society.

♦ Research the market all the time. Consider crowd–sourcing or co–creating services and products with your customers.

♦ Give staff training on time management. "We're going to be on time for meetings; we're going to meet our deadlines; we're going to achieve our targets within budget and within time." Reward according to targets.

♦ Units will only get their budgets if they deliver a proper business plan – another way to enhance a market way of thinking.

♦ Example: a hospital in the Netherlands was bought by a business lady who introduced market culture. She deleted all budgets and all units had to come to her office to plead for a new budget based on a business plan for their unit, whether they were surgery or the laboratory. It was a culture shock in the health care world. She encountered fierce resistance but stuck with this plan until the people got used to it. She forced this bureaucratic, slow, non–efficient hospital into a market culture type that achieves good results now. People who couldn't live with this style, left. The lady herself was a culture intervention.

♦ Check on appraisal and performance criteria. Are employees rewarded for the right things? In market culture, these would be meeting production/sales targets, achieving certain results, safeguarding market share and competitive advantage.

Culture Interventions Recap

Develop your interventions "inside–out and outside–in" and see how you can use the ABCDE levels and elaborate on the implementation phase to help people gain consistency and maximize group leverage. ABCDE levels may help to find the biggest leverage to solve obstacles but also find the right interventions. If there's an obstacle, you can solve it on the higher level. Sometimes the biggest leverage is simply at the Competence level and a skills training will do, next to rewarding people to keep doing it.

Sometimes the biggest leverage is on the Beliefs level and then you do need reflection and executive coaching to change relevant tacit beliefs: otherwise they will not even try the behavior, let alone keep doing it.

Group leverage and persistance

Remember group leverage and learning. It's not one individual learning new behavior, which can be difficult enough – "I have to find the will and skill to change, then I have to practice and then I keep doing it". But the individual is not alone at work. Their coworkers are doing it too. Their boss is doing the same thing. The leaders are encouraging and supporting. Do it together and use group learning to get leverage. People copy, coach and correct each other until a critical mass is doing the new behaviors and you reach a tipping point. Do this in small teams of 10 people, in change circles.

♦ Engage your positive energizers (Chapter 21). They encourage people to go on.
♦ Make change go viral (Chapter 13).
♦ Measure small improvements. Celebrate them.
♦ Anchor new behaviors in daily work life ("Each meeting we..." "Our appraisal is based on...")
♦ Make sure your leaders form a well–trained leadership team (Chapter 19 and Chapter 21) to BE the change and support it. They encourage people to do it.
♦ Plan an event after three months to keep awareness and attention high...

The next step is consistency: people must keep doing it. Anticipate the obstacles you might encounter, like people getting tired or frustrated or bored. It is easy to fall back in our comfort zones, to rely on old behavior. See what interventions are necessary to stimulate people to keep doing it. Make it fun, if possible!

Persistence

Persistence can be the tough part. Many people like new beginnings, everyone loves happy endings, but the tough part is in the "messy" middle... The organization encountered a challenge, came up with interventions, people tried some new behaviors, there were a few small successes and then what? People get tired and long for their comfort zones and business as usual.

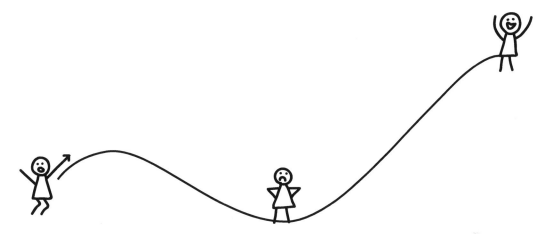

fresh beginning - messy middle - happy end!

It can happen in any change process. The exciting part is over and people simply have to repeat and practice. It comes down to discipline and persistence. Jesus spent 40 days in the desert. This is often used as a metaphor for change: it takes 40 days to acquire new behavior and automate this behavior into a habit. Some use it as a rule of thumb to spend at least six weeks for sustainable change to grow roots.

Research on the brain shows that habits need regular repetition to get "wired" in the brain. Indeed, it does take time for us to acquire new habits. We're not striving for one action but we need continuity: culture.

Scenarios

When you're developing sustainable change, think in scenarios. Research shows that people who have a plan on how to overcome difficult moments when they're trying to stop smoking or stop overeating, succeed more often. If you anticipate what may go wrong and find solutions for difficult moments or obstacles, you have a much better chance to succeed.

"What if people get tired, bored or frustrated? How can we keep attention for the change? What if people are too busy to practice new behaviors? What if one department succeeds while the others give up? What if nothing has changed and the CEO has to give her New Year's speech?"

Think scenarios, think solutions. Use "positive energizers" to give the change another boost. Keep playful metrics that symbolize the change progress. Challenge people to be the first department that successfully works according to the new culture. Temporarily take away work pressure so people can practice. Make choices: focus on culture now and postpone some strategic goals – you can't do everything at the same time.

Take this into account when you work on a change program and interventions.

Repetition

Leadership helps people persevere. Leaders have to repeat the message over and over again and show the change time and again in their own behaviors. This may be boring but it is necessary. Remember that beliefs become behavior. Leaders must communicate the change in every way, especially in their actions, which speak louder than words. Thus they make it easier for others to follow and be acknowledged for doing so.

Engage leaders to attend a tailored management development program or change training to help them change themselves and acquire the beliefs, skills and behaviors to help others change. Aim for a collective leadership team (see the case in Chapter 21).

Look back if ahead is discouraging

Because change can be slow, especially in large organizations, prepare for good old virtues like patience and perseverance. Value any progress towards your goal. "Practice progress, not perfection". Don't emphasize the long road ahead for that could be a recipe for discouragement and frustration. Focus on the progress you've made so far. Look back and see what you already achieved. Celebrate small milestones!

Positive Feedback

It's important to give positive feedback. Focus on positive leadership– emphasize change that seems to work out fine. Don't dwell too long on failures or "learning events". Learn from them and move on quickly.

Research has shown that people who get negative feedback are susceptible to feeling insecure and more negative. When you get in this mood, it's harder to accomplish things and be creative. From a negative mindset it is difficult to access helpful resources in the mind, like optimism, perseverance and the full use of your capabilities. A negative mood can really make your people less effective.

You can never give enough positive feedback, at least when you really mean it. Genuine positive feedback can leverage a whole organization, especially when it becomes viral and people "lift" each other.

Summary

Every organization has to find their own mix of culture interventions. There is no easy recipe – you have to do the work and customize general advice to make it work for your situation. You have to be creative and engage people to participate and find out what works for them.

Consider tools like the ABCDE levels to find obstacles, solutions and the right interventions. Remember to include the two directions of change – outside–in and inside–out – to stimulate the right behavior backed up by beliefs. Prepare for the sometimes messy "middle of change" and stimulate persistence and positive leadership.

I hope this gives some inspiration to develop a successful change process. Keep reading and see if the next cases will bring ideas that are applicable in your organization. Make sure to check out Chapter 19 and Chapter 21 about Change Leadership and Positive Change...

Chapter 17 Case at the University Library. Does the new librarian emerge?

Ready for more cases to get an even better look and feel of OCAI culture change projects? Welcome to the University Library, dedicated to the service of university staff and students. They have 2 locations with over 2,000 study places, they annually lend out more than 55,000 books and people consult over 1.2 billion articles in e–journals.

Staff satisfaction rate is 90% and 75% of the students are content with their service. So maybe there is no need to change from that point of view...But they are facing a major change due to the same technological and societal factors that we all face: international relations in a global world, the digitalization of information, increasing diversity amongst students and researchers, information being present anytime anywhere, people expecting customized service.

The old ways of searching and storing books and scientific magazines are over. The old librarian is gone. The new librarian is a skilled communicative professional with excellent digital literacy. The library's mission is to facilitate the creation of knowledge and stimulate fruitful collaboration by providing an inspiring place to meet. They want to be more visible and inviting to staff and students and they want to distinguish themselves as a great library. That is an interesting goal, judging by their current dominant hierarchy culture...

They are structured in the units Media, Systems, Staff (in the library office), Education & Research Support and the Information Center with a total of 100 personnel of whom 73 participated in the OCAI. We have calculated separate culture profiles for all units, but they look alike. We decided to work with the overall culture profile for this workshop.

Current behaviors

We're in a room with 30 people: the director, the managers and staff who are interested in culture and who joined voluntarily. We're going to discuss their culture assessment and see how far we get with the OCAI workshop.

They deliberately chose to come with 30 of them... emphasizing the value of doing this process together. This way, the workshop can give insights and a shared reference, but we can't change individual beliefs or pinpoint specific actions that people will take after this meeting. People might lean back or hide in such a large group. But they want it this way to kick off their change project.

They recognize their culture profiles instantly: current high scores on clan (31 points) and hierarchy (32) culture, a desire for more clan (38) and adhocracy (32) cultures – but they immediately doubt if this is what they need to execute their strategy and goals. Should they keep the focus on clan culture to this extent if they want to stand out, serve their clients (university staff and students) and make a difference...?

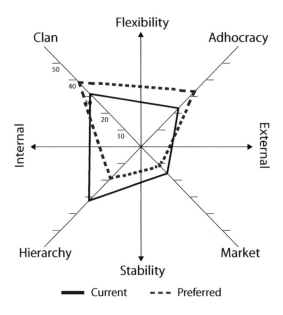

After this plenary discussion, they start elaborating on their current culture in small groups. They have to find the behaviors that make up their culture.

Current behaviors and events:

♦ Meetings: every new idea must go through several meetings and get signatures – it takes too long
♦ Too many regular meetings; we don't have time to do our jobs
♦ Last meeting's notes are being scrutinized for details – it takes the pace out of the next meeting
♦ Too many emails; we cc too many others – just to be sure...
♦ We're too polite and nice to each other
♦ We don't give negative feedback; we're afraid the other gets hurt or angry

- We prefer to work within our own sub–unit, it is a safe silo
- We talk about each other behind their backs
- We are loyal and support direct colleagues with chores
- We have fun at work and make jokes
- Things are organized in an ad hoc way, incidentally, not well planned in advance
- We have to collaborate with other silos... we have different norms... about jokes, formality, replying to email etc
- We don't have a clear overview, who's responsible for what?
- Our processes are in a "phone book" (so many...)
- University introduced 360 degree feedback – some of us refuse to do this
- We wait and see...
- But we are committed to our library work
- "If you don't bother me – I won't bother you" – some of us believe this
- Old stories are repeated; it used to be not done to disagree
- "Everything should stay the same" – some of us believe this
- Employees like to blame certain managers, "us and them"
- We generate lots of new ideas – but we never get to the stage of implementing them. The meetings and processes to go through are discouraging.
- We hide, saying "It can't be done" but we don't tell you why and who said No
- We try to have discussions again after they're closed and try to dispute the decision again
- Attachment to entitlements: The right to drink coffee for 15 minutes

Everyone recognizes their current culture. These are typical events and behaviors in less effective clan and hierarchy cultures. Like not being open, not giving feedback and saying what you think, hiding behind procedures, us and them images, the wait–and–see attitude and a culture of meetings, meetings, meetings. But also: having fun with your direct coworkers, being committed to your professional field and enjoying quiet times, hiding in your office.

This first round stirs ideas for improvement immediately. They want:

- Faster decisions
- More trust
- Collaboration beyond units
- Better communication between units (but not through meetings)
- More output – "We are underperforming"...

Future Scan

It's time to look at the future. The formerly quiet University Library finds itself amidst rapid change; stirred both by digitalization and globalization, demanding customers and the need to produce results. Which culture types would help them cope? They decide, as a group, that they need to adjust their preferred culture. The upward shift from the assessment is better replaced by a shift to the right. Their most important focus is to move towards an external focus.

Clan culture is comfortable, but they doubt if they need more of it. They'd like to keep its good things but they want to develop into a more professional, results–oriented, business–like and learning organization, serving their customers well. The decision is unanimous: Enhance adhocracy and market cultures.

Preferred Culture

Again, they split up in small groups and elaborate their preferred culture into specific behaviors. This is not easy to do. Librarians are not trained to discern behaviors, to consciously notice nonverbal signals or become aware of group interaction patterns. Like many people, they think in big concepts and labels. Eventually, they come up with these lists.

Keep doing:

♦ Celebrate birthdays and successes
♦ Show interest in each other, commitment
♦ People–orientation

Note that there is still homework to be done on this list. What exactly do you do with a people–orientation? How do you behave when you are interested in colleagues or show commitment? These concepts could comprise of different behaviors. They need to elaborate on this further. But this one workshop day is too short. They like to move on and gain an overview of their preferred culture first.

Stop with:

♦ Endless discussions! Accept a decision once it is taken.
♦ Regular meetings…!
♦ Emailing everyone. Phone people or stop by their office (some work alongside the same hallway).
♦ Thinking that we know best (towards customers).
♦ Hiding. Just tell them No and why.

New behavior and intentions, start doing:

- ◆ 1 hour a day free scheduling: decide yourself what you'll do
- ◆ Persist on ideas we believe in; get them through the process and implemented.
- ◆ We start learning. Including mistakes, at first.
- ◆ Let's have positive expectations of each other
- ◆ Groups of expertise around a topic. Maybe we could abrogate our fixed units in the end.
- ◆ Give positive and negative feedback
- ◆ Experiment with new services
- ◆ Focus on doing – we tend to talk and talk and think about things
- ◆ Coach each other
- ◆ Ask the client what they want/need
- ◆ Let's measure output: quantity and quality of services
- ◆ Focus on results and rough lines (let go of How exactly and Details)
- ◆ Flexibility in jobs, consider job crafting in the long run
- ◆ Transparency: share considerations and reasons why
- ◆ Smart goal setting and priorities
- ◆ External partnerships
- ◆ Heraclitus: prepare for constant change

These new behaviors are rooted in adhocracy and market cultures. They reflect a results orientation, making choices, getting things done, trying new things and experiencing more space and freedom at work. What they want to keep is their "social capital": loyalty towards each other. But they want to become more professional by adding results, feedback and learning.

The new University Librarian emerges

"Every employee represents the Library, committed to their work and coworkers. Librarians have taken ownership. They own the Library's results and any failures... They feel responsible for outcomes, for facilitating knowledge creation and scientific collaboration. Serving clients and taking full responsibility. If something is another unit's problem, they will make sure the other unit gets to know the problem and takes action. It's no longer pushing problems from one office to the next.

They see and are being seen. They have become visible (no longer hiding behind bookshelves and within units). They say what they need, what they can or cannot deliver, how things could be improved. It's an openness we haven't seen before. They respectfully give and take feedback, without taking it personally. Feedback has been changed from a personal attack that hurts into factual information of how to improve behaviors and outcomes. They are professionals who are willing to learn and improve, sharing problems and solutions.

They have matured into autonomous, highly–educated professionals. They don't play the blame game, but ask themselves: What can I do about this? They dare to take action and they are okay with being accountable for their actions. Anticipating any issues they proactively brainstorm and prevent problems. They have one common goal: to build an inspiring meeting place where knowledge creation occurs so that the academic community will thrive. They feel proud as library employees."

From resolutions to new habits

This is an inspiring image to them. But how can they make it come true? Now we get to the true puzzle: what would have the biggest leverage effect? These 30 people are very engaged, but there are 70 others who are not present in this workshop.

Because they are busy and overloaded like many modern professionals, they can't sustain large initiatives and big change programs and do all of the new behaviors listed above. That's why the Viral Change method appeals to them. The question is: What behavior could make the difference if everyone did this?

The Library's executives decide to look at Quinn's management roles to see if they can change their leadership style and enhance market and adhocracy cultures by focusing on the producer and director roles and the innovator and broker roles.

Employees say they want more "space" and less micromanagement. They'd like to know their exact goals, their executive helping to set priorities, but they'd like to work on their own and achieve their goals. They don't want to attend so many meetings and explain many details to their bosses. The executives in the workshop take it well. They note that it is time to start changing their leadership style as well.

Homework

But how exactly this will be implemented, must be decided yet. Topics for the next workshop are:

♦ Decide on a list of non–negotiable behaviors in the new culture ("must do")
♦ Decide on one small behavior that is easily copied and will spread
♦ Found the non–negotiable behaviors in firm beliefs

- Discover as many obstacles as possible
- Brainstorm on solutions in an "out of the box" session, starting with extremes that are not feasible soon but will stir creativity, like: Abandon all units. Abrogate all meetings.
- How can they make the new behavior mandatory instead of optional (tie it to appraisal forms..?)

Peer Support and Personal Commitment

This workshop is concluded by a public round where every individual states what they will do as of tomorrow and that they are accountable for this. Everyone chooses a mate. The pairs support each other. They write down each other's resolution: "From now on, I will ..." They will check with each other weekly to sustain progress, support each other and solve any blockages.

This group feels very enthusiastic and inspired. They write down ideas and compliments on big paper posters that they will hang in their entrance hall. This is meant to stir curiosity from the others who are not present today. They want to be ambassadors of change, inviting their absent colleagues to lunch and tell them about culture and new behaviors and entice them to attend the next workshop too. Everyone leaves, tired but content. However, the proof of the pudding is in the eating. Will they do as they have said? An inspiring workshop is a condition to kick off the change, but it is not enough. The energy must be sustained.

Discipline must be nurtured to keep doing it. Support and encouragement must be given. Executives must walk their talk. People will observe each other closely for the next weeks, to assess if the others are for real... The Library director is a very enthusiastic and pro–active woman. She plans a second workshop right away.

They are working on their culture change in regular sessions, doing it together, without an external consultant! This creates even more engagement. I facilitated their first workshop and now they are co–creating their own change. This is the way I prefer change. People taking ownership of their workplace. My role is to be a sparring partner, coming up with ideas and sharing experience, if they get stuck.

Progress

The Library made quite some progress, the director told me after 6 months. They held sessions to brainstorm on ideas. They have invited clients (faculty and students) to receive feedback.

That was confrontational but it seemed a right stimulus to improve service and to understand the client's perspective... This way they practice being open to feedback, being open to change a few things.

Some project groups have started to develop innovative products together with clients – instead of "knowing best" and presenting a finished product to clients: "take it or leave it". That is new behavior. Some individuals show examples of new, assertive behaviors. One employee didn't accept the fact that she didn't get an answer to a request. She had been phoning and emailing, but this coworker from another Library unit was out, or needed time to consult coworkers or promised to let her know.

But he never did. One day, when she knew they were having the unit's regular meeting, she entered the room and asked him for an answer. "I have to know now. I can't proceed and you haven't been responding. I thought that we agreed we would be timely and keep agreements as a professional library."

This was never seen before – and though she was polite – she broke the "old rule" of leaving the other in peace... allowing coworkers to hide in their silos and sub–units. They discussed what happened. The others reluctantly admitted that this could be new, professional behavior. Respond timely to requests by coworkers. No procrastination, no hoarding of information, but instead collaborating or debating an initiative if you don't agree – but not responding is not professional. Things don't go away if you close your eyes... No action is not an option. We respond to each other...

The brave employee who broke into their meeting and who broke a rule was used as an example by the director. The director scans for new behaviors and rewards them publicly, hopefully enticing the others to do it too...

Their change is going in small steps, the director says. She sometimes gets impatient. She clearly sees their pitfall to keep talking about the change in culture sessions, but to not DO it. It becomes possible to hide in the culture sessions as well... attending them enthusiastically, brainstorming for new ideas... but daily behaviors remain the same. They somehow got a little stuck – though on the outside it appears that they are still doing well, meeting regularly in sessions.

Change Circles to Practice

We evaluated this and decided they should focus again on behaviors instead of ideas and innovative projects. In one to–the–point session they will focus again on the necessary behaviors that are non–negotiable in the "new library". This will be their reference. Then they will stop having culture sessions, but instead have "change circles".

A small circle (remember, the Power of 10? See Chapter 13) of trusted coworkers will meet once every fortnight. They support each other. They will share one example of new behavior that went well, and one problem. What didn't work out? How could I respond to this coworker, client, situation?

Each individual will get their time slot to solve an issue or share an example of behavior. It will make all of them more aware and more creative to solve old behaviors and practice new behaviors and responses. They will support each other.

The rules are that you have to work with your own behavior or response. So there is no talking about others in general (except as your counterpart in a situation) and the talking is minimal (5 minutes per issue). The biggest part of the session is practicing the new behavior or response in a role play. This way, they find out what works and what doesn't.

The next session, they share how it went. This way, they enhance collective learning every 2 weeks and create a vehicle for personal and collective change. They start with the leadership team first – to help them deal with issues of old behavior and help them BE the change themselves.

They still have to take care of their pitfall: to talk and analyze. But if these sessions are friendly but tightly directed, they can practice and exercise and start doing the behavioral change. To be continued...

Chapter 18 Case of a Merger. Will they transcend Prejudice and Distrust?

Let's take a look at this case of a merger and the crucial role of leadership during change. This merger concerned five organizations in mental health care of very unequal size. A was the largest organization with 1,200 staff and E the smallest with only 50 people. Organizations B, C and D had about 300 to 400 employees each. After the merger, they counted a total number of 2,400 employees.

These five organizations were working in one region. They had many small locations for mental health care close to villages and town centers, all within a maximum of a two hour drive away from each other. One reason for the merger was cost reduction, necessary in Dutch health care because government funding was no longer secured. The government hoped the market would bring more efficiency into the health care system.

Health care institutions had to compete for clients while health insurance companies decided where their clients could get mental health care. They had to compete for the first time in their history! Many organizations responded to that threat by merging. These five organizations also faced new competitors entering their region and their boards wanted to become the biggest provider of health care in that particular region.

However, they held prejudices about each other. They had known each other for decades working in the same region and their images were set. A were known as the bureaucrats. With 1,200 staff they were kind of bureaucratic. Interesting enough, B and D were known as the hippies, because they seemed relaxed and liked people. E and C however, didn't arouse many strong feelings.

They decided to use the OCAI in the process of the merger. The question was not: "Are we going to merge, yes or no?" This decision was already made by the boards. Employees, who were professional therapists, caretakers and psychiatrists, were not happy with the merger. One of the sentiments that was heard in the hallways was "After this merger we're going to be too large as an organization – 2,400 people – to collaborate. How are we going to care about our patients? We employees will be reduced to numbers."

Five Current Cultures

The OCAI could help them get better acquainted, understand their differences and similarities and build a collective culture after the merger. They have five graphs of current culture that differ a bit:

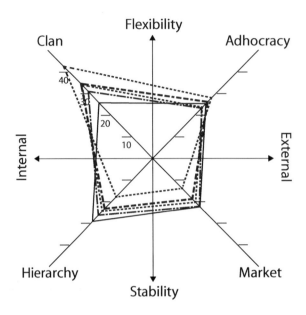

What stands out is the upper profile with a lot of clan culture. This is the smallest organization and in general, small organizations tend to have more of adhocracy and clan cultures. E only had 50 employees and a high score on clan culture. In the middle are B, C and D's profiles that were more or less alike. In the lower left part of the Competing Values Framework one line goes farthest into hierarchy culture. This is the profile of organization A. They had 1,200 employees and were said to be bureaucrats. Their employees indeed gave the highest score to hierarchy culture, but still scored clan culture secondly.

Large versus Small

Let's zoom in to two separate profiles that differ most. On the left is organization A, which was the largest, and on the right is organization E, the smallest organization. The black graph shows their current profile. The dashed graph shows their preferred situation.

A is a more mature organization with more of hierarchy and market culture types. E values flexibility and clan culture. They don't want much change – just a little bit more of adhocracy culture, but overall, they feel fine. In organization A, people are less satis-

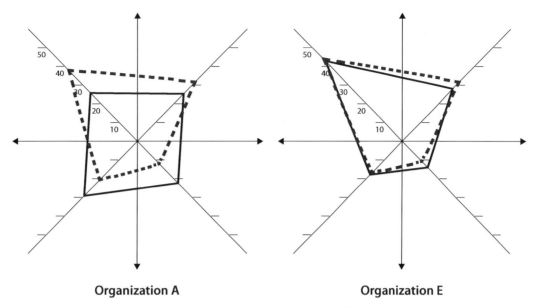

Organization A   Organization E

fied. Positively stated: they are more ready for change. They'd like to have much more clan culture and make an upward shift – more clan culture and adhocracy culture.

The smaller the organization, the smaller the gap between current and preferred culture; the bigger the organization, the bigger the gap. We've seen it before in many assessments. It is understandable: when you're working in a large organization, things go slower and it is harder to control or influence things at work. The smaller the organization, the easier it usually is to have control over your workplace and to change things faster.

What also stands out is that the three profiles above – B, C and D – look alike. They had about 300–400 people each. The size of the organizations seemed to define their cultures as well. B, C and D seemed very similar, so they gained faith about working together.

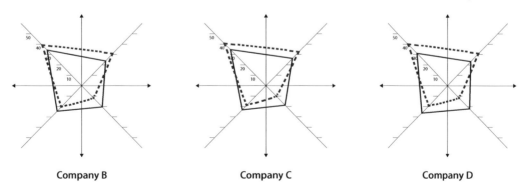

Company B   Company C   Company D

Hippies and Bureaucrats

B and D scored both hierarchy culture and hierarchy culture at 23 points. Their image as being hippies wasn't quite right, because they had just as much hierarchy culture – valuing regulations, procedures, structure, efficiency – as the people–oriented hierarchy culture. And hierarchy culture is not the same as being a hippie, anyway.

Sharing these profiles in the OCAI workshops helped people see through their prejudice and gain more insight. They discovered that, overall, they were more alike than they had thought. This was important because those images were holding people back. They doubted if they could collaborate with hippies or bureaucrats. Discussing the profiles gave them more confidence that maybe this merger could work in the end...

Managers and Professionals

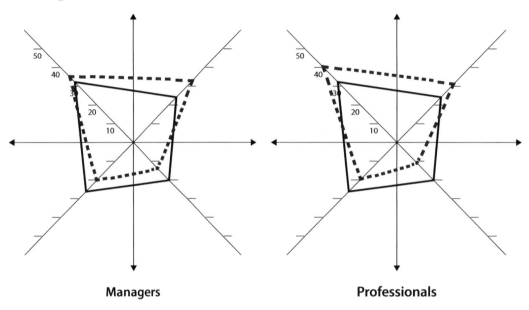

Managers   **Professionals**

Here's another comparison – two different profiles of managers (left) and professional staff (right). Staff means the people who are working directly with clients and patients, like therapists, caretakers and psychiatrists.

The managers have a higher score on hierarchy culture in current culture, as is often the case. The staff experiences less hierarchy culture and they would love to have more of that in the new culture. The managers and team leaders, however, would prefer a big step towards innovation – more adhocracy culture. Both groups show a different emphasis of what is most important for a successful new culture. This gap must be acknowledged, understood and discussed. Why have they scored it like this? What expectations and/or needs do the profiles express? They have to decide what needs to change first. You can't do everything at the same time.

One New Culture: All Agree?

Let's take a look at the preferred culture profiles for organizations A through E. They seem to agree about the future. You can see this in one glance: that is great about the visual OCAI profiles.

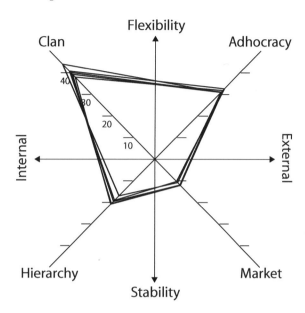

They would like to have the biggest focus on the people–oriented hierarchy culture; they would like to have adhocracy culture. They were all highly educated professionals who liked to work with their clients in their own way. They didn't want to be hampered by hierarchy culture or market culture – results, procedures, smoothly running processes, efficiency – it wasn't their most favorite topic.

We could finish the workshops and say "We agree about the future. We have some slight differences currently, but if we let go of our prejudices which are clearly false, we'll be fine." However, the difference is in the details. The quantified scores and profiles are great to work with, but you need to fill in specific details of each culture type for your situation. Although you might have the same score, you might attach different meanings and behaviors to your typical hierarchy culture. It is necessary to work out the qualitative part of clan culture to agree on. In what way do we want a people–oriented culture...?

17 Workshops

Their managing board had decided to organize open workshops because the organization was so large. They invited all 2,400 people to do the assessment – but the majority did not: 800 people did. Afterwards, they invited everyone to attend the workshops, but only 150 people did. Though they hoped for larger numbers, they decided to give these 150 people an inspiring workshop so they would bring enthusiasm and energy back to their coworkers.

The workshops were held with 17 groups of 8 people. In small groups nobody could "hide". People would be enticed to actively participate and share their ideas. Those 150 participants came from all over the five former organizations. People were mixed in groups because no complete teams attended. It was important to get to know new colleagues and exchange meanings and desires for the new culture. This could challenge their prejudices about each other. They worked a day with the "hippies" or "those bureaucrats". This was the first step to understanding the others and to get accustomed – as a stepping stone toward collaboration.

We had plenary presentations next to breaking out in small groups. After the plenary overview of their profiles, they discussed their current and preferred culture in the small groups, learning from the differences and finding many similarities.

Recognizing Similarities

The people from the large organization A said: "Our adhocracy culture means that we have a lot of discussions on innovative ideas but we don't implement them." B explained: "Our adhocracy score means we start lots of new projects all the time – we actually turn our ideas into projects – but we don't finish projects with results, to be honest."

A wanted to implement ideas they talked about endlessly. B needed to implement fewer ideas and focus on finishing projects they had started – maybe they should talk and think more before they started. They found out they could support each other. Participants discovered more similarities, such as a shared sentiment: "Our core business is helping people with mental problems. But our board of directors comes up with new trendy brands like Internet counseling for youngsters.

But the people who really need mental health care are not on the Internet; they just need a therapist one–on–one. This is our core business. It's not very "sexy". We help people with severe issues and they are not winners in society. We feel that our board of directors is looking for fancy markets and solving luxury problems."

A lot of participants shared this feeling. They didn't support Internet counseling for highly educated people with work stress and other new services that the board promoted. "We want to help people who really need it, who can't help themselves. This is our core business and we feel a bit alienated from our board's initiatives."

Participants said: "The board has their own agendas. They want to look good and do trendy things. We're not feeling acknowledged, working in the primary process with patients. What we do is just hard work with poor people – no quick results, but sometimes even depressing results."

There was a lot of dissatisfaction. "We want a bottom–up process to change and this is why we joined these workshops." Some people were really negative – but all were glad to express and share these feelings.

Sharing Dissatisfaction and Distrust...

The board had good intentions though. The results of the culture assessment had surprised them. They asked the small break–out groups to answer their questions, like: Why do we see this increase in clan culture? The preferred increase in clan culture meant: "**We are afraid** to lose clan culture in the merger. We value relationships and people. Don't take that away from us while you turn our organization into a large mental care factory."

Most people had a history of collaborating like one family; hence the current clan scores. However, that wouldn't work with 2,400 colleagues. "We have to stop working like a family. We feel frustrated, because we can't do a democratic change process and reach consensus. Bottom–up change is not possible with 2,400 people."

The preferred decrease in market culture meant: "**We protest** against too many regulations, top–down obligations and no flexibility to vary our approach with individual patients. We feel restricted and stuck. We have to work through very fixed steps. Sometimes it's necessary to take more time or use another method. We feel that the board and other executives are too much in the command and control mode. They are pushing us and we don't like that."

That was a clear message for the board, coming from most small group–discussions. In the plenary presentation afterwards, these explanations and feelings were shared with the large audience. Some board members were present and discussed strategic decisions they considered, but had not taken yet.

The audience said "Hey, hey! It's not for you to decide. We don't agree with the new brands. We don't like Internet counseling. Why are you taking decisions about our work? We want to decide on the organization's strategy!" The protest–feeling spread. But isn't the board of directors hired to decide on a strategy and convince the organization to execute it? Of course, that is one of their jobs and hopefully, their expertise. You cannot decide on a strategy with 2,400 people and keep everyone happy. Nevertheless, most professionals from the smaller organizations were used to consult colleagues all the time. The professionals from large organization A were used to top–down decisions, but they didn't agree with the contents.

In the Netherlands, especially in semi–public organizations with highly–educated professionals, people like to look for consensus before actually deciding to do something. Some say that this attitude evolved because Dutch people were forced to collaborate in their battle against the sea and rivers that threaten this low situated country. They had to agree on building dikes and accomplish this together.

In this same tradition, these 150 employees wanted to decide on the strategy for this mental health care institution serving a whole region. We discussed different roles within an organization and who is to decide what. I tried to make them accept that you cannot reach complete consensus about everything, all the time, when you're working with 2,400 coworkers, not even with the 150 people in the room.

However, their message was heard – they wanted to have a say. The present board members acknowledged this feeling – and they recognized the distrust against the board. Maybe their biggest challenge was not the Hippie– and Bureaucrat–talk, but the way the board was distrusted. They were seen as chasing their personal interests and trying to look good with modern, sexy initiatives instead of caring for people with mental issues.

Interesting enough, the CEO of this large post–merger organization was a very authoritative person. He embodied a culture shock because therapists seem to appreciate a consensus culture and open dialogue. He was the kind of person who said "No. I decide!" His attitude complicated things and employees found it hard to trust or like him. Unfortunately, he was not present during this upheaval.

The board focused on branding to get used to the new competition, as opposed to former government funding. They were inclined to finding new target groups, making money and keeping things under control. They had to manage 2,400 people and that was a huge challenge. Their line of thought was: "We are responsible for a large organization. We need to control time and costs and find new markets to succeed and be safe."

Professionals didn't acknowledge what the board was trying to achieve with their new strategy. The board didn't pay enough attention to the primary process: the daily counseling of people with mental issues.

The staff felt unacknowledged and they were used to "complain and blame", but not give direct feedback. Their clan culture liked to keep things cozy on the surface. This was complicating their change process, because if you cannot give feedback and people are too sensitive, it's hard to get development or change anything. However, these suppressed feelings of dissatisfaction and distrust came out in the open during the plenary session. They finally said it out loud to the persons it concerned: the present board members.

We need to see and be seen

The small groups had decided that they needed recognition for the primary process. Therapists said "We need to feel that our work is valued though it is not very glamorous. We need to feel that the board and executives are working in our best interests and they understand and represent us. Also, a compliment a day may keep attrition and complaining away."

In the phase of making action plans in small groups, they decided they wanted more communication to bridge this "classic" gap between management and employees because of their different perspective. To succeed as one organization after the merger, professionals needed to know what was going on at top level. They needed to see the board to trust them. The top–guys on the other hand, needed to see what hard work the pro's were doing. A smooth flow of information in both directions was missing – and needed to be restored.

The staff liked to get self–organization within teams. It was voiced as a protest against top–down command and control structures and leadership. "Give us the opportunity to organize our own work within our teams. We don't need detailed orders but just a rough framework and budget boundaries. You can tell me **what** I need to do but not how I should do it. Just give me some space as a skilled professional."

The board should refrain from micromanagement and controlling every detail. The board and higher–rank executives had embraced this leadership style even more after the merger, people felt. They focused on measuring quantitative output while caretakers wanted to include quality. Therapists didn't want a performance indicator like "spend 30 minutes with a depressed patient and do 5 intakes and 20 consults a week", they wanted quality. "Are the clients satisfied with our help? Are we doing a good job as professionals?"

A challenge with these action plans was lack of faith that this was going to work. The workshops helped people from the five organizations see how much they had in common. The prejudice that remained however, was about the board and some top–executives. The staff found each other in their distrust. "Do they care for clients?..."

Indifference and Dissatisfaction

Then there was a large majority who felt indifferent. They were just doing their jobs and didn't seem interested in the organization. "I don't care what logo we wear", someone said. "As long as I can help my clients and get paid."

The 150 people who attended the workshops wanted to express their concerns and some wanted to make a change. But what about the others? The majority was not present. The Power of 10, where people support and influence each other to change in small change circles of direct coworkers, was not used. The board chose open workshops – they hoped the best of it.

Those 150 attendees were not all positive energizers either. There were some change agents present, who could pull the others in a chariot of change. But many people were complaining and wanted to confront the board of directors with their views. But they didn't want to change their attitude, let alone behaviors. They still felt: "The CEO is an authoritative person and I don't like him. Let me tell you another thing he did...[continues to complain]."

Another challenge in a large organization is keeping up momentum. Things tend to go slow past many levels and this might demotivate people who like to get things done. If you work with the small change circles, you can accomplish a lot by yourself (The power of 10 coworkers together, focusing on their own behaviors in the team). But eventually, you need approval and alignment with other levels or departments. You need patience and perseverance. And often, unfortunately, you need political insight in large organizations.

Though participants valued their workshop day, the exchange in small groups as well as the plenary discussion with the board, this was only a starting point. The gain was that people adjusted their prejudice. Back in their teams, they reported "that the "hippies" and the "bureaucrats" too, were people just like us."

But the pain was that this day turned out to be a sole event. Employees got what they expected and feared: The board led the organization and didn't further engage the staff...

The Board drops Culture

This was partly due to organizational politics. During the board meeting after the culture workshops, some board members backed out of the culture process though they had agreed to work on developing an overall culture for the new post–merger organization.

Having seen the outcomes of the workshops, they changed their minds. They didn't want to change their leadership style and they didn't want to discuss the quality of mental health care with staff or go through the trouble of explaining strategy over again. Some had had doubts about the "culture thing" before, but never expressed them. Some simply thought that now was the time to go back to business as usual; weren't they busy enough?

Some board members made deals like "I will resist this culture thing with you – if you support my budget plans", etc. Maybe they were scared by the protest–feeling that had spread amongst professionals. For other board members, quitting was a disappointment. They were truly enthusiastic to consciously create a new culture and improve the organization as a whole after the merger.

But after a vote, the majority of board members decided against further culture development. They chose to not take the expressions of distrust too seriously – though it wouldn't go away by ignoring it! After all the efforts, time and money spent so far, they decided culture wasn't one of their top priorities.

Their train of thought was: "Our desired culture profile shows that we agree on our future, basically. That is enough to know. We can collaborate on this basis. Of course, people complain in workshops if you ask them for their opinion. Therapists like to talk and always know better." And there was nothing we could do or say to make this majority in the board change their mind.

The overall outcome was that some teams worked on culture – depending on team leadership. Culture was a topic in their team meetings, they kept track of their own performance indicators and supported each other with new behaviors. But the majority didn't change much. The only remainder was a general softening of prejudice against other organizations and an annual company day, where employees discussed interesting mental care topics – because they had so much enjoyed the dialogue with unknown coworkers during the culture workshops.

7C Conditions for Success

As a consultant, I was not content with what we achieved. The merged organization didn't seize the opportunity to develop an overall culture and make a fresh start while solving the distrust. The board buried the issue, longing back for their comfort zones. It's not always easy to assess the will and skill of the leaders before you start. Like all people, they can change their minds during the process. They can simply believe that a new logo and mission statement will be enough to operate as one organization after a merger.

Condition 1, commitment from the top, was no longer present. This was partly due to the distrust from professionals that the board discovered. It represented too huge of a challenge at the time – the board was already challenged by the merger, the financial requirements and the sheer size of the new organization.

It appeared hard to reach clarity, let alone consensus about the desired situation: C2 and C3. Should they involve innovative services and brands or stick with their current core business of helping clients face to face once a week? Because they got stuck here, they couldn't proceed to C4 through C7, from communicating, to copy–coach–correct, achieve critical mass and carry on. C1 and C3, commitment from both the top and the employees, represent trust. Trust in each other and trust in the process of change. If they are not sufficiently present, there's a lot of work to do.

But the organization must be willing to commit itself to this process... That requires being open and letting go of comfortable prejudice and projections – and see what emerges, in terms of trust and commitment. Which are, in fact, other words for certain beliefs and behaviors.

What didn't help either was that their system was very large – enhancing a certain distance or even indifference. It would have been different if they had chosen a team approach; keeping it small and having team leaders work with their teams on daily workplace culture. However, in that case, the prejudices were not dismantled. The more important impediment to a successful merger seemed to challenge the Us and Them images and to collaborate with both Hippies and Bureaucrats.

Though we achieved that goal, another big Us and Them issue popped up: a somewhat classic Managers–Workers gap that turned out to be so fierce because it had been ignored and built up for years – deriving from "old–fashioned" top–down leadership at the largest organization (A, affecting 1,200 employees). This gap flourished in a conflict–avoiding clan culture that kept the flame of dissatisfaction secretly burning through the grapevine but that smiled and obeyed in public. Projections became reality. People saw what they expected. Within a framework of distrust, everything the managers did was attributed a meaning as "opposed to the professionals".

I feel it is important to share this case with you. Many consultants, managers and employees have experienced these change programs that didn't deliver what they promised. We have felt the resistance of organizations, bouncing back like rubber, the tardiness of changing systems. The change ambassadors can become tired and give up pushing and pulling the chariot of change.

New priorities, with direct pains and gains, seem far more urgent and important than the long–term effects of culture. People have to choose what to spend time, energy and money on. Sticking with change is not always easy when others and other choices are banging on your door. And your good, old comfort zone looks so comforting, indeed. Enticing us to go back to the way we were...

In summary – large organizations require more effort to engage because of the number of people. When you can't work with all team leaders for reasons of time, budget or feasibility, you cannot reach and influence everyone. The Power of 10 (Chapter 13) can't be applied and amplified.

Leadership is key. This case stresses the importance of the will and skill of leaders (from top executives to team leaders); it's about what they show, not what they tell. We need to assess this before getting started but it's never 100 percent under your control. The dynamics of the board or executive team can change. It would be best if you have some idea about them before you start.

Last but not least, this case is an example of giving up or quitting too soon. Having had the workshops, some people feel they've spent enough time and effort on culture. But you're not done after the workshops. It comes down to perseverance and practicing new behaviors every day, by everyone.

Supporting each other, sticking with the change, counting successes, building the bridge, walking your talk, adjusting plans, trying again and reinforcing new behaviors until you reach a tipping point, and everything becomes natural and comfortable again.

Chapter 19 Why is Change Leadership a Challenge...?

As we have seen from the previous cases, the role of leadership is crucial during the change process. Let's discuss leadership, assess examples of insufficient leadership and understand some personality traits that align with the culture types and the management roles that leaders can adopt if they want to enhance a specific culture type.

Leadership is crucial to change. Edgar Schein said: "To distinguish leadership from management, one can argue that leaders create and change cultures while managers live within them." This definition helps us distinguish what we need during change. Many organizations seem to be run by managers.

Not many are aware of culture, let alone that they consciously co–create a culture. But managers, executives, members of the board, team leaders, supervisors have a leading position – they have a chance to become true leaders once they understand what it takes: they must balance 2B's. Beliefs and behaviors.

Deep Change for Leaders: BE–lief

All managers, executives, team leaders, supervisors, must become true leaders. As global change continues and even accelerates, they have to lead their people instead of being busy with daily business routines. Change is the new normal. They have to become the change they want to see in their workplace.

Remember, how belief becomes behavior. Something you strongly believe, whether you are aware of it or not, becomes visible in your nonverbal communication. People will pick up your mood and your tacit beliefs. You may not consciously notice it, but we all have good radar for nonverbal communication and facial expressions. If I lead a change process, but I have a shadow of a doubt, I will communicate this in my tone of voice, my face etc. You'll notice one way or the other. This will affect the outcome. You may feel less motivated or convinced – you may not even know why.

The thing is that when we're busy we tend to operate on automatic pilot. Automated scripts in our brains help reduce complexity and deal with busy reality. The scripts installed in our minds are rooted in beliefs. We may consciously practice new behaviors or rationally reflect and verbalize new ways – but in "automated situations" that occur under pressure mostly, our beliefs will direct behaviors. The shortcut of mental scripts takes over.

Facial expressions and other nonverbal signals are directed by our subconscious mind, especially when our conscious mind is busy with something else. People reveal what they truly believe through these nonverbal expressions. This is why leaders have to change deeply – including relevant beliefs – or they might communicate the wrong signals when taken by surprise. BE–lief provides a strong foundation for successful change.

What we believe is displayed in behavior. Leaders, whether they are a top executive, supervisor or an assembly line team leader, have to BE the change. They have to be a role model. This is a subtle but crucial process between people and its importance is often underestimated. It seems too simple. But one unattended moment of acting another story based on an old belief and credibility may be gone.

One sigh that "It's not going to work", one frown at a crucial meeting, and doubt may start to spread in the system. In spite of all the change efforts: beware of the forces that strive to reverse the change like the human tendencies to hang on to our comfort zones and to test the others: "Are you for real?"

Check and Change Beliefs

I recommend that leaders, consultants and change guides check their beliefs first. Do I believe that this change is going to work in this particular organizational system? Do I believe we can do it? How do I personally relate to change (more positive or negative memories and sentiments)? Many commonly held beliefs are in fact hampering change. Some of these beliefs emerged when we were kids, reinforced by what our parents said and they were true and helpful at the time. We adopted some of these beliefs in school and, even, business school. Others are based on specific experiences with change or with this organization. Not all of them are true and helpful in our current lives and work...

Some examples of non–helpful beliefs:

♦ Change is dangerous.
♦ I can't do this. New things are scary.
♦ People resist change.
♦ Culture change is painful and difficult.

♦ These employees can't do it.

♦ I can't trust the leaders or authority figures

♦ People stuff is fluffy.

♦ A rational, linear step–by–step change approach will do.

♦ I need to control change or I'm in jeopardy.

♦ I am who I am and I can't change.

♦ Change projects fail in this organization.

♦ We are hampered by our people – it won't work with them.

♦ If I ask for help – I am seen as incapable.

♦ Change will reveal that I am not worth anything.

♦ We've tried everything before – it never works.

♦ People won't really change.

♦ People are a nuisance – getting emotional, making mistakes, slowing me down.

Imagine what you will communicate if you truly believe some of the above examples. People will sense and perceive your doubts or lack of faith. The seeds of failure are subtly sown, maybe without anyone being aware. Imagine, if you believe that change is fun and exciting and that you and your people can do it! If you truly believe this, your behavior will reflect this and reinforce this. People will see you as genuine. They might get inspired, too. Your message is powerful because you literally embody these beliefs and subsequent behaviors that affirm and radiate: "We can do this." What you do is what you say. You gain trust. Others copy you. Believing, saying and acting it: We can do this change.

Imagine what you will experience yourself – if you hold the limiting beliefs above. Remember the power of beliefs as filters through which you see the world. Beliefs may turn into self–fulfilling prophecies, because we tend to focus on what we expect, looking for proof. "You see!" "My people don't believe in this change, I will never get them to do this new behavior." "I can't stick with the new behaviors either. I doubt if one small behavior can make such a difference."

Especially other's nonverbal signals and behaviors with ambiguous meanings and multiple interpretations, can fuel beliefs. It is so easy to see what we think. Beliefs can cause projections; seeing the world not as it is but as you are; we interpret behaviors in the way that suits our personal line of thinking. This is why leader's beliefs are crucial when they lead change, both for themselves and their people.

C1–B1

Remember, successful change starts with C1: Commitment from the top. C1 is crucial. Work with top executives one–on–one to check their beliefs that could either reinforce or hamper change. Assess their will and skill and help them make the change. Call this B1: Leader's and change consultant's beliefs first. If they don't believe that people can change, that organizations can change, that they themselves can change and that they can do this particular change...then they are probably right. They will get the outcome they fear or expect, deep down. Find a method to change these foundational beliefs into helpful assumptions. This could be NLP, a provocative coach or a Psych–K facilitator. I prefer these methods because they address the subconscious mind that stores deeply held beliefs.

The danger in hiring a random executive coach is ending up with many sessions of verbal insights and talking, but no deep change. When you're talking to the conscious mind, you're talking to the wrong person. It's not effective to talk about beliefs – it's best to change them. That can be done by re–programming the "hard disk" or the subconscious mind.

Essential Skill for Leaders: Respond to Behavior

Beliefs are a great foundation for change. But we need to balance 2Bs: next to beliefs, behavior is essential to change as well. Leaders need to show (new) behavior but also respond to behavior by others.

Managers and supervisors are often educated and rewarded for "the right numbers" – getting the output right, getting the product delivered in time, making lots of calls, producing enough invoices etc. But an essential skill for anyone in a leading position is to have enough people skills to notice and respond to behavior. Managers are often not trained in interpreting nonverbal communication and behaviors, let alone intervening to change anything. They are not always aware of interaction patterns like copy–coach–correct. Those skills seem reserved for school teachers, anthropologists, health care workers and therapists.

That's curious, because in organizations, we work with people as well. People produce those numbers that managers like to control in Excel–sheets. In my opinion, leaders, whether mangers, supervisors etc, must be interested in human beings to lead them effectively. If you're interested in humans, you can learn how they think and behave and learn to lead them.

Copy

People will not "do as we say," but they will "do what we do". Our brains are wired to copy non–verbal behaviors – using the older and faster brain circuits for nonverbal behaviors that existed before the verbal, rational neocortex. This is an oversimplification, but it may make things clear.

In my trainer's education, our teacher announced: "Raise your hands above your head" while he stretched his arms in front of him. When we looked around, most students had stretched their arms in front, instead of obeying the spoken command to raise them above their heads. This is why role–modeling works. This is why leaders must be the change – so the others can copy them. The subconscious mind tends to copy others – people will do as we do.

People tend to copy their leaders but also their team members – copying behaviors that provide an advantage in one way or another. All behaviors that we do have a reward. Otherwise, we wouldn't bother to do it. Behaviors fulfill our needs. The reward for behavior could be recognition (in case of new behaviors). But if someone sticks to the old behaviors, their reward could be comfort. Or belonging, if the whole team resists the new behaviors. In that case, it's time to coach and correct people towards the new behaviors.

Coach and Correct Behaviors

Behaviors can change if you:

◆ Add a valuable reward to new behaviors – (for instance: give positive attention)
◆ Take the reward away from old behaviors – (what's the use of doing it...?)
◆ Add punishment/disadvantage to old behaviors – (for instance: give negative attention)

People will look at their leader and assess what they really value: "Do you BE–lieve?" They test how leaders respond – assessing their free space: "Will you let me...?". Don't think of calculating, manipulative employees. Think of any human being: we all do this, consciously or not. This is why leaders must learn to 1. notice and 2. respond to behavior.

If you have children or if you have a dog, you know this process. If you say "no" once, they will probably try again. You have to repeat "no" and implement "no" by not admitting the dog into your office. If you let the dog into your office once, next time the dog expects entrance again after some persistence.

Dogs and children are not grown–ups. But the process is basically the same. People will try you. And though we all have rational minds and we know what you mean, we still respond automatically to behavior and nonverbal signals.

Your team may understand that you're serious about starting meetings on time. But when you let a late–comer in nevertheless – this will be noticed. One other person might try it too, next time. The new behavior that the team agreed on, will slowly but surely be undermined by these old habits. Leaders have to be alert and respond to behavior, even small seemingly insignificant actions, and yes, even with rational adults...

6 C's of Leadership

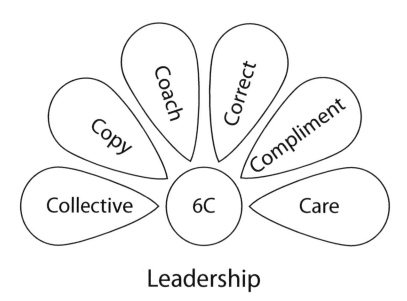

Leadership

These 2B's of culture change can be recalled as six crucial Cs of leadership, easy to remember. They consist of the people skills that you need as a true leader.

1. Collective Purpose

The first C is: envision a collective purpose and keep an overview of what everybody in your team or organization is doing. One of your most important jobs as a leader is that you are responsible for a collective purpose and to communicate that – a collective vision for everybody. It goes without saying that you have to BE–lieve this vision as a leader.

Ask your colleagues, your shop floor, your departments to tell you why the organization exists and what its main goals or strategy is for the next years. You might be surprised. As leaders or consultants, we tend to think that everyone knows this. In reality, the collective purpose is often not clear or there's no consensus about it.

So how can it be inspiring? How can it give direction to the organization's daily business, let alone a change process? A sound, shared and energizing collective purpose acts in a group just like a true be–lief in an individual. It directs collective behavior and thus results.

2. Copied by your people

The second C is to be a role model that people can Copy. People will do what you do, as we discussed. This will only work if you've got your personal beliefs to be helpful and aligned with the change – so you show the right, new behaviors yourself.

3. Coach your people

The third C is to coach people. Facilitate the people in your organization or your team to give their best. Tell them what behaviors you need. Show them yourself. Reward the ones who already do it: "Peter, that is exactly what we do in our new culture. Well done." Support those who can't or don't just yet. "What else do you need? How can I support you to do X? How can the team be of help?"

4. Correct your people

The fourth C is to correct people if necessary. Respond to undesired behaviors. You have to be alert, like when you are raising children or training your dog. Leaders must execute their position power and intervene if necessary. Otherwise, people will get the message they can get away with it. If one of the agreed new behaviors is that people will be on time for meetings, what do you do when somebody is 10 minutes late? It would be best to correct the late coming and say: "No entry – remember? We have an agreement. If you have a great idea, make sure to be on time next meeting." You have to respond to behavior to show that you are serious about this culture change.

5. Compliment people

The fifth C of leadership is to compliment people. A compliment a day may keep attrition, demotivation and problems away! To give true and "effective" compliments can be an art, because you have to mean what you say and be authentic. If a manager is giving compliments as a trick they learned in some management course, people will notice immediately whether this compliment is genuine. Because the manager's nonverbal communication, tone of voice, facial expression – will give away if they really mean this compliment or they're just trying to motivate and influence.

Giving real, genuine, effective compliments is a very important skill for leaders. In fact, it's one of the most important things for positive leadership and change and it is underestimated quite often. The brain is wired to pay attention to negative things – because it wants to avoid pain and wants to protect us.

Corrections and negative feedback will be remembered more easily than things that are going smoothly. Research shows that people need 5 times more positive statements to outweigh 1 negative statement. So, be generous with positive feedback and make sure you mean it. Read more about this skill in the next chapter.

6. Care for people

The sixth C is to care for people. It's great if leaders produce good numbers and deliver their targets, but the key of leadership is working with people. Numbers won't be loyal and follow you – people will. Numbers are an outcome of collaboration – by people.

Leaders have to create a safe space. In a safe group team members dare to speak up and they can give their best to produce the overall results. In an unsafe situation, people tend to hoard information and hide themselves, there's lack of trust, no transparency ("What is he up to?"), fear ("I will be ridiculed if I disagree") and no will to collaborate and support each other. It's easy to see how such a group will not produce the best of results.

You can't create a safe group if you don't care for people. Care means that you're interested and committed to your people. It doesn't mean you have to love or "pamper" them.

The first thing to make a group feel safe, is to be trustworthy as a leader. Be the change and express your be–lief in behaviors: be genuine, authentic, share information, do what you say and say what you do, keep promises, let yourself be seen as an individual. No games. No lies. No secrets.

The second thing to make a group feel safe – and thus enhancing trust and collaboration – is to "see" the group members. If a leader acknowledges individuals, they send a signal that they are in control. They have an overview of the group or situation. Though we may be autonomous, professional grownups, we respond to this kind of leadership and feel safe by being acknowledged.

Next, leaders have to respond to every action that makes a team or an organization unsafe. This comes down to safeguarding basic respect for others and intervening whenever respect is at stake. If team members ridicule others openly, make bad jokes, call each other names, label them according to prejudice, don't take each other seriously, gossip secretly, exclude others, mock, intimidate, lie, bully or other such behaviors – confront them publicly, in the group. This sends a strong signal that these behaviors are not tolerated.

Ask the group to take responsibility for these behaviors as well (empower them to give each other feedback) – but lead by example. Of course, other measures may be necessary as well, including one–on–ones with the joker or the bully etc. If people are afraid, reward them to reinforce new behaviors. Compliment them when they come up with new ideas – thus becoming visible in the group. Compliment when they are brave and safe enough to share doubts or mistakes.

When you care for people – when you show respect for other people's opinions – your team may start to copy that behavior. You teach them how to do that because you are respectful as a leader. You can build an inclusive culture with diversity; you can utilize differences between people and achieve great results where one plus one equals three – but only if the group is safe and respectful.

These are the six crucial C's of leadership – of any leadership, but especially leadership guiding change. Please note this fact: there is no seventh C. There is no "control" and there is no "command" in this list. We already have some of that in our package – probably.

What if we could let go? We would enhance autonomy, professionalism and ownership/empowerment in others. They might control and command themselves more effectively than we ever could do as leaders.

Insufficient Leadership

The six C's don't seem to be common traits yet for all leaders. Many organizations suffer from insufficient leadership. In any discussion forum you hear people complain about their managers.

Apart from the fact that it's easy to blame and some people like to complain, there's justified negative feedback on leadership. Think of the lack of integrity around the credit crunch – and how some leaders don't walk their talk. We have seen leaders with a big ego who are guided by personal interests and power, opposite to the collective purpose. Sometimes it's not power or unethical behavior, but a lack of people skills.

People suffer from financially or technically oriented managers who care about numbers more than people. Trained in technical education, a leader may not see when it is necessary to intervene. So when this coworker arrives 10 minutes late with "a great idea" – this leader may let them in because they value information. But by doing so, they spread ambiguity on the desired behavior and what our agreements are really worth. "Is it okay to come late if you deliver good ideas?"

Remember those seven success conditions and you'll know what to do to improve leadership. Be committed (C1). Be clear (C2). Walk the talk and be the change... Try to work on consensus (C3). Envision and communicate the collective purpose (C4). Remember C5: Encourage people to copy you.

Coach your people, correct and compliment them. Research has shown that people who are complimented work much better. If people feel confident and capable of doing their jobs and they are acknowledged by coworkers and their boss, they tend to give their best. Care for them – and they might just dazzle you... Reach critical mass (C6) and go on until the new behaviors are solid and sticky as culture is (C7)!

People Skills for Leaders

What to do? Six C's of leadership may be easy to remember. But what matters is HOW you actually DO it. How to practice the 6 Cs of leadership? Let's discuss seven people skills to keep in mind, just to give you an idea. You might find it useful to engage in personal development or hire a coach to become a great leader in change when you practice these seven topics:

1. Be yourself

Don't pretend to be someone else, don't play roles – remember how nonverbal communication gives your true meanings and beliefs away and how your credibility is at stake. Leaders are human beings – they don't have to be supermen and women anymore. So, don't worry. We trust and follow authentic leaders – not perfect leaders.

Meanwhile, work on skills that could be improved. Solve any personal issues that may undermine you – secure your emotional intelligence and heal any childhood insecurities.

2. Understand yourself

An important people skill is understanding yourself – what are my preferences?

What is my way of communicating? What drives me? What are my values? What are my qualities? What could be improved? What do I still dream of? What is holding me back? What are deep beliefs? Are they limiting or empowering me? What are my automated responses or behavioral patterns? What needs to be healed? What is still undermining me?

Some managers feel this is exaggerated: "I don't need a therapist". But welcome to today's complex world. We need to be self–conscious to be able to handle complexity, change and uncertainty. We need to deliver stunning services in a fast, impatient experience & attention economy. We must be able to guide others through change. "Because I said so!" doesn't work anymore. You can't understand others, let alone lead them well, until you understand yourself.

3. Understand others

It's essential to understand others. If you have some idea about yourself, your personality traits and preferences and your way of doing things, it becomes easier to understand others and to see how they differ from you. Which values from the Competing Values Framework would they prefer in their lives? Which personality traits and thinking styles appeal to them? How do they differ from you? In what way are they the same? How can you complement each other? What do they need from you? We will discuss the MBTI and Five Factor personality assessments later on in this chapter.

4. Perception: Elephant in the room?

Perception tends to be underestimated. Here's the insight: Your point of view is not THE reality. Other people may have other perceptions of the same reality which are valid, too. Depending on our background, our personality traits, our position in a team or organization and everything we've learned so far, we have a personal view. We don't see the world the way it is, we see the world the way we are. Our perception plays the lead role and we respond to the world from our perception. Distinguishing perception from reality is essential.

When working with a CEO or senior executive, they sometimes tell me: "This is the way it is. My employees are wrong. My staff doesn't get it." This is their perception; the CEO's point of view. It is THEIR reality but not necessarily THE reality.

Some leaders take their perception for reality and this causes problems when they don't accept that others could perceive things differently. Especially in times of change, old meanings become obsolete, ambiguity prevails and people construct new meanings together. In change, things are not true or false, they are evolving.

Acknowledging perception may take the pain out of disputes. People don't have to take it personally anymore. It is not about being right. They all might see different angles of the same thing, depending on their focus. No one sees the elephant in the room. We all see a different part of it, wondering what it is. What counts is finding consensus and constructing new meanings together. People can respect and utilize different points of view to find new insights.

The subconscious assumption that "everyone thinks like me" is probably recognizable. It can make us laugh at ourselves, when we understand how we sometimes wish for clones, who think just like us. It reveals how attached we are to our own perspective. So much so that we take it for reality itself. Understanding perception means you're willing to understand others first before trying to influence them, instead of pushing, in the old–fashioned way: "I am right and we're going in that direction."

5. Listen and respect differences

Listening and respecting differences emerges when we understand perception. Listening may be harder than you think because in the Western world we have been trained in talking and answering instead of being observant.

Extroversion sells, outgoing personalities are rewarded in Western societies, prompt answers get good grades in school – and questioning teachers, parents, authorities and "truths" is not exactly encouraged during socialization. Critical thinking is allowed in academic settings – but behavioral patterns have been strongly formed by the time you reach university. Listening, questioning, daring to respectfully disagree and to differ – for many people they are not natural habits (yet).

6. Communicate and Respond to Individuals

Communication skills begin with all of the above. And go beyond. It is understanding, respecting and responding to people. This field is immense. Enjoy developing your communication skills: You can communicate well if you understand how others are thinking, what part of the message will appeal to them, how you're going to tell them etc. Learn how to use nonverbal communication.

Give positive and negative feedback. Know how to refuse a request and keep your relationship well at the same time. Improve conversation techniques. Become proficient in persuasion and negotiation. Learn how to effectively copy, coach and correct...

7. Respond to group patterns and behavior

Last but not least, train yourself to see group patterns and behavior, next to effectively responding to individual behavior. If you allow one person to break a rule, what will happen to the group?

The others will understand: "I can break this rule, too." Or, in a less equal, safe team culture: "They can break the rule – but I could never do that". They could feel unappreciated and maybe demotivated. You have to be aware of the meanings, beliefs and values, to assess what interventions will cause in the group.

What is happening? How are people influencing each other while they're interacting? Who are the informal opinion leaders in a group? What patterns are visible? Who is being copied? Who coaches the others? Who is being corrected? When do you reach a tipping point and will people see the advantage of new behavior? How can you facilitate them to be more effective as a group? How should you respond when the critics kill the new change ideas? How to respond when they're trying you? How to facilitate new behaviors? How to entice the silent people to share their thoughts? The group interaction level is a fascinating field. Find yourself a training and dive into the theory and techniques of Leary, Belbin, Systemic Work etc. that help discover group patterns.

Especially this group communication level is often neglected in manager's educations. We practice one–on–one communication skills, but the team level is essential. Leaders should lead individuals as well as teams – they may find leverage in responding to and changing group interaction patterns.

They must be able to address individuals one–on–one as well as the whole group, in a team meeting. This requires different skills. You're not a leader until you can lead on the team level, because the collective purpose/vision, shared beliefs and habitual behaviors are developed here.

Help Leaders Change

Let's go back to culture change. Effective leadership, based on the 6 Cs of Leadership helps culture to change. If you're guiding change as an outside consultant or inside HR–manager, it's essential to engage and develop the (other) leaders. They became leaders in the old culture, they are somehow rooted in the old situation that needs to be changed... So, how could they personally develop and change?

Ask them:
How are you personally part of the current culture?

When they understand how, they may be more likely to open up to personal change: 2B Change. Checking and changing beliefs and behaviors, with an executive coach or facilitator. Current leaders are successful in the old situation, apparently appointed a managing position, being rewarded for behaviors, confirmed in their beliefs, developed a typical style of management, trusted by the old boys network, enjoying the advantages of their current comfort zone. Now that is going to change. The stakes are highest for these "old leaders" for they can lose a lot. Yet, they can be an enlightening example of change!

Even when you're tenure is not 20 years, it can take bravery to lead change. You have to change yourself, you build the bridge while you walk on it, with all employees watching and possibly criticizing. Some executives may need a personal coach to work on the first people skills we discussed: be yourself and understand yourself. They may hold limiting beliefs that hamper their personal change process or management style in the new culture.

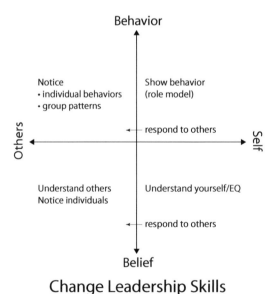

Change Leadership Skills

Turn leaders into a Team

Next to individual coaching, consider a management development program or a specific skills training for all leaders together. Group training can turn managers into a team who help each other – instead of being individualistic achievers – and being rewarded for solitary performance or the achievements of their departments. Group development programs can cover important communication skills, group dynamics and interventions and responses to behaviors in their teams – crucial skills for leaders in change.

Together, managers learn how to shape culture by personal and collective beliefs and behaviors. Make sure they share their bonuses or find other ways to reward group goals and team performance. Top executives tend to be solitary hard–working achievers – that's why they reached the top – where they now comfortably sit. It can be vital to turn them into a true team and foster collaboration. If done well, leaders show collective, consistent leadership to the employees, thus reinforcing the change and each other (read Chapter 21).

Personality and Change

Successful organizational change is personal as well as collective, as we have discussed. The Competing Values Framework can be connected to the work of Carl Gustav Jung, the famous psychotherapist; to the Myers–Briggs Type Indicator, which assesses personality types; and the Five Factor model of personalities. The Myers–Briggs Type Indicator is a survey that assesses dominant personality types. Those personality types align with the Competing Values Framework as research has shown. Jung found that there are three distinguishing differences between personality types.

1. The way that people direct their attention – they could be introvert or extrovert;
2. The way they make decisions – they could be feeling or thinking types;
3. The way they process and gather information – they could be sensing, using their senses in a more analytical way, or they could perceive information as a whole; a "Gestalt" and then they use intuition.

Now take a look at the Competing Values Framework: adhocracy culture, clan culture, hierarchy culture and market culture. The upper part of the Competing Values Framework is focused on flexibility and discretion and aligns with "feeling types" according to Jung. No need to measure everything, they may feel what is right to do and respond in a flexible way. But the bottom part of the Competing Values Framework aligns with the "thinking types" who value stability, control, analysis and research.

The left–hand side of CVF aligns with Jung's introvert people: attention focused inwards, within the organization. The right hand side has an external focus and can be linked with extroversion.

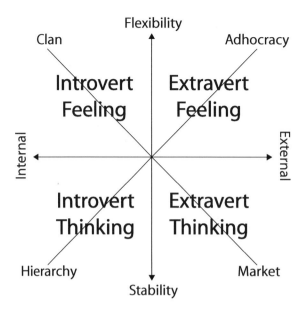

When you look at adhocracy culture, this aligns with the extrovert and feeling personalities of Jung. Find inspiration outside; feel that the market is ready for your innovation, energetic and improvising. Clan culture could seem more introvert and feeling: we are comfortably working together and we are focused on each other as coworkers.

Hierarchy culture aligns with the introvert and thinking type because it is structured, organizing and thinking. In market culture, you expect extroverted people with outward going attention who like to "score". They are the thinking type; focusing on their goal in an organized, rational way. What is missing in the CVF is the Jung perception of sensing or intuition – you could be both in every culture type.

The current leaders can be assessed on their personality traits – how well do they match current or preferred culture…? I don't think that personality types are carved in stone – but they can be tough. This is another discussion concerning basic beliefs: Can people change? Though these traits may seem rather fixed, it can give leaders insight to know their preferences. From here, they work on gradually shifting to another set of beliefs and behaviors, aware that these are not their natural preferences.

You don't have to turn into a psychologist but it's interesting to see what kind of leader types align with the culture types. For leaders themselves, it can give great insight to determine their personal preferences and develop new ways to facilitate change…

Five Factor Model

The "5 Factor Model" assesses five personality traits: openness, conscientiousness, extroversion, agreeableness and neuroticism. Openness is a measure of whether people are inventive and curious, so they're open to new information. Or: they're more consistent and cautious; for instance using proven procedures because they worked well in the past.

Conscientiousness determines whether people are efficient and organized or more easygoing and careless when it comes to details. People can be extroverted or not – so you're outgoing and energetic or you're at your best and most comfortable when solitary and reserved.

Agreeableness is a measure of: Are you friendly? Do you have a lot of empathy? Do you like to relate to people? Or will people perceive you as more cold and unkind? Are you referring to your inner standards instead of adjusting to others?

The fifth factor is emotional stability: whether you are neurotic or not. Some people tend to be more sensitive and nervous during change and challenges, while others have a more secure, rational and confident reaction to stressful situations.

Comparing the Competing Values Framework with these five factors, openness aligns with adhocracy culture – being open to new information, innovative and curious. Clan culture thrives best with a lot of agreeableness: we are friendly and we have empathy because we relate to the others of our clan. Hierarchy culture works best when most people are conscientious – they are efficient and organized, you can rely on them, they check the details as well. In market culture you might see outgoing, energetic people who are extroverted and who want to get things done.

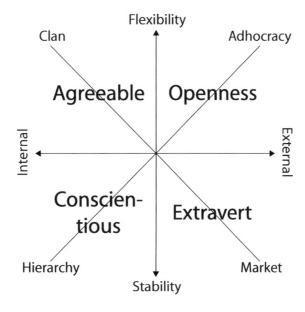

Research has shown that the best leaders are open to new information – they have a high score on openness. They are working carefully with a high score on conscientiousness. They have a high score on being an extrovert – outgoing. They are basically friendly: they score on agreeableness but can be assertive if necessary. The best leaders have a low score on neuroticism – they are emotionally stable.

So, the best leaders show the best of all four competing values. Every culture type has its own merits. There is no good or bad. You need the right mix of those competing values and qualities to get your best results. More proof of the importance to respect the differences... Imagine you are working with an organization with a dominant market culture. Their opposite is clan culture. The market culture leaders tend to see clan culture as something fluffy, but it might help that research shows that you need the features of "Clan people" as well.

What would happen if you enhance your agreeableness as a leader – if you practice to give more compliments and attention, even though you think at first that there's no need – you hired outgoing, competitive, high performing, autonomous professionals. But they might surprise you...and respond by performing even better once they're acknowledged in a personal way.

On the other hand, the clan culture leaders might think market culture is despicable – it's all about targets and financial numbers. "Market culture means those bankers who caused the credit crunch". To the clan leaders, it's the opposite of ethics and human values. Tell them that research has shown that the best leaders are outgoing and results–oriented as well – just like they are in market culture... Clan people could focus on results more, balancing the diagonal axis of the CVF between a people– and a results–orientation. See what will happen to their performance...! It can simply be very profitable to value these differences and to try some leadership behaviors from the opposite quadrant.

Quinn's Management Roles

Personality traits are not fixed in stone but they may be tough to change because people are very attached to them. "This is the way I am". Management roles can be easier to change. Robert Quinn, who developed the Competing Values Framework with Kim Cameron, detected eight management roles that align with the Competing Values Framework. Each culture type has two typical management roles.

The effective manager needs them all. Combine the people and results orientation and find your magic mix in stability versus change. Be flexible and responsive to your market but value some procedures and clear structures. Support people and inspire them to compete... By changing your style of leadership, you can stimulate another culture type. For instance, when you're working in a clan culture and you have a high score on agreeableness and you're a friendly, social person – you might want to enhance your management skills that go with market culture and become more results–oriented. The management roles and corresponding skills are further explained and exercised in the book "Becoming a Master Manager" by Robert Quinn e.a. We take a brief look here to give an idea.

Broker and Innovator Roles

Adhocracy culture likes to create and the management roles are the innovator role and the broker role. The innovator is good at living with change – this is one of the features. They can think creatively and they can "manage" change. The broker role, on the other hand, is about handling power – negotiating agreements and presenting ideas. When there are a lot of innovative ideas and scarce resources to divide, you have to decide who gets the budget. You need the innovator to stir change and innovation and you need the broker role to negotiate resources and outcomes.

Mentor and Facilitator Roles

What do you need to enhance clan culture? Their focus is on collaboration and you need the mentor and the facilitator. The mentor is great at understanding self and others, at communicating and developing employees – coaching them, facilitating to give their best. The mentor role consists of people skills. The second management role in clan culture is the facilitator role. You can build great teams and you notice and influence group behavior. You let people participate in your decisions, build consensus, get them motivated... You know how to manage conflict.

Monitor and Coordinator Roles

Hierarchy culture likes to control. The management roles are monitor and coordinator. The monitor can manage an information overload. You look at your dashboard and you analyze your core processes. You're good at processes, information and separating what is important from what is not. The monitor role measures quality and job performance – is everything delivered in time? Is it good enough? Do we have consistent results here? The coordinator role is great at managing projects, designing jobs and teams – good at organizing and structuring across functions. Hierarchy likes to run smoothly – thank you, coordinator.

Director and Producer Roles

Market culture likes to compete. Your management roles are the director and the producer. The director is creating a vision and communicating it. You set goals, you design and organize. The director directs people to achieve the collective purpose. The producer role means working productively yourself because you are the role model. You foster performance, and you manage time, stress and competing demands.

Summary

To bring about successful culture change, leadership is essential. Leaders must balance 2B's: Beliefs and Behaviors. The key figures in an organizational system could check their beliefs and change those if they are hampering change. Next, it will be easier to display genuine, authentic behavior that supports the change.

Leaders, guiding change, should be aware of 6 crucial C's as well as check on a broad range of people skills including group dynamics. Leaders should notice and respond to behaviors, by individuals as well as in groups, to create the right environment for new behaviors to thrive.

The six C's of Culture Change Leadership are Collective purpose, be Copied, Coach, Correct, Compliment and Care for people.

Next, we briefly visited the eight management roles that align with the four culture types, the MBTI personality traits and the Five Factors.

We can help leaders be ready for change by one–on–one coaching (beliefs) as well as management development (practice people skills, group dynamics, behaviors and support each other as a team).

Further reading

Competing values Leadership: quadrant roles and personality traits by Alan Belasen and Nancy Frank in Leadership and Organization Development Journal Vol. 29 No. 2, 2008 pp. 127–143.

Chapter 20 Case: at the maintenance unit. How to let go of tight control?

Here's another case that illustrates the crucial role of leadership. It shows how an "old–fashioned" CEO is controlled by his fears and how one division considers to empower themselves and take ownership for their change. This organization has machine maintenance as its core business, next to process optimization. Let's call them MM for privacy reasons. They have locations all over the country and their 400 employees can be divided into mechanics and engineers. The specialist mechanics work at the client's site to do machine maintenance. The engineers give advice and guide more complex projects around process optimization.

MM is organized in a traditional hierarchical structure, with a strong CEO on top. They are organized in four divisions throughout the country. The managing team of one division, supported by two companywide HR advisors, does the OCAI assessment and gets together for a one day workshop. Their CEO is an older man who has been with MM for ages and he practically IS the company. He likes to control everything and he is concerned about their deteriorating profits and worsening numbers. The 4 division directors report to this CEO, who means well but gives them "little space" as the division director explains.

Each division is organized in locations, with a location manager who is fully accountable for the budget to spend and the turnover that their location generates. There used to be a foreman, who reported to the division director every day, but now they have a location manager who is allowed to "run their own shop". This is a new structure of positions and authorization. The organization is facing increasing competition in a market that is shrinking due to the economic downturn. Factories throughout the country try to postpone their maintenance. They want to avoid expensive hiring of outside mechanics.

The strength of MM's mechanics however is that they are well trained with up–to–date knowledge. They are outsourced to the client's site, but once this factory needs to cut costs, MM's mechanics are the first to exit through the gate. Another challenge is the hiring and retention of technical personnel. There's a shortage on the market for higher–educated, specialist mechanics and engineers. MM invests in their training and education but they leave easily, hired by a competitor. Talking of process optimization during their culture workshop they draw the conclusion that their pipeline from intake to servicing a client is too long. One manager says: "We operate in spite of our processes, instead of thanks to them". This is a painful conclusion for MM which is selling process optimization...

Dream of Change

They recognize their current (dark side of) hierarchy culture instantly and they admire the preferred active adhocracy culture, wondering if they will ever get there – it looks more like a dream, illustrating the need for change at this point in time. They don't really consider this much adhocracy culture for machine maintenance but it depicts a feeling. They currently have a dominant hierarchy culture of over 42 points, softened by around 32 points clan culture. The CEO is a people–oriented man; that's why people matter. The mechanics form close pairs when they are working on machine maintenance with a client. Colleagues know each other well. Only their hierarchy culture evolved to its dark side and is "over the top".

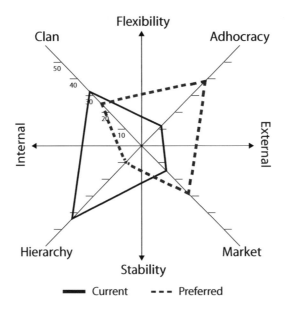

Current behaviors are:

- ◆ You can't do anything without a signature.
- ◆ We shift accountability upwards, so it's never our fault, but our boss's.
- ◆ We respond by procedures when we want to arrange something, we don't make

an exception for one mechanic, but we try to rewrite a procedure so all possible circumstances are covered, turning the procedure into a phone book.

♦ We spend 2 pages on explaining why a request was declined, trying to be correct according to the rules and keeping our relationships well.

♦ We spend our valuable working time on solving issues that should not have happened in the first place. Because no one has a clear overview (phone books!) there's a lot of confusion and discussion.

♦ You have to deliver your numbers the fifteenth of every month, no matter what. Even if it would be wise to wait until you get that crucial information on the 16th. People tend to manipulate figures to make them look good on the 15th. This is not efficient. The pressure to deliver detailed reports to the CEO and answering his questions is keeping us from doing our work – dealing with challenges and actually increasing our turnover... His fear of declining turnover is turning into reality this way...!

♦ We now have 15 autonomous location managers – we hold them accountable but we don't reward them. Moreover, they are being treated as children who are called in to report and who are patronized.

♦ We shift accountability to other levels: 3 others after me will check the document, so I don't read it but simply sign it. The thing is, the other 3 think that I checked it and might sign the document too, without properly reading it...

♦ Our mechanics can get all the technical courses they want, but 2 miles extra driving on their declaration will be declined by the accounting department, explained by 2 pages – that took about 2 hours to write down. Who is "penny wise and pound foolish"?

♦ We cannot make mistakes. All executives focus on details. Details are important and should be correct at all times.

The CEO

These behaviors and examples illustrated their workplace. They sighed: "Isn't it incredible how we still make money in spite of producing all these papers and reports...?" We do this to reassure ourselves and each other and most of all, our CEO. The division director said: "Every time I plead for more freedom and trust, the CEO says to me: 'I am responsible for this shop! I can't take risks and let anyone experiment with anything or we will all go down. You have the biggest division so if you fail, this company will go broke'."

"Out of fear, the CEO loves micromanagement and he can't let go. He freaks when your numbers are late (not on the fifteenth). He wants to know all the details about staff, he is a people guy so he remembers names and circumstances and wants to know everything. He is nice, really, and he means well."

What can I do?

I asked them to reflect on what they, the managing team of the largest division of MM, said about their CEO. They didn't get it at first. They said: "You mean we shouldn't talk about him like this? Not tell you how he's doing the wrong things?" No. I meant this: They made themselves dependent on the CEO. They responded just like their employees, shifting responsibility for the situation upwards, to their boss. They discussed how he should change. And they were probably right. But the most empowering question is:

How can I change? What can I do about this situation?

The division director said he'd talked with the CEO many times but he couldn't convince him. Of course, the first step is to talk with the CEO and suggest executive coaching to work on the CEO's deep beliefs and fears. And yes, the CEO might do better after an excellent leadership training. Once more, the director could point out the advantages of "letting go". But that would be just talking – trying to convince the other to change.

Don't talk, change yourself

The director could take responsibility for the situation and take more action himself, instead of just talking to the CEO – which didn't produce any effects. He could consider responses like:

◆ Negotiate a date range ("second half of the month" instead on the 15th sharp) to deliver the numbers and claim trust and respect for his professional autonomy as a division director.
◆ Or, simply not deliver the numbers but reassure the CEO that turnover was all right and he would get the Excel sheet as soon as he got time to finish it (but he was too busy making money right now)...
◆ Or, prove how the turnover increased after letting go of pennywise regulations that took too much time. Simply abrogate some detailed regulations and prove how well it works.
◆ Take responsibility for his division and "hide" his division from the CEO, giving his people more space to perform and surprise the CEO with great performance...

How about that? That would be shocking...! Yes, but it could make a difference. Or it would get him fired. If you feel a strong "No, we can't do that" – it means that you are touching on a core value. In this case, they held strong clan culture values that dictated: "Be nice to the CEO. The poor man is scared and we will obey to reassure him."

On the other hand – a clear action could make a difference. This is open for discussion. Take such action, yes or no? The group has to assess this and decide for themselves. It scared and excited them to think about taking ownership and changing yourself: to become the change you want to see. To actually do it, instead of just talk about it.

Questions for reflection:

♦ How do you role–model current behaviors? How are you currently part of the culture...?
♦ Is there anything you would dare to do without a proper signature?
♦ Do you dare to make a visible but useful exception to a rule?
♦ Do you dare to say No to the CEO?
♦ As a professional, do you feel accountable for your results?
♦ Do you feel comfortable – knowing that everything is controlled by the CEO? Is it reassuring, in a way?

Current core beliefs

While discussing this situation, they realized they shared key beliefs that kept the situation stuck:

1. Everything must be uniform. Uniformity is king.
2. Control keeps the danger away. There is danger outside uniformity.
3. Details are important because the devil is in the details.

I asked them to take a moment to "breathe in" these collective beliefs. What did it feel like to be working in a workplace founded on these beliefs? Coming from a technical background, the division's managing team waved this exercise away.

But the two HR ladies said: "It feels tight and burdensome. It is the opposite of inspiring and wanting to get things done". And they all nodded... Yes, right. This was not what they needed when they wanted to conquer their challenges and improve performance in a downturning market. Practically, they were always checking in the back of their minds: Are we doing things the right way? This was their current culture. They should turn that around completely. They needed the opposite:

Are we doing the right things?

They engaged in a dialogue and agreed to always ask this empowering question. For yourself and to others. Am I doing the right things? Are you doing the right things? Keep an open mind at all times and discuss things like: "Should we focus on details or move quickly with this prospect, departing from rough lines? Can we make an exception to speed this project up? Afterwards, can we abrogate the rule or simplify it to speed other projects up as well? Can we loosen control? Is uniformity client–focused or does it serve our needs? Can we benefit from diversity? Can we change, improve and learn? Can we go ahead while waiting for an official signature? Can you trust me with this...? etc."

They decided that accountability and autonomy were needed as low in the organization as possible and as high as necessary. They wanted to work with rough outlines without specific details on how to do something but simply stating "what" needs to be done. They decided to give their location managers more space as of now, emphasizing their qualities of being entrepreneurial and accountable. The managing team of this division decided to stop micromanaging and to role–model "professional empowerment". They realized that they needed courage to do this. The courage to let go...

They agreed to these things:

- ◆ Daily ask yourself and others (and when taking decisions): Are we doing the right things?
- ◆ Respect and reward the location manager's position as intended: a fully autonomous professional.
- ◆ Stop executing detailed prescriptions, reconsider what we could let go. What is the worst thing that can happen? Is that acceptable? Preserve a bottom line of procedures and quality standards that are non–negotiable but try to let go of non–essentials.
- ◆ Allow our subordinates to deliver numbers in the last 2 weeks of each month (instead the 15th)
- ◆ Consider the decisions and documents that need our signature. All other things will not be signed by us anymore. We'll explain this to our people once we have the list.
- ◆ Consider to reward and compliment on the "What" as opposed to "How".
- ◆ Be honest in meetings with employees, saying things like: "I don't know" to role–model new, learning behaviors, giving others permission to learn too.

After this first workshop they did the division's change project on their own, taking ownership and focusing on "letting go and daring to be different".

Summary

This case shows the effects of the dark side of hierarchy culture and a controlling CEO, creating what he fears: a badly performing organization. They have a typical focus on "Doing things the Right way" instead of "Doing the Right Things". It feels shocking for them to consider taking ownership – What can I do myself? This is an empowering question, but more typical for their opposite: adhocracy culture. The group gained many insights, like this common one: We tend to talk – instead of doing something about it.

Chapter 21 How to co–create Change with Positive Energy?

In this chapter, we discuss the Rocky Flats story as an example of "positive change". It is a story of success because they used an abundance approach: based on faith and high expectations (as opposed to the fearful CEO in the previous chapter). This case was researched by Kim Cameron and Marc Lavine, and described in their book "Making the impossible – possible". It is an excellent illustration of positive leadership and using the qualities of the Competing Values Framework. We will also have a look at positive energy networks that can fast forward your culture change.

Rocky Flats Case

Rocky Flats was a nuclear weapons plant full of plutonium in the United States of America, close to the city of Denver. By 1995, the plant had become obsolete. They had to break it down. The US government estimated it would take 70 years and $36 billion to demolish this plant and to make it a safe place again. They hired Kaiser–Hill and this company did the job in 10 years at $6 billion. They did it 60 years ahead of the deadline and saved $30 billion on the budget. They started with 7,000 employees and the last people closed down the plant in the year 2005. How did they do it ?!

The abundance approach

Kaiser–Hill used an unusual abundance approach to change the situation and facilitate this collective peak performance. Most management theories focus on the problems and challenges one encounters when it comes to organizational change. It is assumed that to achieve a goal, all kinds of obstacles must be overcome. Leaders learn to recognize and solve problems.

The usual problem–solving approach consists of the following:

1. Identify and analyze problems
2. Generate alternative solutions
3. Evaluate and select the optimal option
4. Implement the solution

Following this usual approach means getting out of trouble and reaching a "normal" situation. The organization is changed, reengineered, and operates smoothly again. The abundance approach supplements this traditional problem–solving approach by going beyond the normal situation to reach an excellent situation. Its basic assumption is not to solve problems but to enable everyone's highest potential to be reached.

Isn't this a bit too optimistic? Not per se. Research shows the "heliotropic effect" of abundance. It's an upward positive spiral of improvement. When you expect more, you achieve more. This is a fascinating effect that works with individuals ("What you can conceive and believe, you will achieve") and within groups. See here what changing beliefs might possibly bring about... Remember, how beliefs operate as filters and self–fulfilling prophecies. Do you choose to believe in your organizational culture change... or not? Research by Marcial Losada shows that people in excellent organizations make five times more positive than negative statements (think of compliments, encouragement, trust, and optimism). John Gottmann discovered the same patterns. Positive communication will produce positive results. It is a reinforcing circle.

This effect also works the other way. Downsizing and laying off employees will produce negative performance. Interpersonal relationships are finished when people leave; trust and loyalty diminish, secrecy and fear increase. When a negative spiral has started, performance will deteriorate. Abundance has amplifying effects. The benefits grow because positive emotions are developed, social capital is formed, pro-social behavior is demonstrated and resilience is created. Research also shows that people are able to access more competencies when they are in a positive state of mind than when they feel insecure, negative and scared. Fear narrows us down and we can't find solutions as easily as we would from a positive mindset.

Collective, positive, paradoxical leadership

Let's go back to Kaiser–Hill. Their success story at Rocky Flats is a story of leadership success. Complex changes derive from a combination of factors that are often difficult to discern separately and are certainly difficult to repeat. But the Competing Values Framework leads to some clues about their success. Kaiser–Hill brought 50 managers to the project. They excelled in leadership. Cameron & Lavine state that the one–strong–leader story is actually a myth. Effective change is produced by many formal and informal leaders. They tell and show the same message over and over, each one of them in their own authentic way.

It doesn't depend on one man or woman. Their successors take over if managers leave. Effective leadership is a strong collective with shared values and goals. To align so many leaders into a coherent way of thinking and acting, you need a clear and inspiring vision. These leaders actually share a "leadership culture" that gives continuity and consistency to the organization.

Think about the change leadership requirements in Chapter 19; you could build such a leadership culture during a collective management development program where leaders work on "2B Change". Sustainable change demands multiple leaders, consistency and continuity in the long term. So, in fact, effective leadership derives from multiple individuals who skillfully respond to the behaviors in their (not too big) teams and help new habits take hold. Moreover, Cameron & Lavine concluded that successful change often requires conflicting, paradoxical strategies. That's why they used the Competing Values Framework. It identifies the basic orientations that emerge in almost all human activity. That is, all organized human activity has an underlying structure that can be categorized into four quadrants, based on the two polarities of (a) flexibility versus stability and (b) internal processing versus external positioning. In order to achieve success, you often need all four quadrants:

1. Clan culture to collaborate
2. Adhocracy culture to create
3. Market culture to compete
4. Hierarchy culture to control

This was also the case at Rocky Flats to change from a predictable, safety–obsessed and efficient nuclear plant into an innovative and effective shutdown project that resulted in an environmentally clean site. So, what were the key enablers to make the impossible possible? Cameron and Lavine found:

In summary, this extraordinary change required the following:

◆ Collective leadership, executed by multiple individuals in multiple ways
◆ Positive leadership departing from an abundance approach
◆ Paradoxical leadership: the pursuit of simultaneously conflicting strategies from four quadrants and utilizing all three necessary leadership roles for change

Positive Energy Networks

The Rocky Flats and Kaiser–Hill story is exceptional and inspirational. It shows how collective, positive, paradoxical leadership can bring forth incredible results. Let's take a look at positive change from another perspective: Positive Energy Networks. This example is taken from Kim Cameron's book "Positive Leadership" that is a very inspiring, positive book about positive leadership in organizations. A must–read... Research performed by Baker, Cross, and Wooten (2003) shows that people can be classified as energizers or energy drains, and this makes a lot of difference. Energizers stimulate vitality in others; by interacting with energizers, others feel motivated and inspired. Energy givers are optimistic, attentive, reliable, and unselfish. They attract others.

Energy drains, on the other hand, reduce good feelings and enthusiasm in others. They absorb energy and weaken or tire others, reducing motivation. Studies show that energy drains are critical, inflexible, selfish, and unreliable. You might know them from personal experience: coworkers you tend to avoid because they are always complaining, criticizing every new idea with negative arguments, and simply not getting involved in anything. I hope your colleagues radiate enthusiasm and make you feel that anything is possible so you want to go to work. Remember the ones who pull the chariot of change? They might well be the positive energizers in your organization. It is this group we need for successful change. Baker, Cross, and Parker discovered that energizing is an acquired talent, not a character trait. For example, there is no correlation between giving energy and being an introvert or an extrovert. It is possible to learn how to become an energizer, no matter how spontaneous or extroverted you are by nature. Good news...

Energizers

Energizers help organizations because they enable others to function more effectively. Research by Baker (2004) shows that employee success can be predicted more reliably by their belonging to a "positive energy network" than by their position in the information network (who is receiving information from whom) and the network of influence (who influences whom).

In the capacity of an energy giver, people prove to be four times more successful than if they are the primary figure in the information or influence network. This success is also "contagious" for people who are in contact with these energizers. By interacting with them, these people start to become energizers as well and achieve better results. Baker discovered that organizations that excel in their endeavors have three times the number of energizers of organizations performing at an average level.

This is understandable because energizers will have a positive influence on the strength of the interpersonal relationships in an organization, as well as affecting cooperation, coordination, and working efficiency. Executives can be important in this process by behaving as positive energizers and by consciously stimulating "positive energy networks." Identify the energizers within the organization, and acknowledge, reward, and support these people. Because energizers have a positive effect on others, they should be positioned in places where a lot of interaction is required. This allows many others to come into contact with the energizers' "vitality." Energizers can also be used to coach their colleagues.

Spread positive change

For change to occur, it is essential to have as many "relay stations" as possible on all levels of the organization. Just having top management get on the soapbox will not do much good. All executives will have to collectively communicate the same message and stimulate the preferred behavior in true "people manager" style. You will also need enthusiastic colleagues: positive energizers or propagandists, change agents, early adopters or sponsors, any of the names professional literature calls them. These are the people who embrace change and sell it to others, who lead by example for as long as it takes to reach a critical mass and get most people to behave according to the new culture.

Every organization needs these people to get moving and to keep moving until the desired change has been achieved. Our positive energizers do revolution by evolution—one step at a time, repeating why and what we want to change and showing the way. These are the people we are looking for to take part in the change groups, project groups, and committees that will be formed to guide and pioneer the change. Ask a number of people (or as many as possible) to provide you with the names of three energizers. Think of people who demonstrate the following characteristics:

♦ Are open to change
♦ Are enthusiastic
♦ Tend to look for possibilities (rather than limitations)
♦ Find ways to solve problems (rather than look for objections)

- Think of solutions (rather than problems)
- Are focused on what you can achieve (rather than what you can avoid)
- Are active and work hard (rather than think about things endlessly)
- Are energetic
- Have a lot of ideas
- Do what they say (or promise) and say what they do
- Attract others, people who will motivate you

Ask those people whose names are mentioned most to take part in the change group. They will think along with you, look for possibilities, and get others going. Preferably, these people come from all parts of the organization. Representation of departments and levels is great, but pay particular attention to the criteria mentioned above. These positive energizers will help you pull the chariot of change and reach a tipping point while they spread their energy through the Network–ocracy. They might help bring about "Viral Change" as we discussed in Chapter 13, so new behaviors get contagious and everyone starts copying them – showing one small, new behavior that can make a huge difference if everyone in the organizational system is doing it. We have included a case with positive energizers in Chapter 22. Get inspired and see how positive change can help your organization.

Summary

This positive chapter gave you inspiration, I hope. We have seen how the abundance approach departs fundamentally from other beliefs than are normally held and taught in business schools. These positive beliefs and high expectations were transferred to the employees in the Rocky Flats plant by multiple, adequate leaders that used all competing values–styles and were well aligned as a leadership team.

We also examined networks of positive energizers in the Network–ocracy (the organizational system) that can help new behaviors spread through the system because they are easy to copy and those positive people are simply so... energizing and inspirational. Try the abundance mindset and the positive energizers to the advantage of your organization's change...

Further Reading

Making the Imposssible Possible – Leading Extraordinary Performance, by Kim Cameron and Marc Lavine.

Positive Leadership – Strategies for Extraordinary Performance, Kim Cameron.

Chapter 22 Case: at a National Bank. How to wake up in a positive way?

Let's take a look at this "positive change" case from Zelda, a change manager who got her inspiration from the Positive Energizers concept in the previous chapter. In spite of the fiction writing style, this is a true story and on her request I leave out her last name and her employer.

Welcome to the IT Department

Please meet Zelda, an internal change manager at a large national bank. She's working in the bank's IT Department, hired to guide some IT change projects. But this time it's different. She is taking up the challenge to change the culture of the IT Department. "We really need a change", Zelda laughs. She is a very positive minded, optimistic kind of person.

Imagine this IT Department: "We have a total staff of 164 and I see immaturity everywhere", Zelda explains. "I see grown–ups with a childish, individualist attitude, comparing themselves with colleagues all the time and thinking: 'I have to have what you have!'." But that isn't the major issue. The thing is that this IT Department seems to be providing bad service. The other bank departments are dissatisfied and are giving a lot of negative feedback. This goes beyond the normal clichés and prejudice of "those IT geeks can't communicate when they fix my computer".

Zelda says: "Actually, we're at the forefront in IT, but we're not communicating it. Everyone working here is fairly highly educated in IT. But the culture is not customer focused at all. I have to say I agree with our internal clients. The help desk is not good enough, though the programmers are OK. But if you have a technical issue like I was having the other day, you call your techie friends instead of the help desk.

I couldn't open my project plan after saving it – and one of my friends fixed it for me. Just like I was trying to show a YouTube movie in my presentation and after two (!) weeks our help desk reported they couldn't help me. We really need a wakeup call over here."

"In the bigger scheme of things the need for a different way of delivering IT is also on the charts – instead of us telling our internal customer what they can and cannot have, the new way of thinking is – how can we educate them on the latest technology that could be useful to them and how can we make our services better."

The IT Department has a history of lifetime employment. "One of the tacit beliefs is: If you stay long enough, you get promoted," Zelda explains. "We have a culture of avoiding conflicts and zero consequence if you don't deliver as you promised.

The older IT guys tend to dress formally in suits and ties, the youngsters are wearing pink shirts to work. This is a new generation coming into our workplace, but our bank is slow to catch up. We're falling behind. If our top executives attend an international conference, they want to have the newest gadgets too. We want to have iPads or you don't look good when you're abroad. But our IT guys seem to be reluctant to educate us on these cool gadgets.

And they don't like to slice and dice our customers, like professional service departments do. They emphasize everyone should be treated the same. But sometimes there's a national issue and you have to give priority to a high authority! Whether it's against your principles or not."

Change made compulsory

How will Zelda wake up their IT Department? How is she going to change this conservative culture into a customer focused organization? "I've been thinking about that", Zelda says. "This is IT and we like to work with numbers. So I figure that we need a survey or an assessment to determine our status quo. Now I've found the Organizational Culture Assessment Instrument online and decided we're going to use the OCAI to get started. But whenever we had a survey before, we only had a 30% response rate. I think that wouldn't be good enough."

Zelda takes her idea to Barry, the Head of the IT Department who is fairly new to the organization. She's lucky that Barry is a very reasonable, open–minded guy. They talk about getting their IT guys to move and Barry supports Zelda right away, because he agrees that changes are necessary. He's responsible for improving this department. "What if we organize culture sessions and make them compulsory?" Zelda proposes. "That would be tricky. It grows resistance", Barry objects.

"But maybe we could get all their issues out in the open... If we do it the right way"

Zelda pleads. "Think about that. We can organize some interesting sessions where people can speak their minds about things. We need to trigger them or their response rate to anything remains low and slow. I think it is exciting and I'm a bit nervous about making it mandatory as well. But I feel that we have to try it this time."

Barry hesitates. But Zelda has a point. They need to break through this indifference or this habit of we–have–always–done–it–this–way. Get them out of their comfort zones. Shake them out of the naturalness of staying–long–enough–and–doing–it–the–same–way–so–nothing–changes–and–get–safely–promoted. Maybe they should stir a reaction. Something will happen and people might wake up.

"What if I put sheets on the wall?" Zelda continues enthusiastically. "Everyone can choose which session they want to attend. They can choose their mates to go together. But you have to pick one of the sessions that we schedule. There's no negotiating that. OK?"

She has thought this through, obviously. Barry is impressed. This ambitious girl might facilitate him to achieve his performance targets for the IT Department. He gave her the assignment to come up with something, a bit halfheartedly, not expecting much of a change manager dedicated to IT projects. "Zelda, go ahead. I'll support you. We have to make a change." Barry smiles.

She's a bit tense, because it's exciting. But she does it. She actually explains in an email that they're going to have culture sessions and that Barry wants all staff to be there, working on culture with Zelda. She hangs the sheets of paper on the wall. She's ready for take–off. Expecting a storm. But they start filling in their names, some reluctantly, but obedient. Some are even excited with expectations… So is Zelda…

Culture sessions

They enter the room slowly. It's Zelda's first group coming in for a culture session. She has everything set up for them: A bunch of computers displaying their OCAI assessment page. Pens and papers. Her smile and lots of humor. Zelda knows she needs to entice them, reassure them and listen to them. They need attention. And she's ready to give them her full attention.

Yes, there is some resistance. One man frowns. They sit back with their arms crossed. Before she can begin, someone asks how long this is going to take. "I'm extremely busy. I have no more than an hour."

'Let's make it worthwhile", Zelda says. "We're all busy. But this is important."

Someone laughs, another coughs.

"Don't you think so?" Zelda asks them.

"Listen, I don't mean to hurt you, but I think this is [peep]. It's a waste of time. Nothing is ever going to change in this bank and the other departments will look down on us anyway. You can pimp your help desk or your service, but things will always be the same."

"I challenge you", Zelda says. "To make a difference this time. This is your opportunity to share your thoughts and to improve things. If we start to change, the others will have to change to respond to us. If you don't collaborate, you won't get anything changed at all, ever. So who wants to have things changed?"

A lot of hands are raised. "OK guys, let's get started. I want you to make a list of everything that sucks if that's a relief."

"How much time have we got, haha!"

"OK guys. It's a match. You've got 5 minutes to write it down. And next I want you to outcompete yourself. Make an even longer list of great things that are so good at that you want to keep doing them."

"Wait a minute, Zelda. Who is going to see all of this information?"

"Trust me guys. Our head Barry is going to see this. But not with your names on top of your list. But we have to work on ourselves, because we don't want everyone complaining about us, now do we? I think we need to change."

Zelda has very intense sessions with her IT colleagues. All employees do the online OCAI assessment in one room together, trusting that their privacy is secured. They share their lists of good and bad things. And they give lots of qualitative feedback. Especially about their 8 managers. They are very outspoken, it even feels a bit like manager bashing.

Zelda has a way of enticing them, influencing them and speaking her mind. She even addresses immaturity because they notice it themselves.

"So you don't like the managers, because they are controlling you as if you were naughty children."

And one of the senior IT guys says: "Yeah, it's like we're having a parent–child relationship or something. He's dominant, OK. But I think we need more self–respect. That is our part of the equation.

We can help the clients and we have the information. No need to be dependent on the managers and behave like kids. We can take decisions and be accountable for them. We can give and take feedback, aren't we adults?"

That's an impressive moment in one of the groups. They recognize it and agree. Something is beginning to move. Little sparks of insight start to challenge old habits and attitudes. Why not look at it in another way…?

Zelda is tired after the sessions. She's fully alert and aware of everything that happens in the room. She loves it, but it is so intense… She needs to guide this very skillfully.

The OCAI serves its purpose. It's a great and easy reference framework to start thinking and talking about habits, tacit beliefs, the way we do things around here, about tensions and irritations. It gives an idea of what should be changed. No IT guy was ever educated in people stuff, but the majority likes the sessions without the ordinary jokes about "fluffy stuff and feelings".

Zelda took a chance with making the assessment obligatory and doing it with a group in one room. But she managed to give the participants faith and enticed them to open up. That's quite an achievement.

She somehow combined doing the assessment with the OCAI–workshops afterwards, when you fill in the generalist culture types with your specific examples and add qualitative information to the numbers and profiles from the assessment.

OCAI results: Revolution calling

The outcome? Zelda counts 150 people out of 164 that joined the assessment and the culture sessions. That's 91% They did not only join, but also made a difference during the sessions. They started to think constructively and started to discuss improvements. She has started a culture intervention already. It's often therapeutic to give attention to staff and to respectfully listen to their views. It's a way to open up and get started.

The outcome of the OCAI assessment speaks louder than words. The IT guys are currently experiencing a dominant hierarchy culture (43,85 points). The focus is on Control, valuing procedures, clear structures, efficiency and reliability (treating all your customers the same way). They have results–oriented market culture that

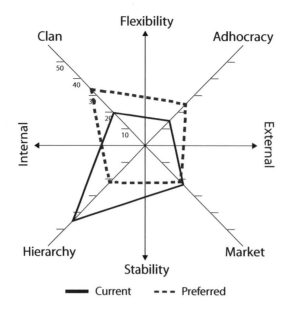

values competition and getting things done (22,73) and then some minor elements of people–oriented clan culture (19,05) and entrepreneurial, innovative adhocracy culture (14,37). That is recognizable.

Their preferred culture calls for revolution. A shift of more than 10 points in this Competing Values Framework is extraordinary and calls for radical change. They are through with their own hierarchy culture and want it diminished with 20 points in favor of clan culture. They vote for a people–oriented clan culture to be dominant in the future (32,82) followed by professional freedom and dynamics (24,29 adhocracy culture) and an equal basis of results (21,29 market culture) and procedures and lean processes (21,60 hierarchy culture).

They want a huge upwards shift to the quadrants that value flexibility above stability. This might help them strengthen their customer focus, though they might also need more of the externally focused market culture. These results align with the mood in the culture sessions, including the manager bashing. When Zelda studies their OCAI report, she sees that leadership deviates from the overall dominant hierarchy culture.

Interestingly enough, the separate profile for Organizational Leadership, one of the 6 culture factors that is assessed, shows a different graph than the 5 other factors. (Those are: Dominant Characteristics, Organizational Glue, Management of Employees, Criteria of Success, Strategic Emphases). The IT workers perceive their managers as very results–oriented, stressing the importance of targets and results. They are seen as hard–drivers, producers and competitive people, managing from a market culture perspective.

Employees want 11,65 points less of this attitude in favor of a people–oriented manager who supports and facilitates their staff (+ 5,95 clan culture), but above all they want more innovative managers who are not afraid of experimenting, risk taking and trying things (+9,73 adhocracy). That's interesting. Zelda knew people were not satisfied, but she didn't know it was to this extent (something has to change soon) and that leadership is considered differently.

Being open about the change

"Barry, what do you think?" Zelda asks.

"I think it's impressive", he says. "I think we have to take this to a higher level. Show the other directors what we are doing in our department. How our employees feel."

"Really? That would be awesome!" Zelda says. "I'd love to give a presentation in the board. Can you get me there? We will show them an example of walk our talk. We open up. They can laugh at us, they can look down on us, they can get all of their prejudice confirmed, but they will respect us for having the guts of telling them openly about how we are trying to change."

"But first, we're going to discuss the results with the managers. They must know how staff is feeling about them."

That is painful. The managers take the negative feedback. 65% of the IT staff has considered quitting their jobs because of their leadership. It's time for some changes. Thanks to Barry's support and networking, Zelda is allowed into the Bank's Board meeting to present the outcome of their culture assessment. The board is impressed by their openness (it is a brave thing to do) and is interested. They consider taking the culture change further, to include other departments as well. Zelda feels she is supported.

An important outcome of the board meeting is that they determine 4 strategic goals for the IT Department. That's great because most IT staff didn't know why they were doing things. Zelda and Barry can now start to communicate those goals to their staff... And the other departments might start to have culture assessments and sessions as well, following the great example of IT. That's important branding for the IT guys, who used to be the black sheep of the bank.

Network of Energizers

Zelda is in her office, reflecting on the change process she started. She's reading through the extra materials from OCAI Online. She particularly likes their white paper on Positive Energy Networks. Research has found that some people energize others while their opposites feel like energy drains. It's best to give the "drains" solitary tasks. Give the energizers positions with lots of interactions because they are contagious: They spread positivism, enthusiasm and hope through the organization. That's no wishful thinking but proven in research. You can learn how to utilize your energizers in change programs, having them "sell and pull" the change, energizing the majority to try it until a critical mass of people is changing so you reach a tipping point! The change becomes real. You want to reach that point where it's more advantageous to join the change than to resist.

Finding the positive people

Would that work with her IT guys? Zelda wonders. Why not try it? She certainly needs ambassadors for change. So she starts composing an informal email.

"Hi guys, I am looking for people who have the following characteristics: They are open to change and enthusiastic. They tend to look for possibilities rather than limitations and think of solutions rather than problems.

Do you know anyone who is focused on what they can achieve rather than what to avoid? Active people who work hard? With lots of ideas and energy? People who do as they say and that you can rely on? People that energize and motivate others? Please email me their names. I'm curious to know the co–workers who can support us make the change." She hits the send button. And she's excited when she starts to get replies. She makes a list of the names that are mentioned once, twice, more. And she ends up with a list of 20 people. She has identified the positive energizers of their IT Department!

Positive Change Squad

They come into the room, 20 people, not knowing exactly why they were invited. Zelda welcomes them and says: "It's not me who invited you. Your co–workers did. They thought you are open to change and enthusiastic. You look for possibilities and solutions and what to achieve rather than what to avoid. You are active, energetic and you work hard. You do as you say and people can rely on you. You energize and motivate others."

It's as if a light starts to beam in the room. They all smile and take this as a huge compliment, which it is. "So your co–workers chose you. Do you want to join me in the Change Squad? Will you help our department make the culture change?"

They all agree. Zelda has her change ambassadors! She has trumped herself with creativity. She's had so much fun with compiling a goodie bag for them, to emphasize her message. She now gives them chocolate coins to put their money where their mouth is. She has "smiley" sweets to eat when life is bitter. Then they start working on ideas. How will they stimulate the change?

Ideas for interventions

Action speaks louder than words. Now they must come up with some ideas for interventions. What will they do to make the change? People tell Zelda in the hallways: "All our hope is on you". But she refuses to take this burden on her shoulders.

She answers: "It never depends on one person. It's this whole group that must make the change." Come on guys, take some responsibility. Stop being dependent on others and grow up! They are immature, Zelda thinks again.

This is like some of the behaviors that she had identified during the culture sessions. Zelda found that OCAI Online's manual with the ABCDE scheme of culture was quite inspirational. She focused on behavior (the D–level of change) and she discussed what the IT people wanted to change in behaviors, in what they DO.

They discussed what is in your span of control to influence: for example – the way I speak to a customer. "My manager has nothing to do with that, it is the way how I speak to, and treat a customer." This notion leads to ownership and them eventually taking responsibility for their own actions.

Zelda wants them to stop being a victim and start taking control of what they can influence. But she needs to be patient. They want to give her "their monkey". She hands it back. They have to start to think and act differently. She cannot change **them**.

And how to enhance clan culture? One quick win is to start sending birthday cards to staff, an idea from the energizers that's easily implemented.

Zelda is going to make an HR booklet for managers, helping them improve. She seeks the support of 2 HR consultants in the bank, who help her do this. The HR booklet is "branded" with the IT Department's logo. Zelda feels it is important that IT communicates what they do and proves that they are good enough...

It may enhance pride within the IT Department and brand some positive associations about IT with the other departments. She asks everyone to email her ideas. Clan culture is all about participation. So far, she gets 40 ideas. She is doing a World cafe session with the staff on two topics: A calendar for the year that promotes and educates people – technical and Bank staff. Example: Getting in a futuristic IT speaker; optimal utilization of your Blackberry etc. The second topic is on branding and communication for our IT department.

Zelda asks the IT people what they want to see in their calendar. Because they love gadgets (they are in IT!) they organize a "Bring our toys to work" session. Showing each other the latest, coolest stuff. Creating awareness at the same time that technology moves forward very fast and that they need to change. And have some fun together, exploring the toys / gadgets.

The most important intervention is starting a leadership program and a staff program, by an external provider, to work on immaturity, as Zelda puts it. The program follows important competencies that have to do with emotional intelligence. The EQ program is the core of the change, Zelda says. It comprises of topics like Managing people, Performance coaching, Communicating, Building high performance teams, Client experience management, Relationships, Enhancing Engagement and so on.

"The other stuff is nice, but these programs are key", Zelda feels. She's writing a submission to get permission for the budget, supported by one of the "top guys". "He's great at finding funds and he offered to help me", Zelda explains. "We're writing in business language, no IT language this time. I'm confident that it will work out."

It's been 3 months since Zelda started the challenge of changing the IT Department's culture. She's surprised about the progress so far. "I've come further than I expected. It's very promising. We'll reach a tipping point where more and more people get into a winning mood. Positive energizers support this. We're starting to have fun while we change. We get recognition from the Board. Barry backs it up. Without his support, we couldn't have come so far. I'm excited!" Zelda: Well done so far!

Do you feel inspired? Or challenged? Do you feel like competing or collaborating? Whatever it is – send us your cases of OCAI culture change as well! Share them in our LinkedIn group or email us. We can inspire each other and learn from each case. If you want to, connect with the OCAI change community on LinkedIn [add link].

Chapter 23

What does the 21st Century Workplace look like?

In this chapter we will take a look at the future of organizational life. In our online, global database with culture assessments we see an interesting desire for more adhocracy and clan cultures in the future, across countries and economic activities. What does this mean...?

Let's explore the desire for innovation, mastery and autonomy and other needs in our young 21st century. Let's meet Generation Y and dream of the future. Let's see how many organizations still work in an old–fashioned way, while the "only way is up" in the Competing Values Framework, according to today's professional employees.

More Flexibility, please

When you take a look at our database, it's no coincidence anymore: there is a strong tendency towards more adhocracy and clan culture types in the future. It's every-where around the world, in all kinds of organizations and teams, in all economic sectors: people want an upwards shift. The only way is up, in the Competing Values Framework.

We took the results of 5700 random participants from the United States of America (update September 2012) and drew their collective culture profile. The black graph is the current culture and the dashed graph is the preferred culture type. People want over 10 points more flexibility, towards clan and adhocracy culture. What does it mean? Does it have anything to do with our current era?

Voting for more adhocracy might mean: People like more innovation and experi-ments. They'd like flexibility to organize their own tasks in their own way. They like variation in their jobs and some professional freedom.

From their increased clan culture score, it seems that: People like a more people–oriented workplace. This could represent a desire to be acknowledged at work. They like friendly coworkers and managers, they appreciate coaching and development, team spirit, engagement, inclusiveness and feeling safe within a group or team.

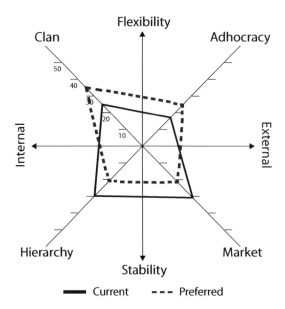

People want less hierarchy culture – they want less control and less focus on efficiency, uniformity and processes. They might feel hampered having to wait for permission and the right signature.

Less market culture could mean: People want less targets and work pressure, feeling that results are all that counts, clocking in and out. They don't like too much of a competitive culture, with the risk of losing face, constantly outperforming the others and keeping track of their reputation. Everybody wants more flexibility. Everybody wants more people–oriented clan culture and entrepreneurial, innovative adhocracy culture.

Majority: Managers who Measure

However, the majority of organizations from our database still have hierarchy and market culture types! They are focused on stability – like mature organizations in an industrial area. The thing is, we're not in an industrial era anymore. Technology accelerated and connected the world...

But many managers still love the paradigm of total control, measurement and stability, even though Frederick Taylor, who started the innovation of measuring labor times and labor division, was fashionable one hundred years ago. Taylor's worldview is convenient: reducing complexity to small, controllable tasks. His main assumption is that reality can be known and planned for. From this point of view, negative deviations are called failures, improvisation and professional freedom are undesirable, standardization is king and new regulations are the answer to diminish uncertainty and the variety of reality.

In such a designable reality, you only need to do your job and do as you're told. You have a distinct position in hierarchy and a long–term perspective: if you work hard, you will climb the ladder and be rewarded for years of compliance to this system. The boss knows best, because reality can be known and he has the room with the (over)view, at the top of the building.

Things don't move at the speed of light – yet – and he sees them coming. Boundaries of knowledge, capital and geography still determine the playing field. Those were the days. Knowing that reality was under control and someone knew best – "knowledge is power". In this mechanistic, material world, we used to have:

The old way of change:

♦ top down design and decisions about change
♦ by exclusive teams (mostly top executives)
♦ who order the others to change their ways (by command and control)
♦ and often don't want to change themselves
♦ focused on the organization
♦ in a linear way: big initiatives for big change, small ones cause small change
♦ with a clear beginning and end ("unfreeze–change–refreeze")
♦ based on the belief: we know what's best because we have all the information – and we analyzed it thoroughly

21st Century Facts

Get the picture? Remember? However, we have now reached the 21st century. In Western Europe, the United States and parts of South America and Asia, we have largely developed into a servicing economy while the products are being manufactured in China and other emerging markets.

Our information society is complex. Technology developing at a high rate enables us to network more easily and to work from anywhere. Social media lets us virtually enter in office buildings and follow employees online.

When we look at our workplaces, we notice that people are higher educated than ever before. The workforce consists of more and more professionals who know how to organize their own jobs and can work independently. We need to be well educated in our complex and technologically–driven world. There is a change in the workload, the pace, the complexity and the nature of work. In these Western societies we're mostly working with people. We're providing services and information to one another.

The global economy and technology make innovation necessary because there is increasing global competition at an incredibly rapid pace. If you want to survive as an organization you need to be fast and respond to future needs.

The 21st Century workplace is:

- technology development at an amazing pace
- making life and work more digital
- enhancing globalization because information and services travel at the speed of light
- inviting global competition from emergent markets
- making the need for innovation and performance even more apparent
- while reducing costs – which is a case for standardization – but
- delivering complex products and services to critical, demanding customers
- who want a solution right now
- so you need to retain talent and
- engage your highly educated professionals
- who thrive on purpose, meaningful work, autonomy and mastery in their field
- or they will leave and become self–employed contractors
- while the baby boomers get ready to retire and leave all the work to
- fewer people who collaborate all over the world in huge diversity
- using technology to its max, including social media showing the inside of the workplace to the outside world

Flat or big organizations?

Some organizations respond to these challenges by becoming flat and flexible, changing their structure to facilitate projects and temporary work. They foster self–organizing units that facilitate professionals who know how to work independently and motivate themselves and respond quickly to rapid changes. It's flat, participative, democratic and complex, if you will. Their culture consists of interesting combinations of people–oriented clan culture as well as results–oriented market culture and dynamic, open–to–change adhocracy culture.

The other organizational reaction to this rapidly changing world is becoming big and powerful by merger and acquisition, hoping for large–scale advantages. They try to become a powerful player in this market with divisions everywhere. Their professionals are necessary to manage the complexity of operating in a large–scale organization, focusing on strategy and research and global marketing, solving the puzzle of complex logistics, implementing efficient processes, designing companywide procedures and structures to align uniform activities worldwide and keep control. It's necessarily top–down, well–thought of, and complex. Their main culture types seem to be control–oriented hierarchy and results–oriented market culture.

Interpreting these facts about organizations and professionals in a rapidly changing world leads to some suggestions of why so many people desire more clan and adhocracy cultures. We have seen how change becomes necessary from the outside: our 21st Century technology accelerates and connects the world. Organizations have to adapt to this changing environment, whether they like it or not. From our database it appears that many organizations have not yet adapted to our new world – they still have dominant hierarchy and market cultures.

But there's also change from within organizations because employees have a higher education and want to work as autonomous professionals. Let's explore this inner world and motivation and see why so many professionals prefer clan and adhocracy cultures.

Evolution: Maslow's Pyramid

The need for more flexibility derives partly from within – says motivation theory. You've probably seen this well–known pyramid by Abraham Maslow:

Maslow's hierarchy of needs

At the bottom are the physiological needs that need to be fulfilled first. Next, you need to feel safe and have a sense of belonging. Once you've got that, people are ready to develop their self–esteem. An advanced need in the hierarchy of motivation is self–actualization. You'd like to develop yourself into the person that you are, manifesting your potential. You'd like to explore your possibilities and use your talents to achieve your goals and make you dreams come true.

This kind of "advanced need" emerges when people have enough to eat, feel safe, belong to a group and feel confident enough – to explain it very simply. When we look at Western societies, we might conclude that our basic physical needs are fulfilled by now. Most of us feel safe and we belong to several groups, more than ever before if we take social media into account.

In our individualistic societies we have developed self–esteem and our educational system stimulates personal development and self–actualization. You need to learn and develop longer than ever before, to gain access to our professional knowledge– and service–economy. More individuals than before are entering the top of the pyramid and they value self–actualization. "I'd like to develop into the best possible person that I could ever be." This slogan is even found in lady's magazines; "Live your best life".

Looking at the pyramid one might argue that clan and adhocracy culture types match the needs of the upper part of this pyramid very well: "I want to be connected with other people, develop myself, participate in decisions, commit to a group, but also need my professional freedom to work independently in my own special way. I'd like to learn new stuff, experiment, be innovative, entrepreneurial, and independent. Just give me space and I will blossom!"

Weggeman's Research: Give Professionals Space

The upward shift is not only visible in OCAI Online's database but was also found by Dutch professor Dr. Mathieu Weggeman. His research shows that higher educated professionals prefer more professional freedom and responsibilities. They like to have some space. Only from time to time, they appreciate more attention from their managers and colleagues. (His book has not yet been translated into English, title: *Don't manage professionals!*).

Weggeman states that professionals and organizations would be better off if managers would stop telling them how to do their jobs and would restrict themselves to telling professionals what needs to be done by when—just like the new contract Kaiser Hill negotiated (see Chapter 17). It gives more freedom and more responsibilities, but professionals are well trained and can live with that. To ensure quality, performance, and efficient production, Weggeman recommends a strong collective ambition and peer reviews, with colleagues checking on each other's work.

Intrinsic motivation and passion for your profession is much more effective than external control, procedures, and targets. Professionals have chosen their profession, like to be good at it and tend to work hard. If you organize them well, organizations can have better performance, says Weggeman.

Knowing this, it's interesting that there's a movement towards more external pressure, control and management. In many industry groups, we see increasing regulations. Governments and society demand good governance, transparency and accountability. Demanding customers want good but cheap products and services that are delivered on time.

To meet these outside requirements, organizations and executives rely on the "good old" lower two quadrants of the OCAI model: they emphasize and appreciate hierarchy and market cultures. They love the paradigm of control. But Frederick Taylor is dead: the industrial era is over and we have entered a new league...

Professionals currently adapt to the rules but start to dislike managers with Excel sheets trying to keep track of output and results. Professionals leave their passion, creativity and innovative ideas at home. Weggeman shows this in his book. In the Netherlands, more professionals than ever before are currently self–employed. They have left their organizations because they couldn't bear to be managed. That could be different. For instance, in clan and adhocracy cultures.

Daniel Pink: Mastery, Autonomy and Purpose

Weggeman's results align well with Daniel Pink's motivational theory (read his book: 'Drive: The Surprising Truth About What Motivates Us'). Pink says we have reached so much material wealth that other things start to motivate us. Now that we have salaries or profits that will enable us to pay our mortgage or rent, we're going to the next level. At this level, other criteria than money make a difference to the workforce.

So, what will motivate people to work hard and give their extreme best? Pink found that what motivates us are mastery, autonomy and purpose. Professionals like to get better in their profession step–by–step. Mastery of skills is motivating. They like to get better at doing their job and conquer new challenges. Mastery is constant learning. See the parallel with adhocracy culture? Pink states we also like autonomy. We are motivated by professional freedom to schedule our tasks and do our jobs the way we like to.

And we love purpose. If you want to get people to move, give them meaning – a beautiful purpose. The Kaiser–Hill leaders gave this great vision to the discouraged workers of Rocky Flats. If you give people a greater purpose than just making money for yourself or the organization – they work hard.

We don't just want to make a living: we want to make a difference! We like to contribute to the world. We thrive on hope and positive meaning. Kaiser–Hill created a wildlife refuge and a great space for 2,000,000 people living in the Denver area. Looking at mastery, autonomy and purpose as the motivational needs of the modern professional, this aligns pretty well with what the OCAI database is showing us. Connect and create in clan and adhocracy cultures!

Generation Y

More change from your own staff derives from Generation Y: the people born after 1980, who have finished their education and started a career in your workplace. They are a very digitally–savvy generation, born and raised on technology, if you like.

Descriptions are: They know how to multi–task and may have short attention spans; they need immediate gratification and positive feedback. They would be overconfident and driven by personal growth. Some of these labels are based on research, but some are debatable. What matters is this typical image of Generation Y, who are changing the workplaces from within. This new Y–professional is autonomous. "Live life to the max" – could be their motto. They don't like command and control structures, working in old–fashioned hierarchies and being controlled by a manager or limited by their position. They like to do it all.

They are also called the slash/slash generation because they combine and multitask a lot but don't like to choose. They like collaboration in loose networks. Their values are flexibility, creativity, freedom and social responsibility; a purpose to contribute to the world. Generation Y helps to change corporate cultures, slowly but surely. Organizations will do their best to hire them because we need them...Imagine our workplace in the 21st Century. We live and work in a high–speed, intertwined, complex, globally operating, real time reality. In this network–like, hyper, hectic information world, we need:

The 21C way of Change:
♦ bottom up design and decisions in collaboration with the top
♦ "inclusive" change: including and engaging all organization members
♦ who deliver complex products/services, know and interact with customers
♦ who add their professional views crisscross from the organization
♦ to make this one giant jigsaw puzzle that represents current, complex reality
♦ and who take ownership for the change, so

- ◆ who are willing to change their mindsets and behaviors
- ◆ focused on teams and individuals who support each other to change
- ◆ combining personal and collective change
- ◆ in a non–linear way, using the network–like nature of organizations,
- ◆ knowing that small key changes can have huge effects,
- ◆ looking for tipping points,
- ◆ and you're never done, but constantly changing along, and need to be faster still
- ◆ based on the belief: no–one knows what's best because reality is far too complex – and we don't have time to dig through all the details – so let's change together, do something now and learn!

See how the need for professionals, flexibility, people skills, entrepreneurship, ownership, autonomy, collaboration, co–creation, engagement, mastery, development, innovation and openness becomes more and more apparent?

Change is a core competence

The ability to change must be built into organizations more than ever before. The modern organization simply doesn't have the time anymore, to thoroughly plan huge change programs, designed by the CEO and his exclusive top team. Everything is happening at high speed, everything is connected and real time. Inside or outside the organization are not clearly defined concepts anymore.

The CEO can't control everything anymore. He must trust his professionals who may be present in the office, but gaming on their smart phones or who may be invisible, but outperforming everyone from home. The organization's professionals can't wait for their manager's permission while they connect with customers, suppliers and citizens all the time, getting ideas, solving problems, seeing opportunities, gaining information, spending energy, leaving an impression that will be quickly tweeted and "liked" or not. Information and reputation cannot be controlled.

Providing complex products that need support and explanation, collaborating in organizations, creating and delivering services in interaction with the customer and coworkers, make it matter how we feel at work. Customers and colleagues will sense our moods and motivation before we utter a word.

They respond to our purpose – is it sympathetic or too plainly commercial? Are you here to connect or to sell? Will you give or take? Are you like me? They will turn away if we don't have the autonomy to solve their issues. If we have to ask our boss first, we lose valuable time. If we have to wait for a new procedure, the opportunity is gone. The prospect browsed away, tweeting their discontent.

Even when our business is traditionally manufacturing material goods that are transported at the speed of trucks, the information about our organization travels at the speed of light across the globe. Or the lack thereof. Why didn't anyone hear about our organization? No–one will buy what they can't see or hear about. No–one will like what they don't know. We don't trust what's unknown – "Something must be wrong with your organization if our social network hasn't recommended you".

Others determine our business success more than even before. It's about fans and followers these days, inside and outside of the organization. No–one buys our stuff if they don't like us. No–one buys into our orders and commands if we don't engage them. People want to think for themselves. The boss is just a job someone does. So what is the CEO thinking? We don't have time to wait for his permission to proceed with details. We need to fix this problem now. We need to make this change now. We need to fulfill our needs now. We want mastery, autonomy and purpose. We want to make a difference.

Ownership: the New Professional

We challenge our skills to gain even more mastery, like self–confident and autonomous professionals who like to take their own decisions and do our jobs in the way we think is best. Don't tell us how to do it – we're professionals. Just tell us what you need by when, and we'll deliver. That's what professionals say.

Leaders, give us some space! Stop controlling us and micromanaging us and boring us with Excel sheets. Just give us the vision, the direction, the purpose, paint the dream! And we'll go for it. Better than you could ever imagine. Going every extra mile – and beyond. That is ownership. Managers say they want employees to take ownership as a mindset. To stop waiting for orders, depending on their manager, asking for permission, hiding their mistakes, fearing for their position, hoarding information, making excuses, saying "That's not my job", complaining, gossiping and blaming head office or the other departments, justifying why they didn't do it.

Ownership is: To see it, own it, solve it and do it (definition by Roger Connors and Tom Smith in Change the culture–Change the game). Embody your organization. Be the change you want to see in your workplace. So if you see a client who's lost in the hallway, it's your problem – if customer service is a core value. You see it, you feel responsible and you solve the situation by asking them how you can help, even though you're not the receptionist but the CEO.

Taking ownership is an attitude; an awareness and motivation to actually take action, take charge, expand your locus of control and influence whatever you can't control.

It's dealing with complaints. Preventing problems from occurring. Delivering more to customers. Innovating faster than your competitors. Sharing information, inspiration and energy between departments. Collaborating smoothly. Solving complex issues. Creating the perfect customer experience, worth a tweet and a re–tweet. Making others feel welcome, served, appreciated, rewarded. Being likable, productive and positive.

The first crucial condition is that leaders must be willing to let go... of control, fear, managing by details etc. They must have faith in our professional attitude and accountability. The second crucial condition is that you have built a strong culture that sets the stage for flexible behaviors and change, based on firm values and beliefs that stand the test of time. Turn your organization into a "tribe" with a shared purpose. Use this flexible, invisible but strong collective glue that gives focus, direction, meaning, norms about what (not) to do and criteria for decision making.

Culture is Key

The thing is, most people will draw the organizational chart without hesitation. But when asked for the image of culture... The direction, strategic goals, criteria, values, norms, key beliefs and behaviors are often tacit knowledge or, worse, not known. No wonder that organizations need structure and rules and control to keep people together and get things done...! They have to push buttons and give orders and measure progress or no–one will know what to do or they won't be motivated.

However, depending on command and control mechanisms may be the hard way to get some results. The smart way is using the flexible and cohesive glue of culture and strategy. Research proves this time and again. Just one quote from Harvard Business Review: "As James Heskett wrote in his latest book *The Culture Cycle*, effective culture can account for 20–30 percent of the differential in corporate performance when compared with "culturally unremarkable" competitors."

Culture is the fastest way to get extraordinary results. It takes effort to create a community that will self–organize, change, respond and know what to do and what not to do because its culture is internalized. But once you've got a functional culture, it will make you fast. It doesn't take three signatures over three levels to push the button GO.

It takes just one smart, motivated and authorized professional to GO. They know they're acting in line with strategy, guided by the values, criteria and norms of culture, taking ownership within the broad boundaries you've given them – so they feel empowered and confident enough to take ownership.

No need to test their tolerance for frustration and practice patience – as is the case in old–fashioned hierarchies. No need to demotivate and to have energy, inspiration and ideas drip away. No need to have gifted professionals wait for permission, meanwhile browsing the web looking for a real opportunity, a new challenge that will give them satisfaction.

Once you've got this effective culture, you're different from your competitors. It's easy to copy an organization chart. It's possible to copy products and look–alike–services, to set the same price, to copy your competitor's wages, even to deduct their strategy and follow them. But it's another thing to copy their culture, their leadership, their talent, their creativity and collaboration.

Culture gives an organization a competitive advantage because it's not easily copied. An effective 21C culture fosters creativity, change–ability and collaboration. The ability to collaborate well, to change fast if necessary, to decide fast and to be creative (in relations, decisions or innovations) are key features of successful 21C organizations.

In today's fast changing, complex and connected world, the competitive advantage depends on how well people collaborate and co–create (quickly sharing instead of hoarding information), how creative, open– and change–minded they are, how well they take ownership and use their professional freedom to create the best customer experience.

Winning workplaces are those who:

♦ Care for their people and have managers who coach and give attention
♦ Provide a purpose to contribute to planet earth or society, something beyond material wins
♦ Engage their highly educated employees and entice them to learn more
♦ Stimulate innovation, autonomy, space to learn and experiment
♦ Include everyone, utilize diversity and fulfill our need to belong
♦ With an effective, inspiring culture around core values but with changeable behaviors

Culture gets more important this century... It's the typical way we do things around here, even when we're all working from home... It must be flexible and strong, to bond us and give meaning to our work. Together, we can achieve more. That's why we go through the "bother" of collaboration.

Remember from Chapter 3, culture gives us a collective purpose, a shared identity and belonging, helps determine social hierarchy (leader and follower–roles), reduces complexity (we know what we must do) and provides continuity.

How to build change into culture?

Culture gives continuity, if we're open to changing behaviors, though we stick to our core values. We'd keep the A and B: identity and beliefs. That is our core. But one of our core values is that we are open–minded to change C, D and E in order to respond to challenges.

We must do this together, but if necessary we discuss our challenges, adapt our strategy AND decide to change our competencies, behaviors and environment/ effect (C,D and E). We dress up our culture core with new, typical behaviors that still match the dominant culture type! That is how you build change within your culture.

People and Results

The need for more flexibility seems clear. I expect future cultures to show more clan and adhocracy scores, like our OCAI Online participants desire. But market culture also stays relevant. In the end, organizational cultures must value results as well.

W P Carey Business School did an extensive study based on the Competing Values Framework and actual effectiveness of organizations. They found that organizations with a strong clan culture have the highest scores on employee satisfaction and quality. The market culture–type organizations score highest on profits but also on... innovation. Their research suggests that organizations with a high score on market culture are doing well but not necessarily have satisfied employees. Those organizations have good financial performance and somehow, their competitiveness also leads to innovation.

The researchers Angelo Kinicki, Chad Hartnell and Amy Yi Ou state that the most successful organizations seem to have a unique blend of two opposite culture types: the people–oriented clan culture and the results–oriented market culture. This is a big polarity on the diagonal axis of the CVF, so people need to combine behaviors from the people orientation as well as performance orientation.

We will see... These are indeed exciting times of change!

Summary

Both external, technological and economic developments and internal, motivational reasons cause rapid change within organizations. The OCAI online database shows current organizational cultures to score on hierarchy and market cultures, while people want more clan and adhocracy cultures in the future. This need for more flexibility seems understandable and necessary – when we compare our 21st century challenges with the industrial era we come from.

First conclusions are that change is a core competence and that culture becomes more important in our service/experience economy to add value to the customers and to provide "flexible glue" to the employees – fostering autonomy while still providing shelter, belonging and a meaningful, collective purpose...

The challenge is how we're going to develop new leadership and "flexible" culture types without losing the advantages of control, order and results. How are we going to make a great mix from this Competing Values Framework, taking into account that we want more flexibility and we need results?

These are interesting times. Let's develop some great places to work and really develop the workplace, the workers and the world!

Chapter 24 How to stop Reading and Talking – and start Doing?

Great that you have made it to the end of this book! I know how busy you are, how many distractions cross our paths and this bulk load I wanted to share with you... It can be a lot. Let's do the recap of what we have learned so far. Though I said this book wasn't written to be read, you just did. Now it is time to DO it. Nothing will happen if we don't take action. Beware of the talking trap...!

Above all: BE the change. You can only change yourself. Be willing, authentic and honest. BE the change and change your own beliefs and behaviors. Be open and learn! Be courageous. People will do as you do. Show them the way.

Another thing that stands out for me is: We can't order the others to change. If you want change, you need to involve everyone. Engage them and make it easy to change. The old paradigm is still alive: many consultants and managers are busy with old–fashioned, exclusive change for specialists, assuming they know best. The old way creates partial change at best, and often frustrations, side–effects, discouragement, resistance and the belief that change is hard, unpleasant and tiring.

So, if you forget everything I said in the previous 23 chapters, please take this with you: BE the change, DO it and INCLUDE and ENGAGE the others. The next two things to remember are: Work with behaviors and work in small teams; using the power of 10. Small groups of people who trust each other, support and interact, can change the world. That's why we use the OCAI Workshops as vehicles for change – that's how you continue with your team to support and sustain the new behaviors in "change circles". Be specific – real change comes down to new behaviors/habits and nothing else.

Forget huge change campaigns, keep it small and effective. Honor small behavioral changes, practice one new action and turn it into a habit. Practice change leadership: get skilled enough to notice and respond to other's behaviors (and expressed beliefs) and interact with and influence the others. Invest in training and coaching to be able to turn your team into a "change circle". Be as committed to yourself and your people as you would be to your children and dogs... Respond to behavior.

Beware of the talking trap. After you've reached consensus, the change circle is no longer a meeting, it is a practice playground. Practice, practice, copy, coach and correct.

If you keep these six things in mind, I'd be happy. They go wrong often and bring about the notorious failure rate of change programs.

1. DO it (beware of the talking trap)
2. BE the change (as a team member and as a leader)
3. INCLUDE: engage and empower the others, do it together
4. BEHAVIORS: new specific habits are key to change
5. SMALL TEAMS: engage in supportive change circles of 10 people max.
6. NOTICE + RESPOND to behaviors

The long recap: enjoy the puzzle of finding out what will help your organization change successfully.

The basis is the **7–Step Guide to Culture Change**:

1. Assess the current and preferred culture (15 minutes) as a starting point
2. Diagnose the quantified, visual profile
3. Understand culture better by adding qualitative examples, stories,
4. Raise engagement and awareness and create consensus of where we are
5. Assess the future, vision and strategy to see where we need to go
6. Understand and customize the necessary, preferred culture to thrive in this future. Agree and see this new culture, from values down to behavior and outcomes
7. Together, create a How–to–change plan that people take ownership for because they co–created it. Work in small teams, ocai–workshops or change circles of 10 people max.

During the process, check your **7C's for Successful Change**:

1 Commitment from the top

The top executives need to be committed, not only to the change and its expected gains, but to personal change as well. They must be so committed that they are willing to change themselves if necessary and endure the discomfort of adopting new habits.

◆ Assess the Will of Key Players
◆ Assess Necessity to Change Now
◆ Assess the Skill of Key Players

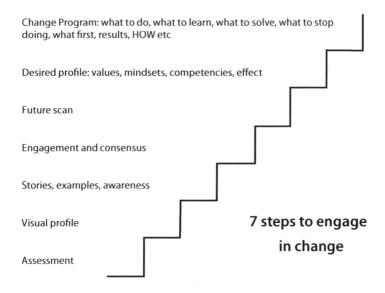

Change Program: what to do, what to learn, what to solve, what to stop doing, what first, results, HOW etc

Desired profile: values, mindsets, competencies, effect

Future scan

Engagement and consensus

Stories, examples, awareness

Visual profile

Assessment

7 steps to engage in change

2 Clarity on current and desired situation and goals

Without clarity, efforts tend to diversify, diffuse and confuse. We need to know where we stand, where we need to go and why we have to move now. Clarity lacks more often than you think. Ask the team leaders or employees to explain your organization's strategy. And you will have your answer if there's clarity for starters.

3 Consensus and commitment from workers

Consensus and commitment, engagement if you will, are vital to change. The CEO can't change 1,000 others, not even 10 of them. He can try to influence them, role model, be the change he wants to see.

But enough others have to change their behaviors or nothing will change in the organization as a whole. You can only achieve consensus and commitment in small teams (the power of 10, see Chapter 13, "change circles"), starting with the OCAI–workshops as the first vehicle for inclusive, engaging change.

4 Continuous Communication

Communicate, have dialogues, ask, explain, exchange. True communication creates meaning and connection. Without communication there will be no understanding, respect, confidence and will to really make change happen this time. Communicate and support each other in small teams.

5 Copy coach and correct (in small teams or Change Circles)

Respond to all behaviors all the time – this is a major leadership skill that seems to be often lacking. Utilize the copy mechanism: people will do what you do. Be the change so others can copy you. Coach them and if necessary, correct old or undesired behaviors.

Be consistent and the change will become clear. People might check if you are for real. Small behaviors can have huge impact. Consistently keep doing it: copy, coach and correct. Organize the change in small teams (the power of 10, see Chapter 13) of people who support each other.

6 Create Critical Mass

If the behaviors are spreading through the organizational system, you are on the right track. Reach that famous critical mass when enough people are executing the new behaviors and it becomes profitable for everyone to do so, even for the ones who resisted so far.

7 Carry on

Last but not least: Carry on. Never, never give up. The minute you let go is the minute people are tempted to go back to old habits and rest in their comfort zones. Help them through the "messy middle" to a happy ending, when "new" has become a habit again. Until the next change...

Yes, we can!

Most things worth achieving are done in a group. Next to a few extraordinary individuals, most people collaborate in teams to accomplish great and meaningful purposes. Too large becomes tardy and impersonal, but the optimal human size is 10. Groups of 10 may become power circles and change the world...

These circles together may form a tribe of like-minded people. Don't hesitate – every one of us has the power to invite 9 others to join. Together, we have a way to change our workplace into an empowering, inspiring place. It's totally worth it... it's where most of us spend the biggest part of the week!

True change means collaboration and co-creation, true leadership is all about followers and fans – both are no longer possible through command and control. Together, we can lead change!

But will you?

There's only one question left. Will you... do it? Check this first.

The next thing to do now, is to team up in a powerful group of 10... Convince the first 9 people who can help you start. No one can do it alone. But together, we can do it and co–create our culture and change.

Personally, I wish I had known this way back... Struggling alone, taking (lack of) progress too personally at the time, working from an exclusive specialist perspective, and getting frustrated. It wasn't enough for me to make a living. I wanted to make a difference. But in order to do so, I needed the others. What didn't work was present the best solution and tell them what to do.

But what did work, was to truly connect with people and invite them to change with me in small groups... 10 by 10, work my way through the organization. Mostly, first the Management team, then the next level of managers, then their teams... Circles of Change, causing exciting ripples in the organization.

You can do it, too! Start small, start with the power of 10

Bring your own will and skill up to date. Next, organize co–creation and collaboration. Win fans and followers. Inspire the positive energizers. Work from the Abundance approach. Engage those who are committed too. Be courageous enough to notice and respond to behaviors – don't act consensus if it's fake – your time is too valuable for plays and games. Be true. Practice new behaviors together. This is about real change. Take ownership and co–create your future!

Don't forget to download your checklists at:

www.organizationalculturechange.com/go/premiumcontent

Chapter 25 Resources & References

There's abundance out there... I read a lot but I am not going to share a list of 100 books: you probably don't have time for that. Let's focus on a few books that have made difference for me and that this book is based upon. The same counts for web links. I've kept it simple and short, but feel free to browse the Internet for more.

Must–Read Books:

1. "Diagnosing and Changing Organizational Culture – based on the Competing Values Framework" – Kim Cameron & Robert Quinn, 3rd edition Jossey–Bass 2011, ISBN 9780470650264
2. "Viral Change" – Leandro Herrero, MeetingMinds 2008, ISBN 9781905776054
3. "Making the Impossible – Possible" – Kim Cameron & Marc Lavine, Berrett–Koehler Publishers 2006, ISBN 1576753905
4. "Positive Leadership – Strategies for Extraordinary Performance" – Kim Cameron, Berrett–Koehler Publishers 2008, ISBN 9781576756027

Additional Reading Books:

"Becoming a Master Manager: A Competing Values Approach" – Quinn et al., Wiley 2007, ISBN 9780470050774

"Lift: Becoming a Positive Force in Any Situation", – Ryan & Robert Quinn, Academic Service 2009, ISBN 9789052617657

"Building the Bridge as You Walk On It: A Guide for Leading Change" – Robert Quinn (Jossey–Bass, 2004), ISBN

"Change the Culture, Change the Game" – Roger Conners & Tom Smith, Portfolio/Penguin, ISBN 9781591843610

"Deep Change – Discovering the Leader Within" – Robert Quinn, Jossey–Bass 1996, ISBN 9780787902445

"Het licht en de korenmaat" – Dutch: Hans Wopereis. Publ: Ten Have, 2009. ISBN: 9789025960384

"Drive: The Surprising Truth About What Motivates Us" – Daniel Pink, Riverhead Trade 2011, ISNB 9781594484803

"Leidinggeven aan Professionals? Niet Doen!" – Dutch: Mathieu Weggeman, Scriptum 2006, ISBN 9789055943524

"The Fifth Discipline: The Art and Practice of the Learning Organization" – Peter Senge, Doubleday/Currency 1990, ISBN 0–385–51725–4 (second edition)

"Collaboration – How leaders avoid the traps, create unity, and reap big results" – Morten T. Hansen, Harvard Business Press 2009, ISBN 9781422115152

Articles:

Competing values Leadership: quadrant roles and personality traits by Alan Belasen and Nancy Frank in Leadership and Organization Development Journal Vol. 29 No. 2, 2008 pp. 127–143

Organizational Culture and Organizational Effectiveness: A meta–analytic investigation of the Competing Values Framework's Theoretical Suppositions – Chad Hartnell, May Yi Ou, Angelo Kinicki, Journal of Applied Psychology, online publication January 2011

http://knowledge.wpcarey.asu.edu/article.cfm?articleid=1989

Web links:

Online Organizational Culture Assessment Instrument

www.ocai–online.com

Online Video Training Culture Change with OCAI

www.organizationalculturechange.com

Linkedin Discussion Group: Organizational Culture Assessment to Change

www.linkedin.com/groups/Organizational–Culture–Assessment–Change–3462687

Facebook

www.facebook.com/Culture.Change.Community

Youtube Channel

www.youtube.com/user/OrganizationCulture

Twitter

twitter.com/marcellabremer

Workshops and training: Culture Change Days

www.ocai–online.com/products/culture–change–days

pre-approved training for PHR, SPHR and GPHR certificates

Printed in Great Britain
by Amazon